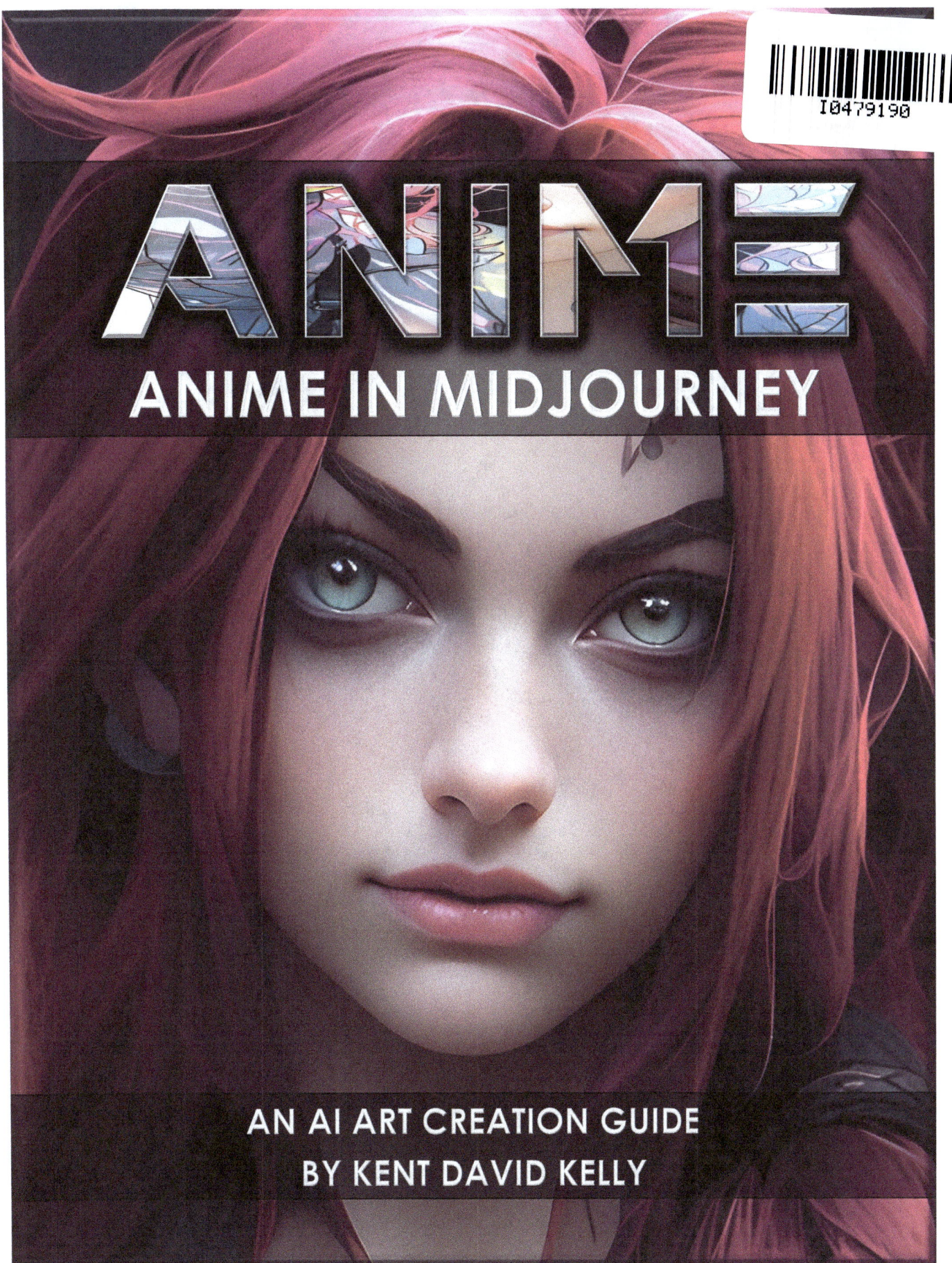

ANIME

ANIME IN MIDJOURNEY

AN AI ART CREATION GUIDE
BY KENT DAVID KELLY

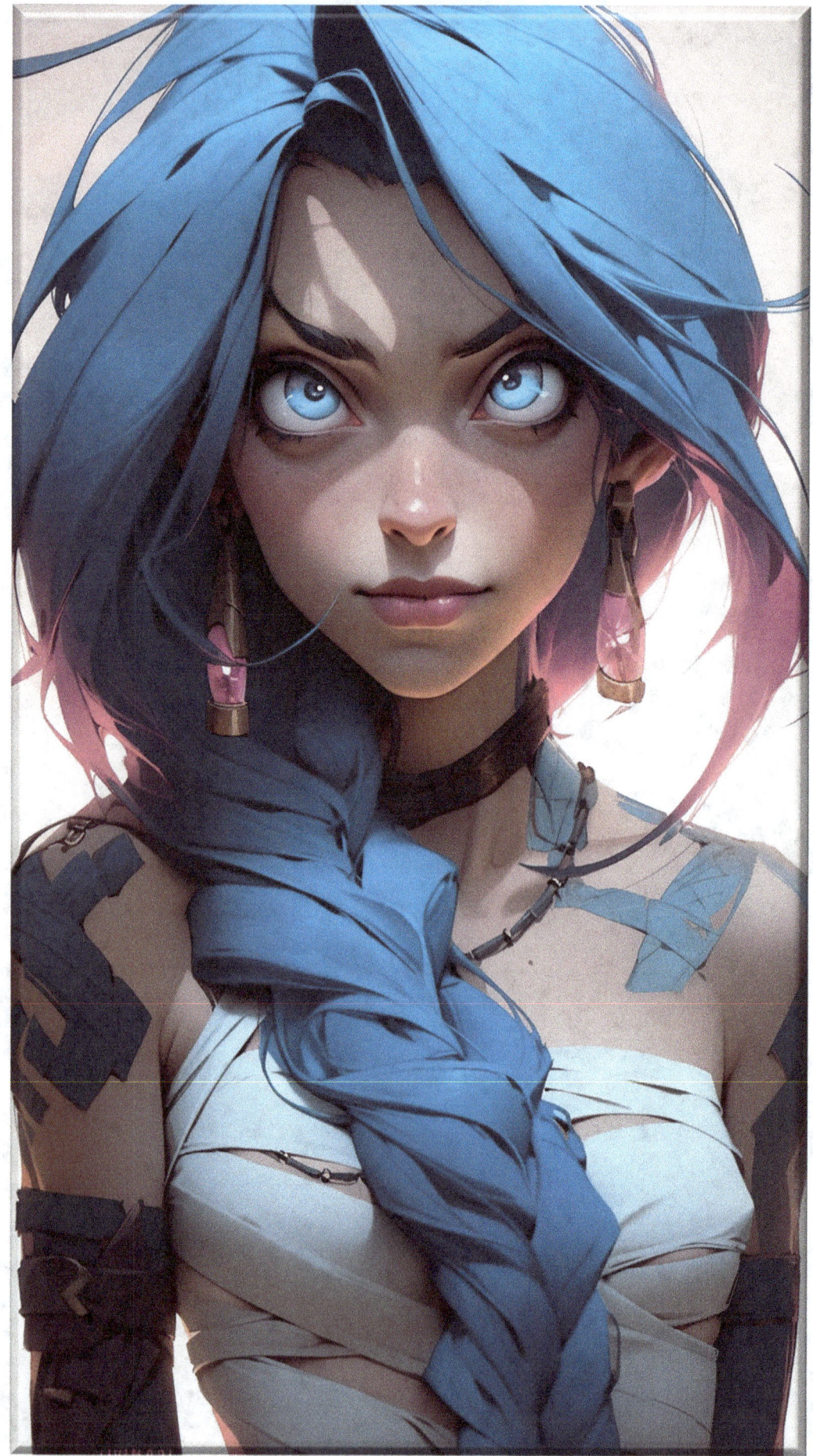

ANIME IN MIDJOURNEY

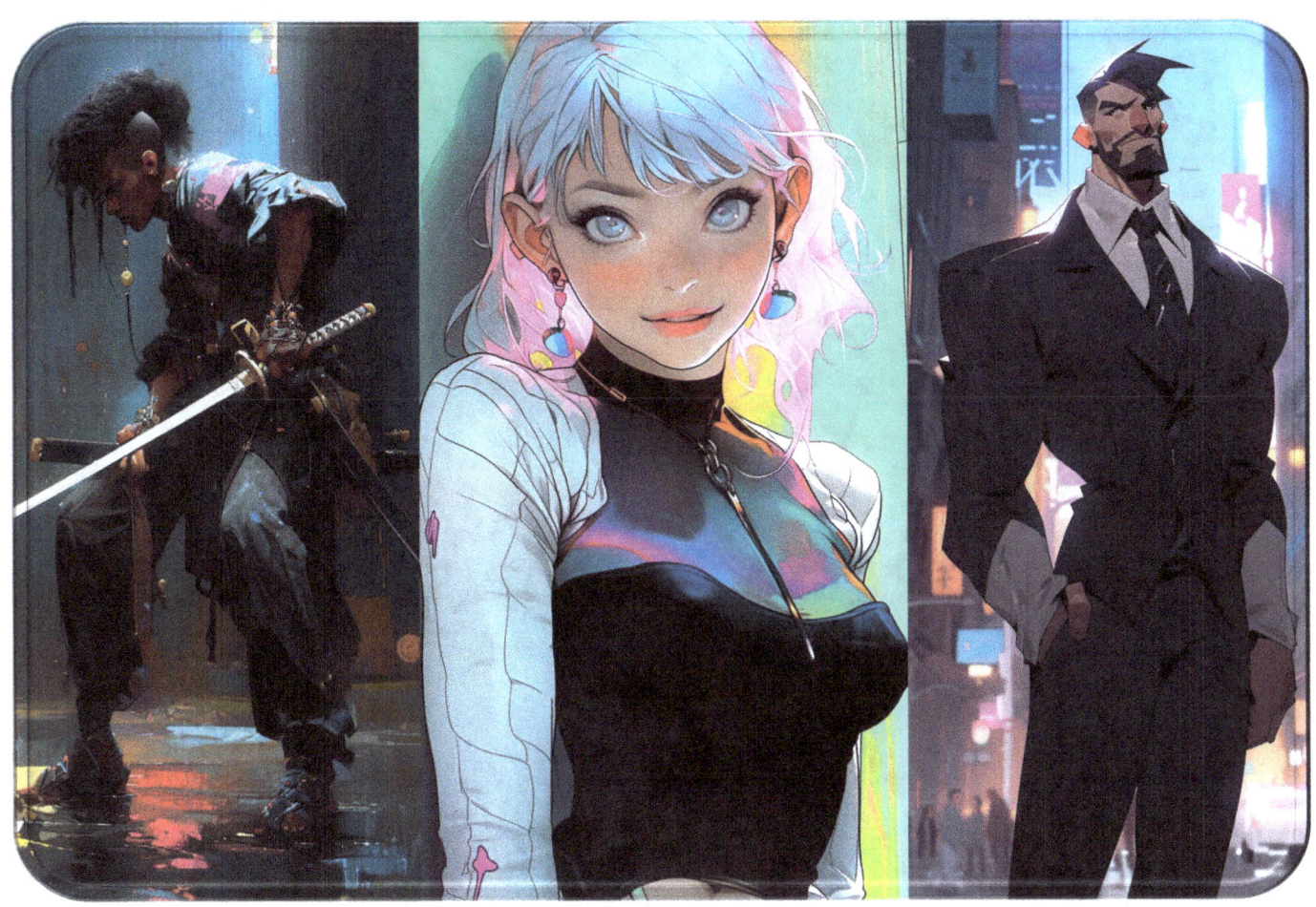

AN AI ART CREATION GUIDE

CREATED BY

Kent David Kelly

WONDERLAND IMPRINTS

Only the Finest Works of Fantasy

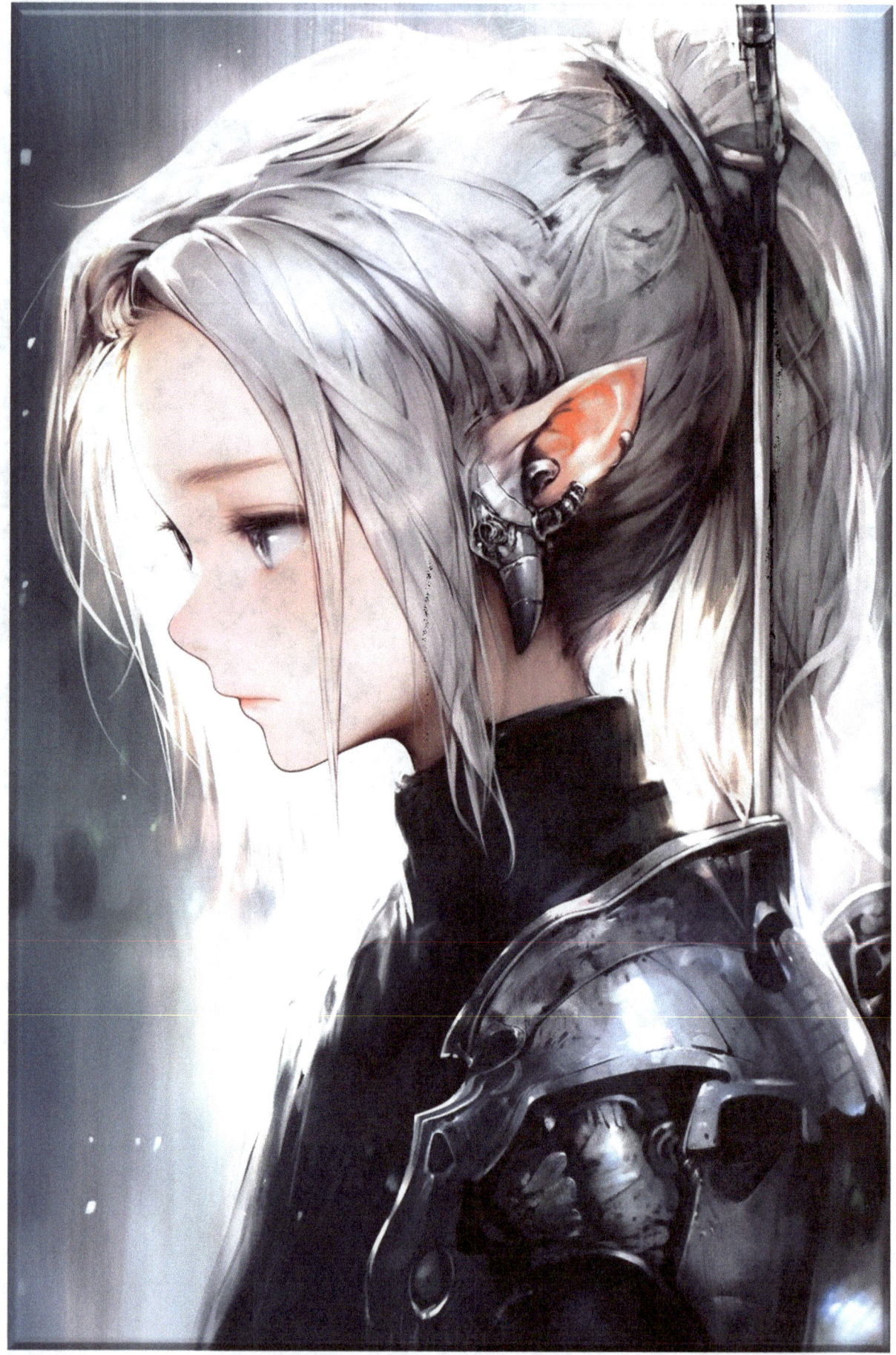

TABLE OF CONTENTS

DISCLAIMER

This is an unofficial and educational learning guide, created by Kent David Kelly. This publication is neither officially created nor endorsed by Midjourney, Inc. or any affiliated entities. Midjourney is a trademark of Midjourney Inc., 333 Harrison Street, San Francisco, CA 94105. This publication is not meant to infringe upon these copyrights and trademarks. In the interests of Fair Use, this introductory e-book has been established for informational, educational, and entertainment purposes only. The author of this volume, Kent David Kelly, is not affiliated with Midjourney, Amazon, DriveThruRPG, or with any other product, celebrity, artist, or vendor mentioned in this book. All artwork featured in this volume was created by Kent David Kelly, 2023, via the use of prompt coding in Midjourney AI.

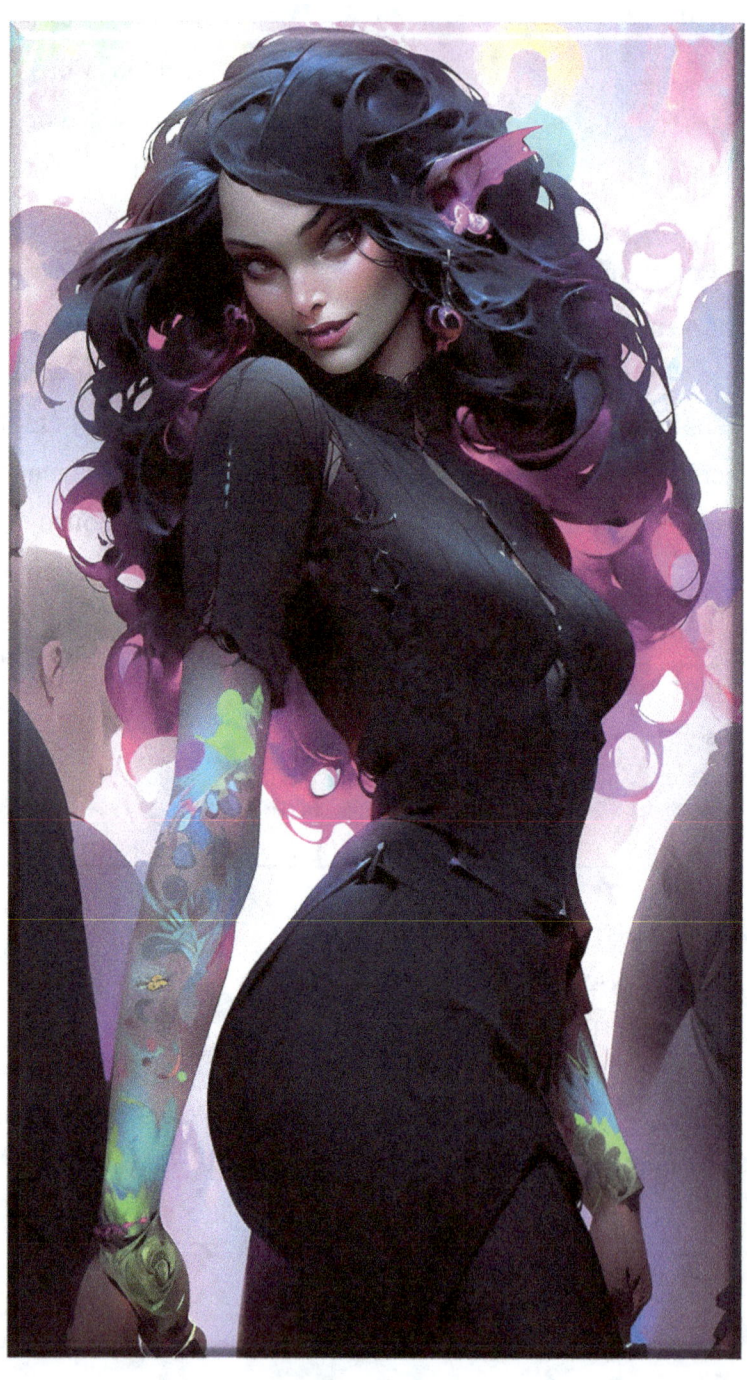

ONE:
JUMP START

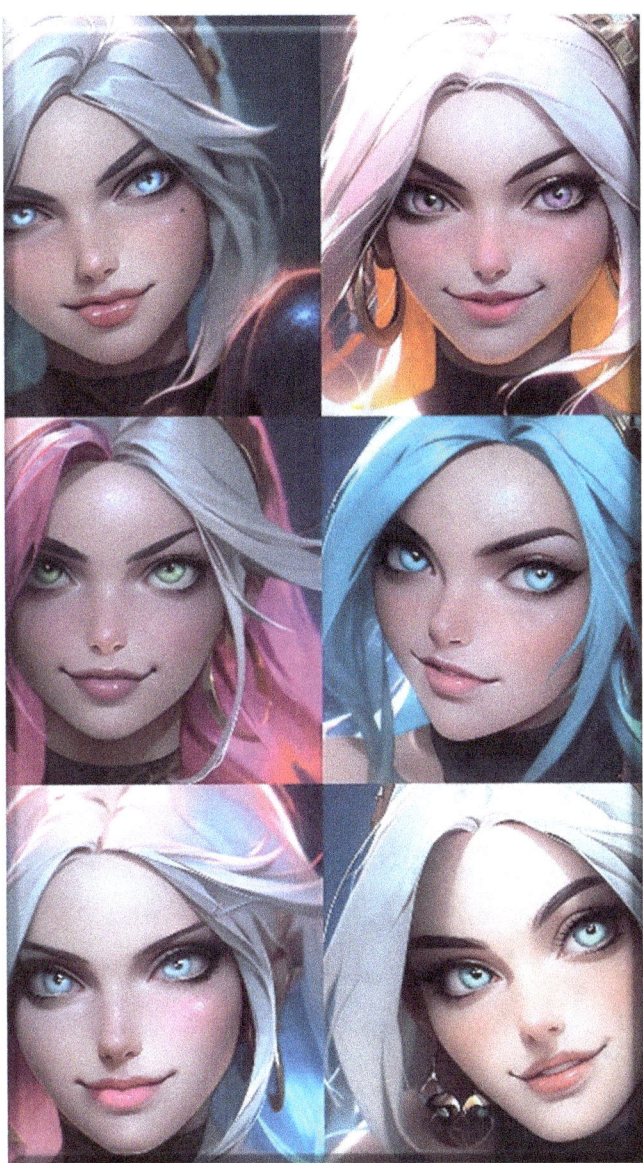

I recommend using my initial book in this AI Empowerment series, **Beginning with Midjourney**, which covers all of the basics of art crafting in methodical detail. But if you don't have that book, the jump start guide hereafter is here to help you get started in no time.

Introduction

Midjourney is an online platform, driven by Discord software. It lets you generate images that are influenced by your word codes (prompts) and a massive database powered by Artificial Intelligence (AI). If you don't know what a prompt is or how to write one, you can copy the ones found throughout this book. The prompt that evoked each image appears in full, in text, below the picture itself. They all begin with one slash-code word, "/imagine". You will find the first example of this on the next page.

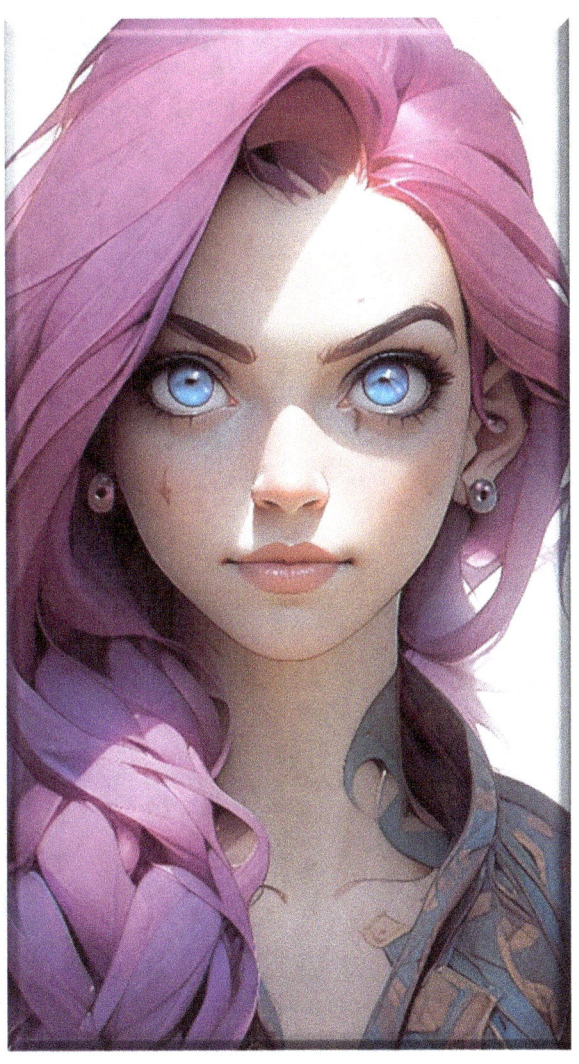

Let's Get Moving

Welcome to Midjourney, and the endless world of AI art evoked by your words and your imagination. If you are familiar with Midjourney already, you can easily skip this section and move forward to image generation. But if you are not familiar with Midjourney, Discord, and their many technicalities, you will want to slow down a bit so that you can make your own images, rather than just looking at the ones in this book.

FOLIO IMAGE 001

/imagine   **A girl like Jinx mixed with a medieval adventurer, the most beautiful woman in the world, the fabulous ladies, close up, looking in camera, mysterious, mesmerizing, gorgeous perfect face with a strong emphasis on character design --ar 9:16 --niji 5 -- style expressive**

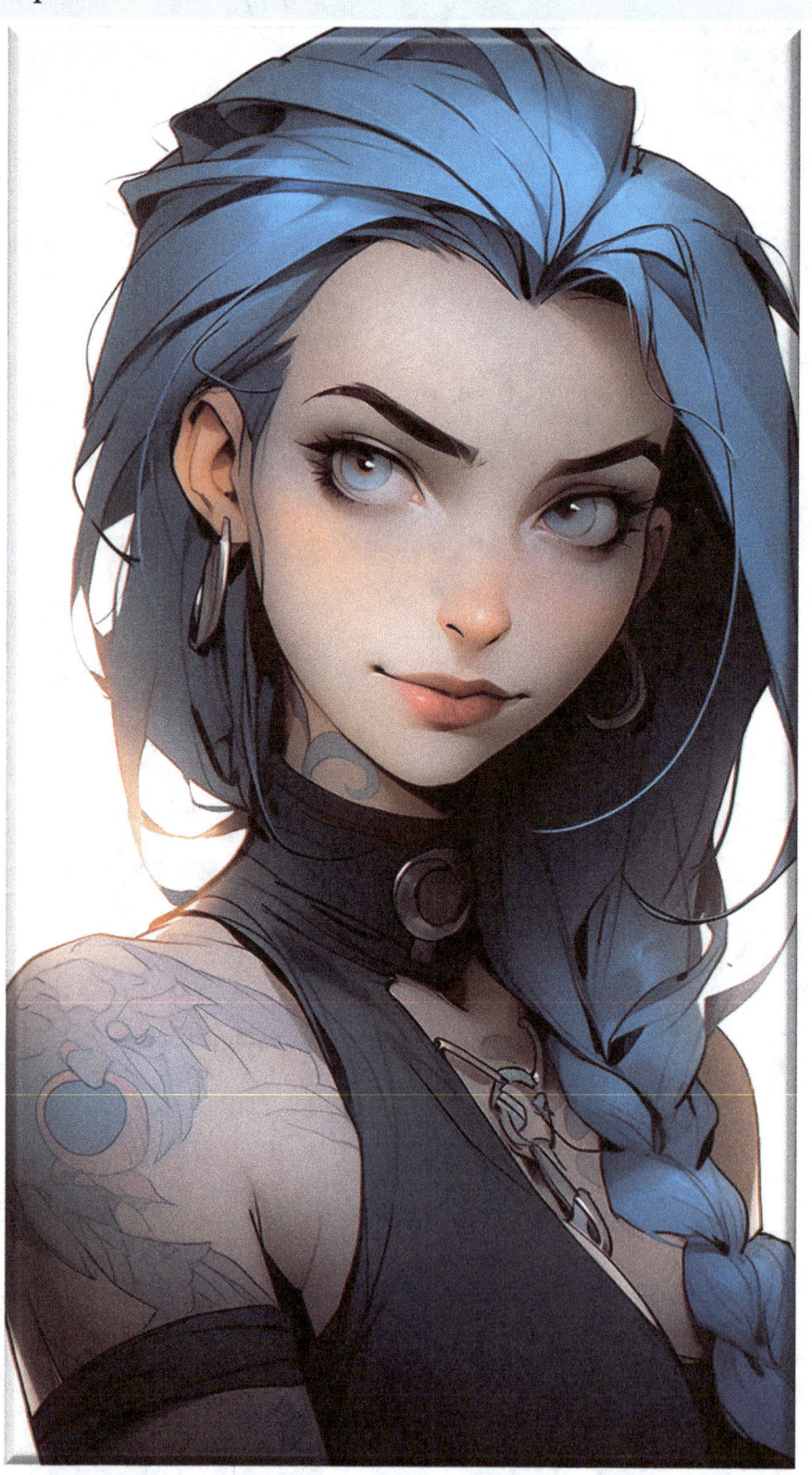

Jump Start, Step 1:

Journey

The first thing you will want to do is this: Go to the **Midjourney** website (which is on the web at **Midjourney dot com**) and sign up for access. The main site page is always changing, but as of this writing (2023) you will want to left click on the "**Join the Beta**" button at lower right.

Then, click on "**Accept Invite**" to create your account, followed by "**Continue to Discord**." (You can create a paid account when you like, as the free trial is very short.) You now have access to the Midjourney AI bot! You will find a paid subscription is definitely worth it.

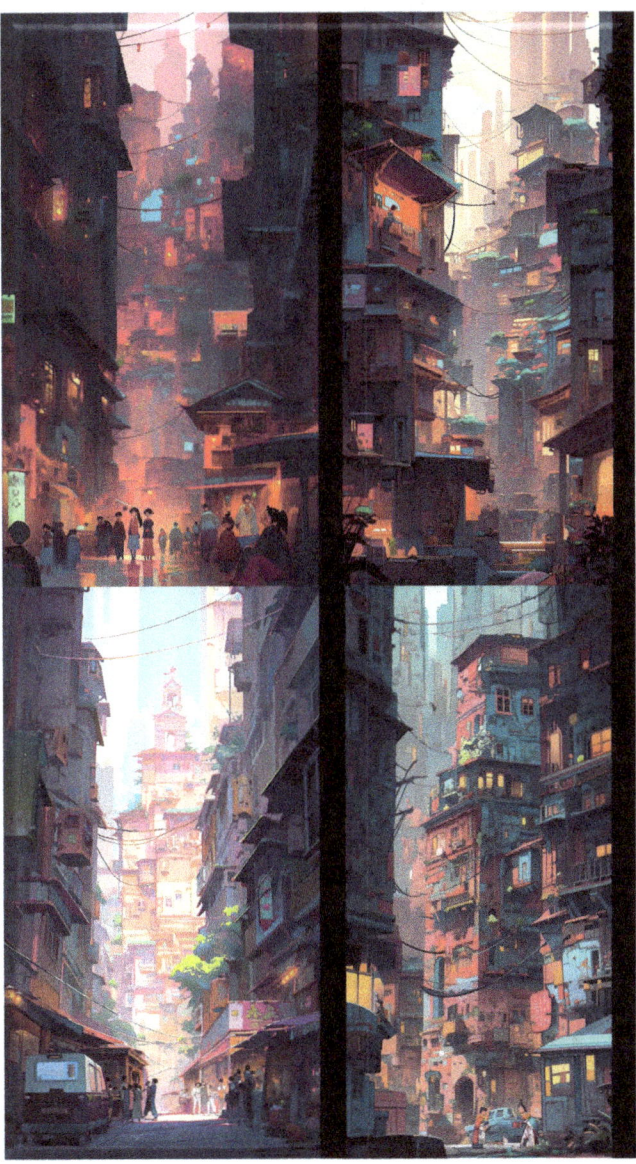

Jump Start, Step 2:

Arrive

Everyone is creating art prompts, and things are moving quickly. You will want to familiarize yourself with the Discord interface.

At first, you will see a wall of text that might look overwhelming.

On the left side, you will see a vertical column of text, titled "**Midjourney**" at the top.

Toward the bottom – you might need to scroll down a bit, using your mouse wheel or the scroll bar – is a section called "**Newcomer Rooms**."

There, click on the first room you see, for example "**newbies-26**" or a different "**newbies**" number that you are seeing now.

Jump Start, Step 3:

Look Around

You are now in the art creation room in Discord, where everyone is making images with typed in prompts.

The center of your interface – the widest part – is now filled with pictures and strange codes such as U1, V2, Upscale and so forth.

You can scroll down in this area to see other things that people are creating.

At the very bottom of this center area, you will see a **plus sign (+)** with a **blinking cursor**.

That's where you type in your prompt codes.

Jump Start, Step 4:

Slow Things Down

To shut everyone else's jabbering off so you can focus, look for the green words that read "**Midjourney Bot**" in the middle of the screen.

Right click those words, and then **left** click on "**Message**."

Now, you are in a quieter place where you can message the Midjourney Bot directly.

FOLIO IMAGE 002

/imagine   **A Geisha woman with hair in a bun style, wearing a red dress, in the style of soft color blending, intense color palette, realistic lighting, close-up, like Angura Kei, photo-realistic techniques, bold character designs --niji 5 --s 100 --ar 9:16 --chaos 9**

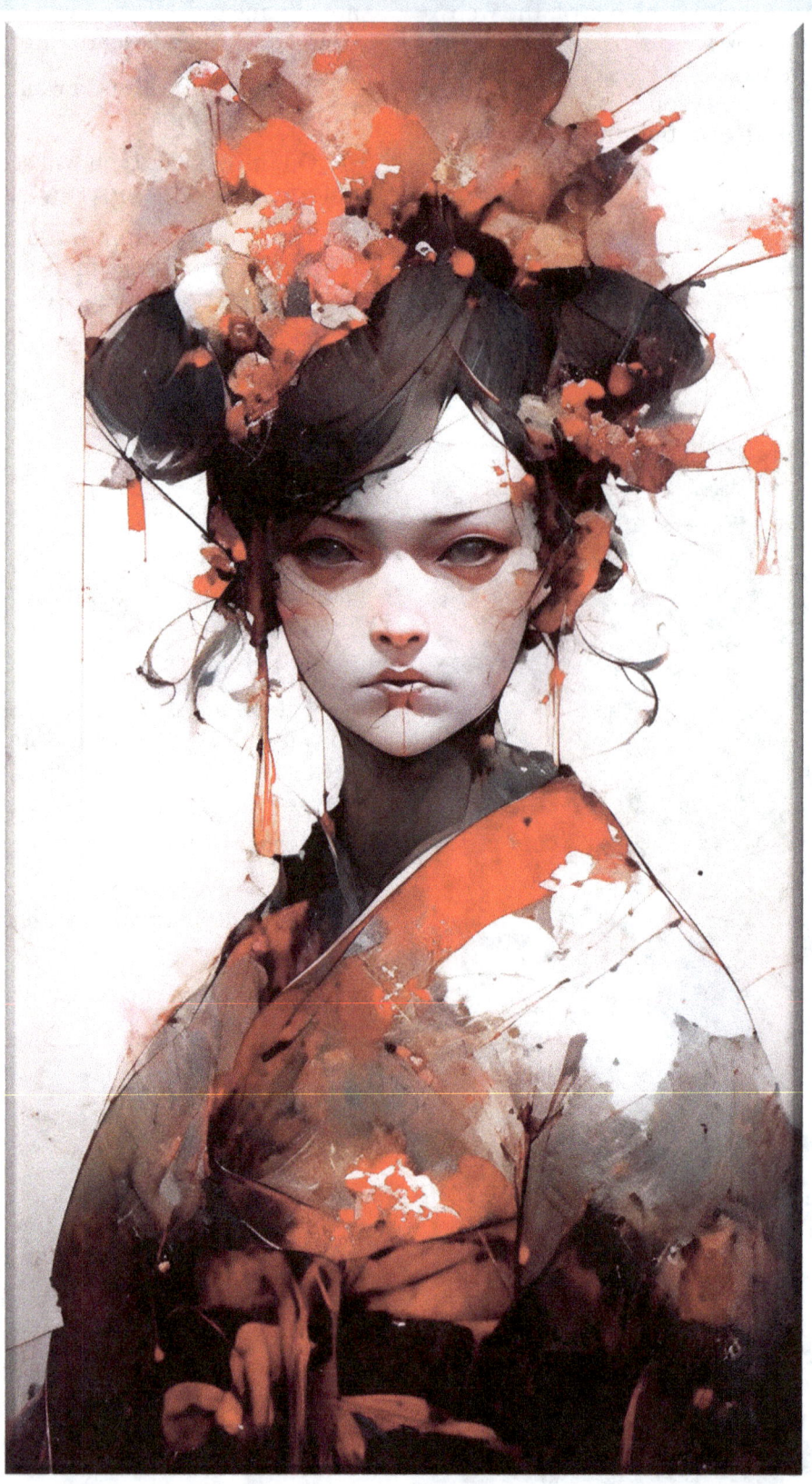

Jump Start, Step 5:

Create

Left click down where the cursor is blinking and type in your first test prompt.

Press the **Slash key (/)**, which is to the right of your Space Bar, over by the right-hand Shift key.

Then type the word **imagine** and press the **Space Bar**.

Your cursor moves to the right, into a smaller window that reads "**prompt**."

Type "**a beautiful world from the imagination**" and press **Enter**.

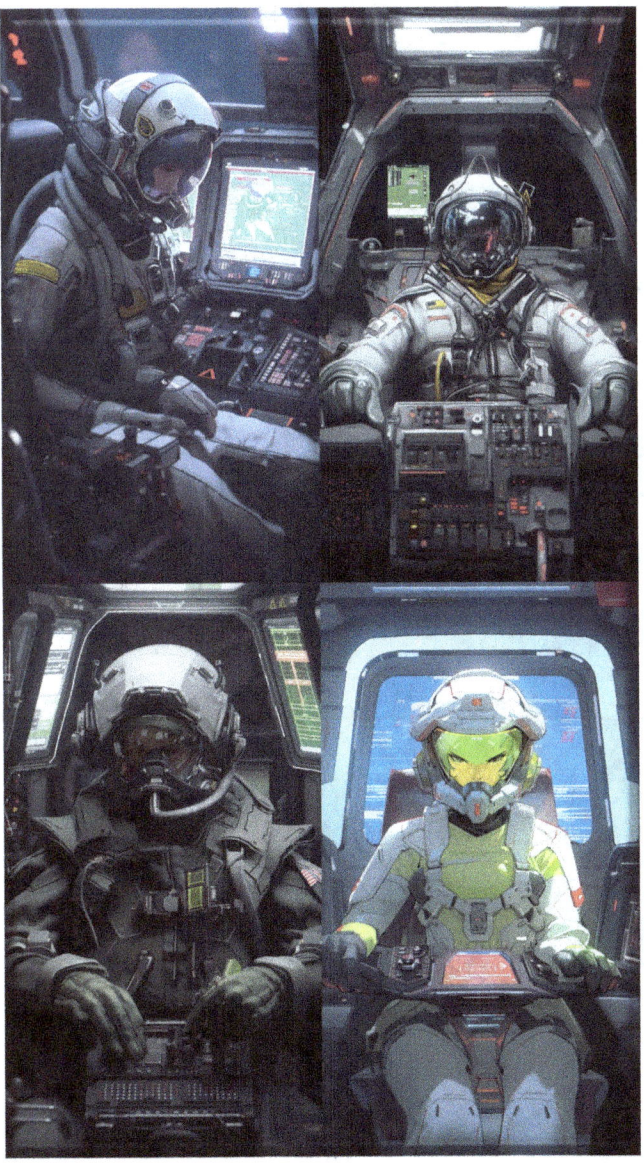

Jump Start, Step 6:

Coffee Break

Wait for your images to be created.

The Midjourney Bot will tell you it is **(Waiting to start)**, but you don't need to do anything else.

It's messaging the Midjourney servers and the database to draw in elements of your prompt request.

It can take a while if you're on a free account and lots of people are doing the same thing.

Soon, the percentage **(%)** of completion text from Midjourney will begin to count upwards from zero.

Wait until it reaches **(100%)**, which is when it presents your first creations.

Jump Start, Step 7:

Explore

The images are ready!

The screen jumps a bit because there is something new to see.

Take a look at the first serving of what Midjourney has offered you.

Here is an example of what happened when I entered this code a few minutes ago.

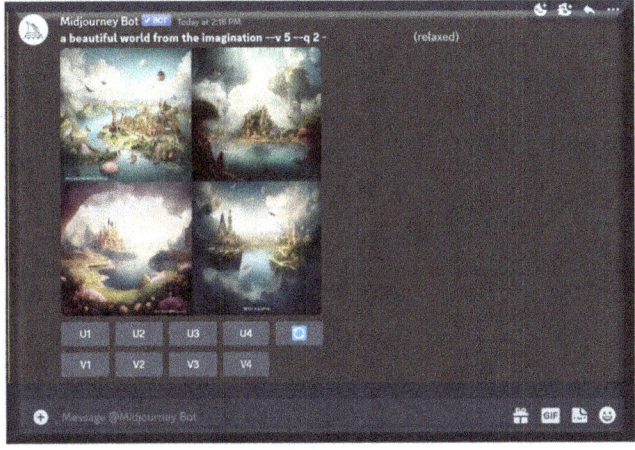

(Screenshot © Midjourney Inc., presented for educational and informative demonstration only.)

FOLIO IMAGE 003

/imagine   **Close-up, King Arthur, a portrait, standing in a castle, photorealism, silver armor outfit, portrait of a male king, singularity sculpted, intense stare, intricate stitching, long black hair --ar 9:16 --niji 5**

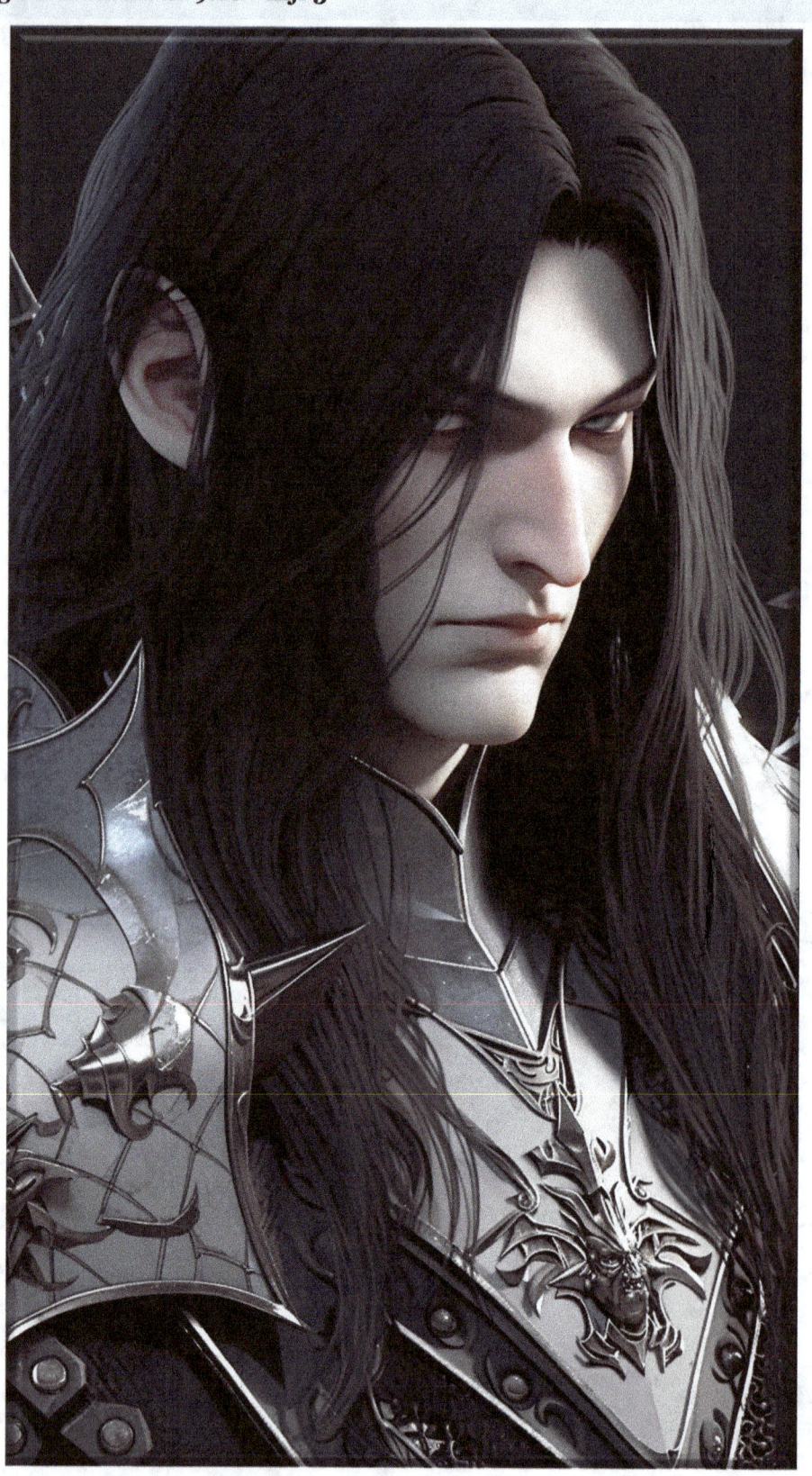

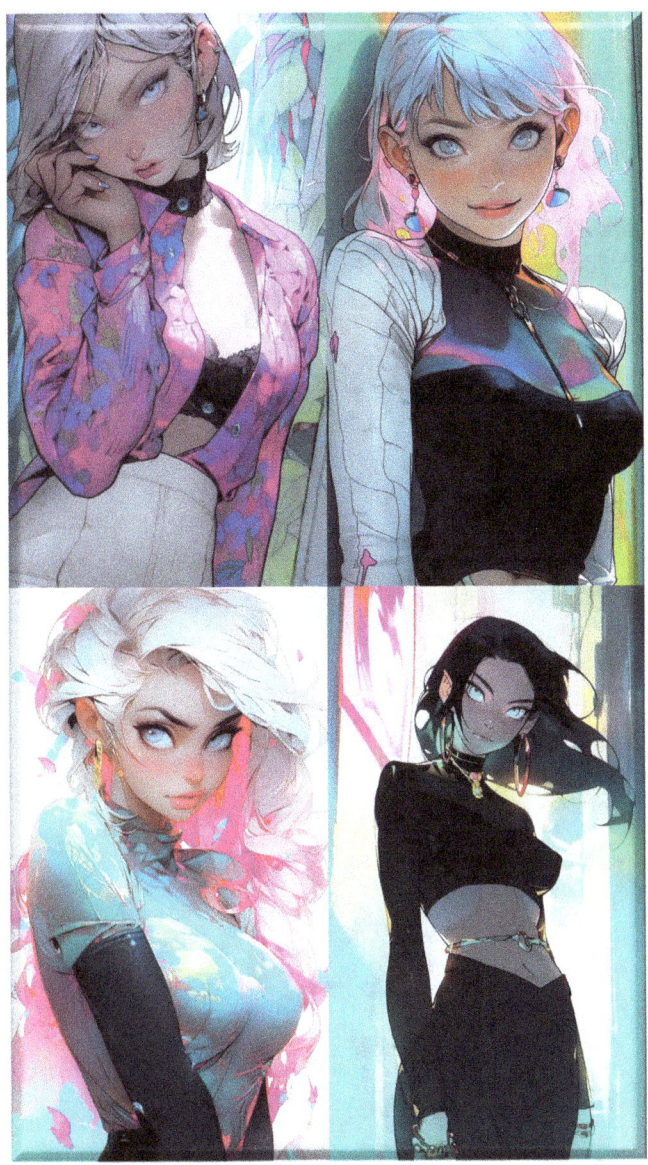

Click on an **Upscale** button (**U1** for upper left, **U2** for upper right, **U3** for lower left, or **U4** for lower right) or a **Variation** button (**V1** for upper left, **V2** for upper right, **V3** for lower left, or **V4** for lower right) to see what other amazing things Midjourney can do.

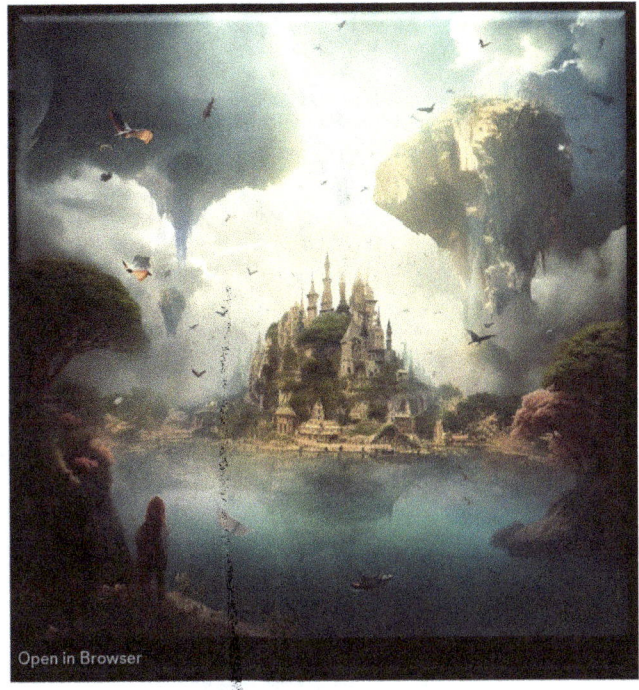

Open in Browser

(Screenshot © Midjourney Inc., presented for educational and informative demonstration only.)

Jump Start, Step 9:

Archive

Save your art. **Left click** on any Upscaled image to enlarge it.

At bottom left, click on **Open in Browser**.

Right click on the image and select **Save Image As**.

Point to where you want to save the file on your computer – perhaps the **Desktop** or a document folder – and then click **Save**.

You can always create one or more folders to save your images in, under My Documents or similar.

This is especially helpful when you're undertaking a new project or working on multiple complex features at once, like character sketches and backgrounds of different imagined locations.

Jump Start, Step 8:

Curate

Customize your images to make them more yours, and more the way you want them.

In this example (pg. 11, screenshot) we see a grid of 4 images, showing imaginary worlds.

If we want to type in a different prompt, or to add words to this prompt, we can type in a new "/imagine" phrase in the bottom + cursor field.

Or we can **Upscale** (make a small image big), make **Variations** (remix an image to change it up a bit), or click on the blue circle to **Reroll** all four pictures.

FOLIO IMAGE 004

/imagine   A girl like Jinx mixed with Emma Stone and Jaina Proudmoore, the most beautiful woman in the world, the fabulous ladies, close up, looking in camera, mysterious, mesmerizing, gorgeous perfect face with a strong emphasis on character design --ar 9:16 --niji 5 --style expressive

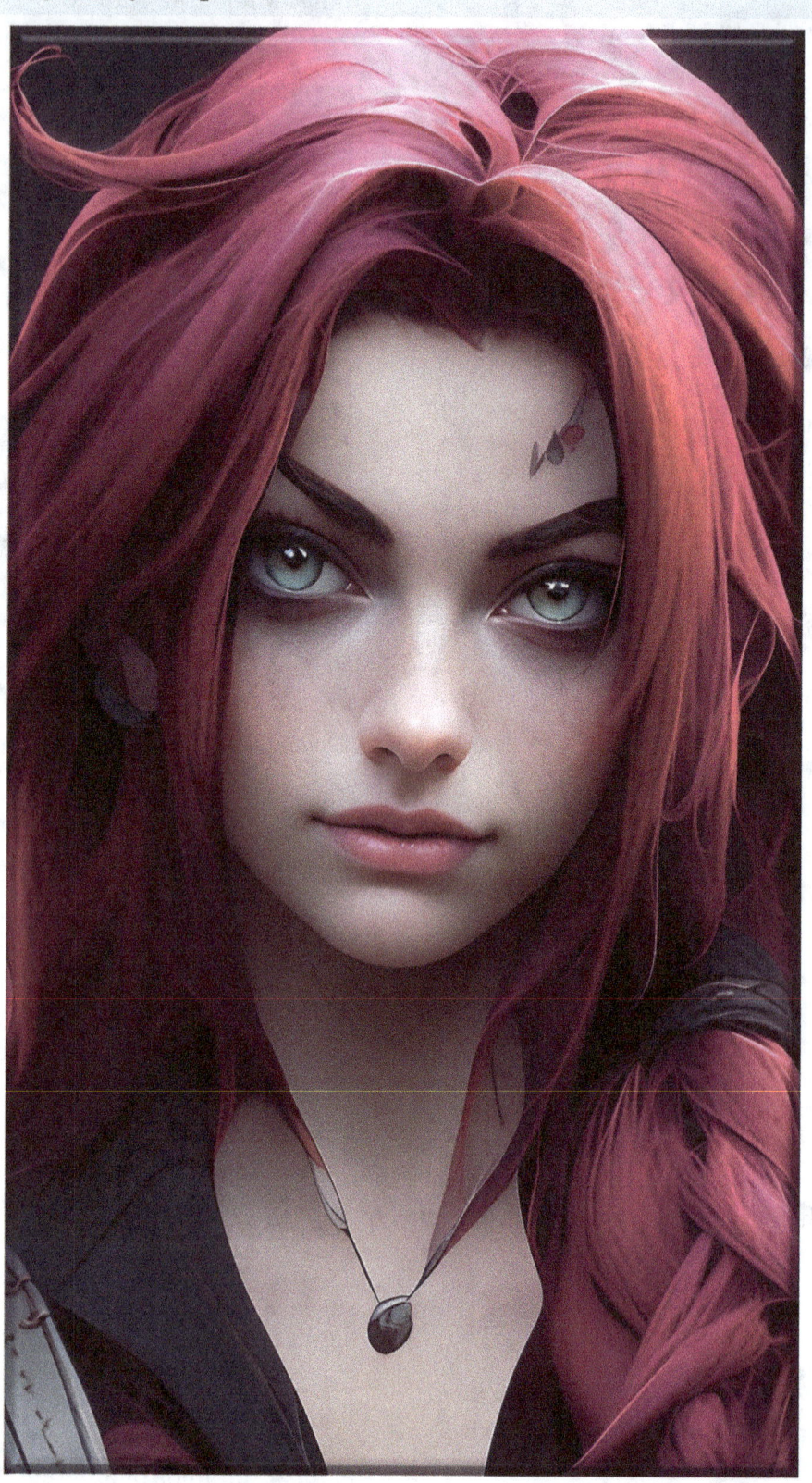

Jump Start, Step 10:

Journey On

That's it!

For much more detail and answers to questions, refer to your artistic companion, **Beginning with Midjourney**.

If you need up-to-the-minute updates to the ever-changing Midjourney web suite, refer to the User Guide on the Midjourney website.

Don't be afraid to experiment, try new things, and let your imagination run wild. With Midjourney AI, the possibilities are endless, and you'll be amazed at the artwork you can create, even with minimal experience. (It took me a few weeks to learn, and then I was off and running.)

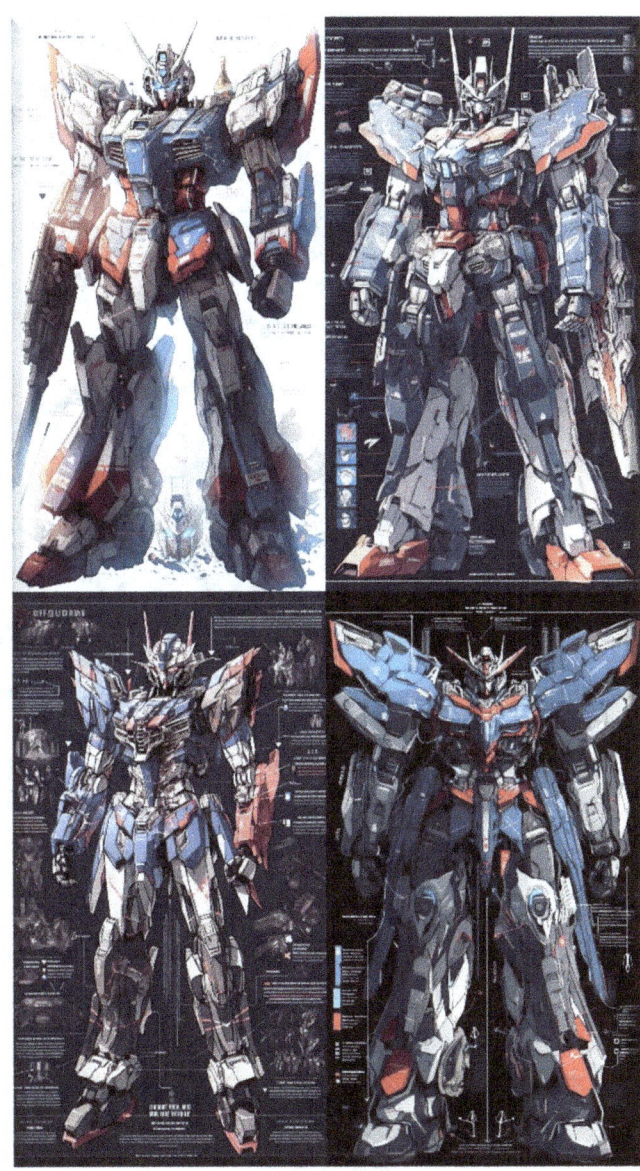

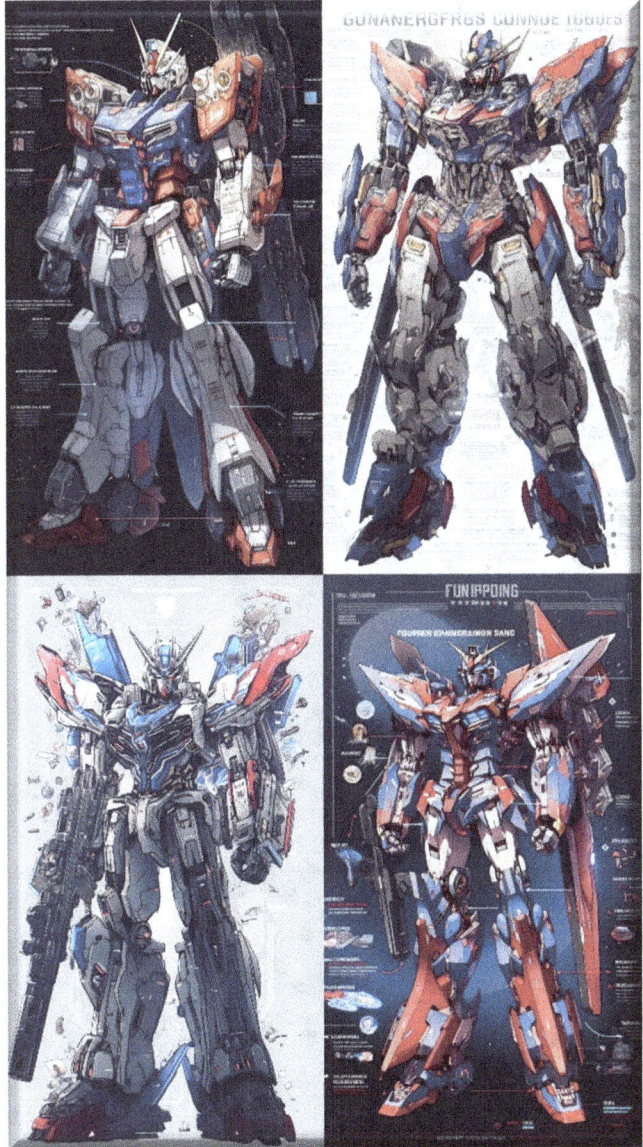

Creating art is a journey, and Midjourney AI is a powerful tool that can help you unlock your creativity and bring your artistic visions to life.

Also, don't forget that you can endlessly reroll new iterations of a prompt code, if you can feel that you are very close to a breakthrough but Midjourney has not quite caught up to your imagination yet. Trying changing the wording a bit, and running some more generations, and see what you can come up with – in the same way that the image grids on this page resulted in the curated image on the next page.

FOLIO IMAGE 005

/imagine   **Dynamic, cutaway infographic, a mecha like Optimus Prime and a Jaeger, or the most epic Gundam in the world, the fabulous mecha, mysterious, mesmerizing, gorgeous perfect mecha with a strong emphasis on character design --ar 9:16 --niji 5**

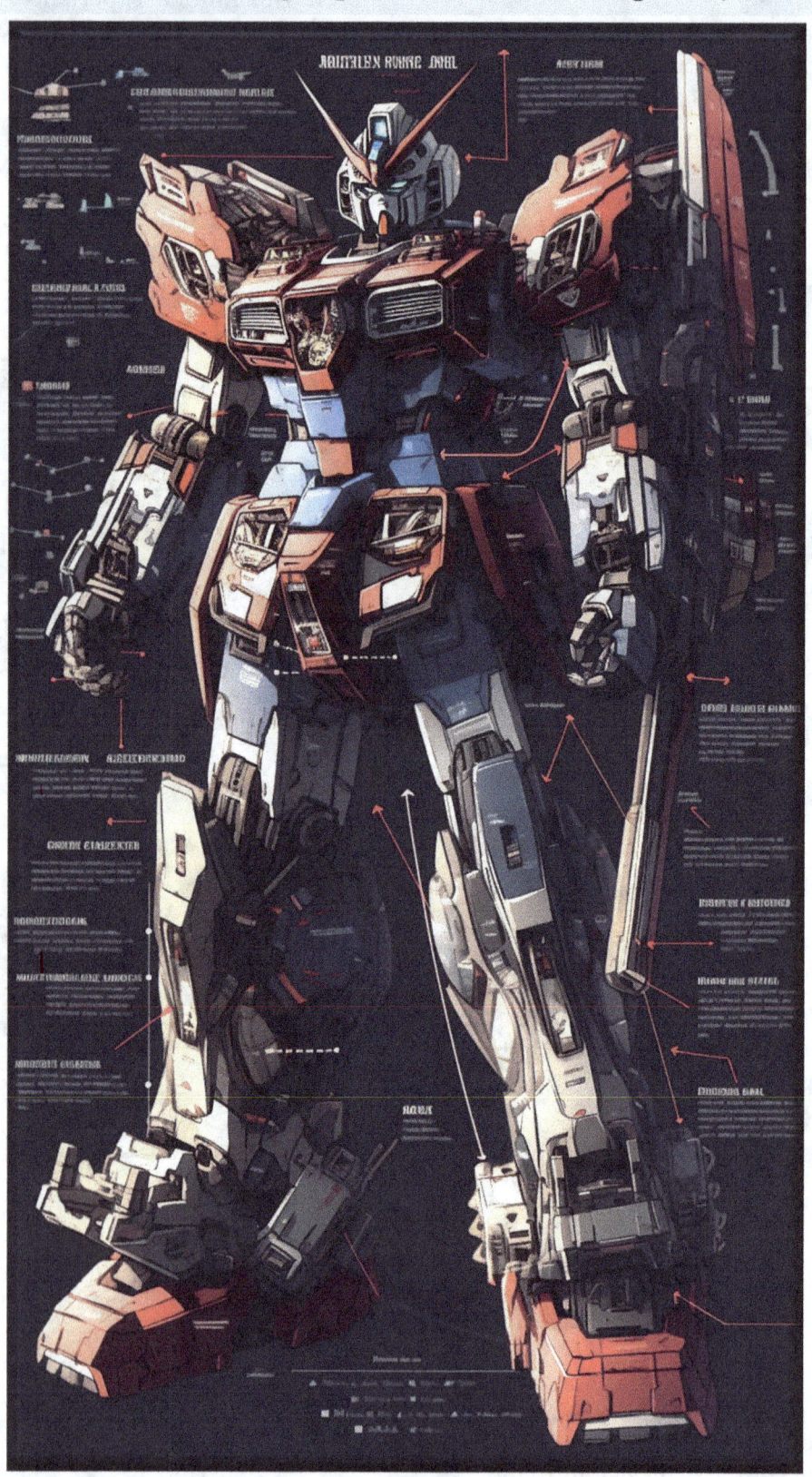

Two:
The World of Anime

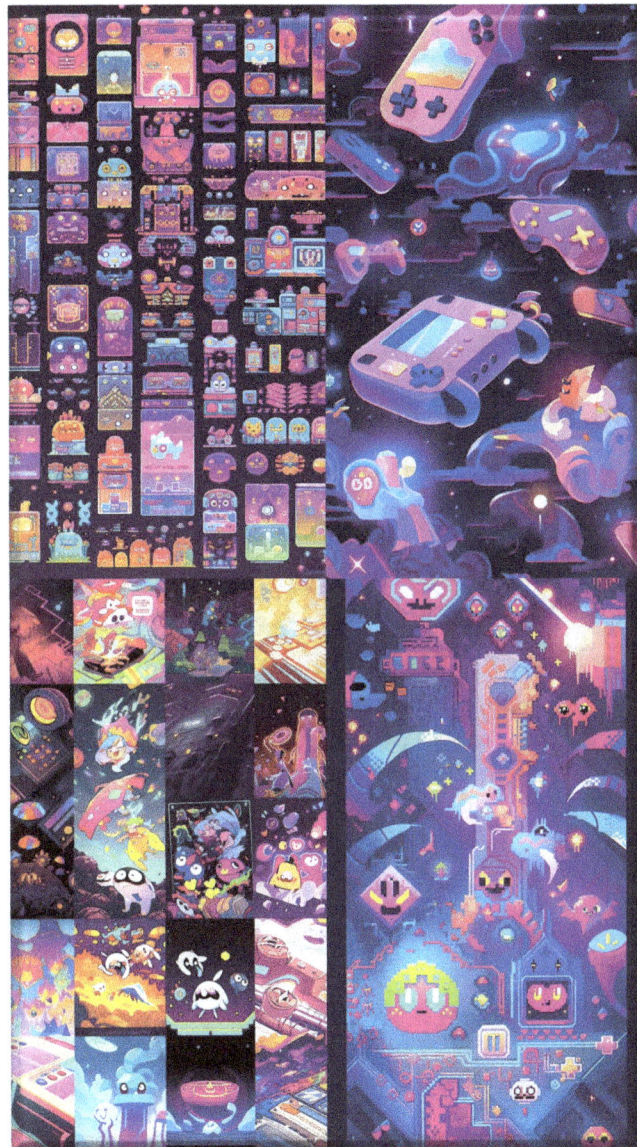

The Importance of Anime Art

So, to be precise: What is anime art?

Anime art is a unique and captivating form of visual storytelling that originated in Japan. Over the decades, it has gained worldwide popularity. I myself experienced and loved the genre – although I didn't know what it was as a child at the time, in Mundelein, Illinois during the 1970s – through groundbreaking "Americanized" shows such as *Speed Racer*, *Kimba the White Lion*, *Star Blazers*, and *Battle of the Planets*.

(I also loved anime-adjacent works and toys, such as *Shogun Warriors*, *Godzilla*, *Big Robot*, and the *Micronauts*. You will find some of these fantastic influences throughout this book.)

Anime is characterized by its distinct style, which often features large, expressive eyes, colorful and vibrant hair, and intensified facial expressions that convey a wide range of emotions.

Anime art encompasses a wide variety of genres, including action, adventure, romance, fantasy, sci-fi, horror, and more, catering to diverse interests and tastes. The great thing about it, in my opinion, is that it is an aesthetic movement rather than a single product or artistic approach.

You can find anime shows, movies, books, art, cosplay, and graphic novels, and even though two sources can be very different from one another, they both share the same recognizable imagery and spirit.

One of the most distinctive aspects of anime art, to me, is its ability to capture the imagination and to evoke strong emotions. Whether it's through the dynamic action sequences, heartwarming relationships between characters, or the breathtakingly beautiful landscapes, anime art has a way of drawing viewers into its rich and immersive worlds.

Anime creates an immediate and direct emotional bond with the invested viewer. I can still remember the first time I rooted for Speedy's Mach Five to beat the bad guys, waking my mom out of her nap, which didn't go so well as I recall …

Another hallmark of anime art, I believe, is its attention to detail. From the intricate costumes and weapons to the elaborate settings and backgrounds, anime artists pour their creativity and craftsmanship into every frame.

Each character is meticulously designed with their own unique personality traits, quirks, and backstories, making them relatable and memorable to the audience. Even specific mecha, vehicles, and anime locations can pull at your heartstrings once you get yourself fully immersed in a good story.

FOLIO IMAGE 006

/imagine   **Close-up, a girl like Ibuki, Yakuza tattoos, a portrait, standing in a Dojo, photorealism, brown ninja outfit, portrait of a masked female ninja, singularity sculpted, karate hands, intense stare, intricate stitching, long black hair --ar 9:16 --niji 5 --style expressive**

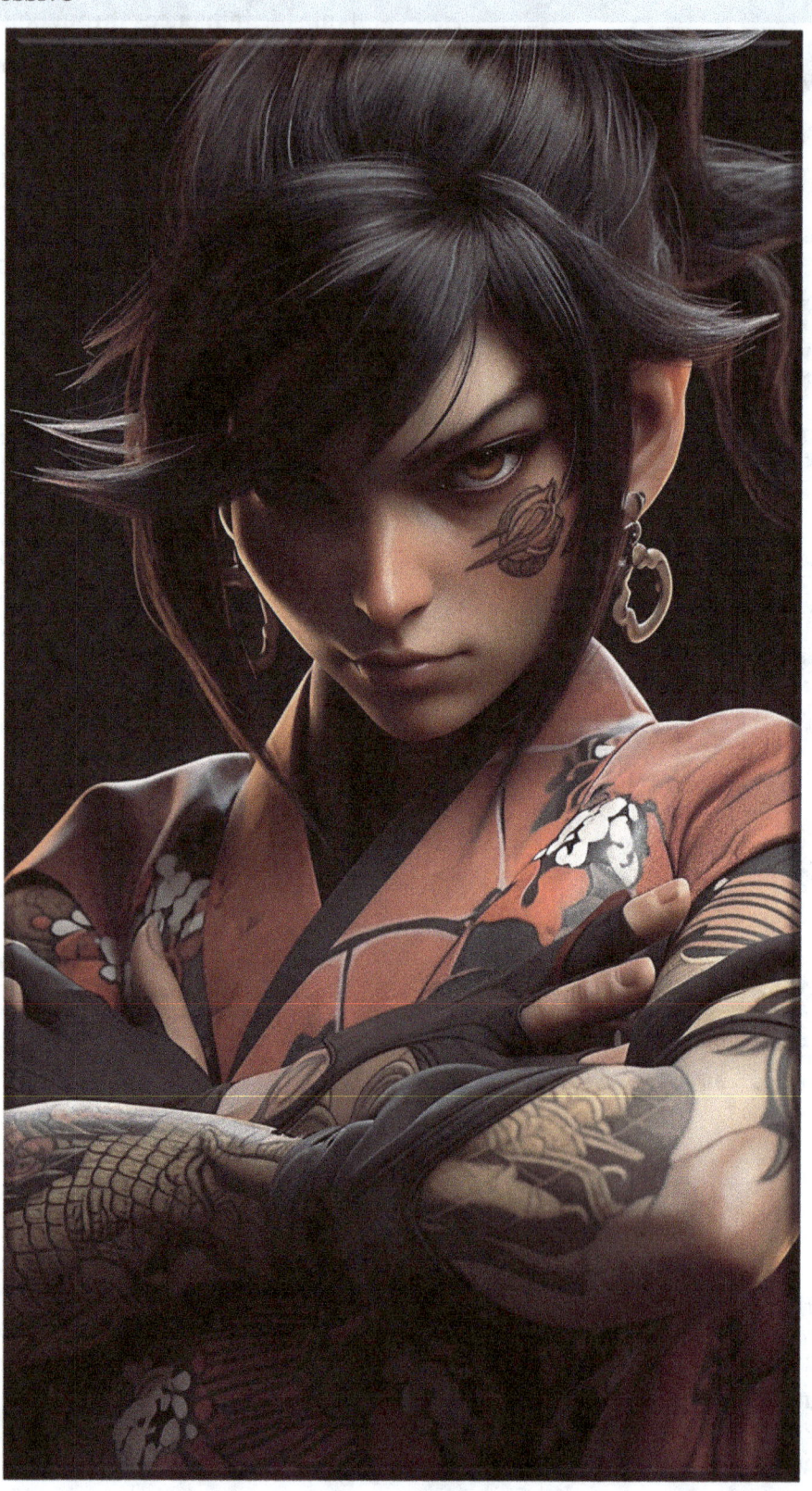

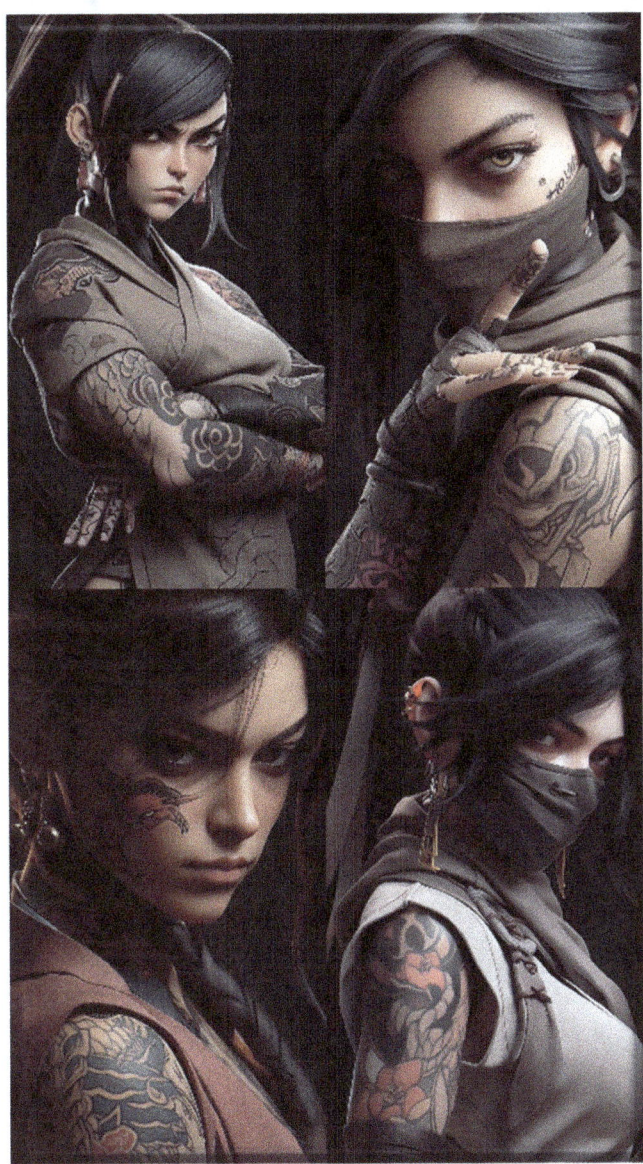

Beyond its visual appeal, anime art also explores deep and thought-provoking themes, addressing important topics such as love, friendship, family, self-identity, and societal issues. Even if you didn't begin your childhood with Gaiking, Great Mazinga, and Raideen – in which case I feel for you – you will learn all at once that anime can be funny, heartwarming, thrilling, or tear-jerking, often leaving a lasting impact on viewers and inspiring them to think critically about the world around them. And it can often make you laugh, marvel, and empathize deeply all at the same time. But it's not just about you and your own love of the form, if you want to reach out. Anime art has a vibrant and dedicated fan community that spans across the globe.

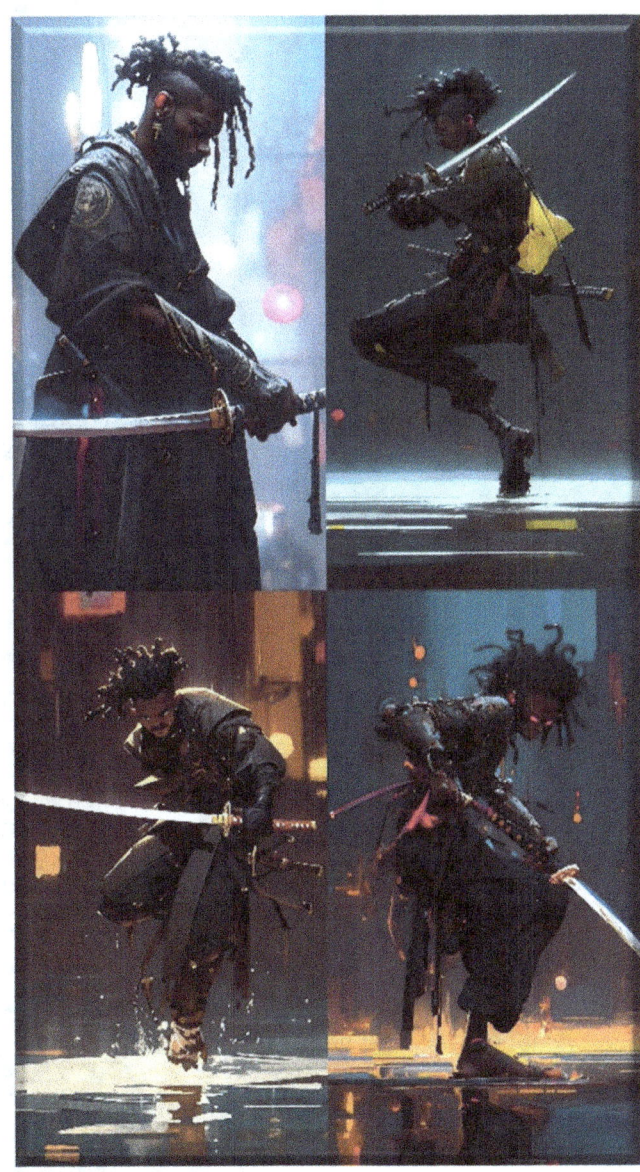

You'll also find that anime art embraces a wide range of artistic techniques and styles, from traditional hand-drawn animation to cutting-edge digital art. This allows for endless creativity and innovation, with artists constantly pushing the boundaries of what's possible in terms of visual storytelling.

And when you're working in Midjourney, you can often create entirely new effects and even concepts that other people have not yet imagined.

That's one of the truly beautiful things about combining anime and Midjourney: It quickly takes on a life of its own, and it does that through your careful and consistent iterations upon a good idea.

FOLIO IMAGE 007

/imagine   **Dark fantasy, a woman like Sylvanas Windrunner, or an elf maiden necromancer, as a Fortnite or other videogame character, 3D realistic render, full body image, dark background, character design --ar 9:16 --style expressive --niji 5**

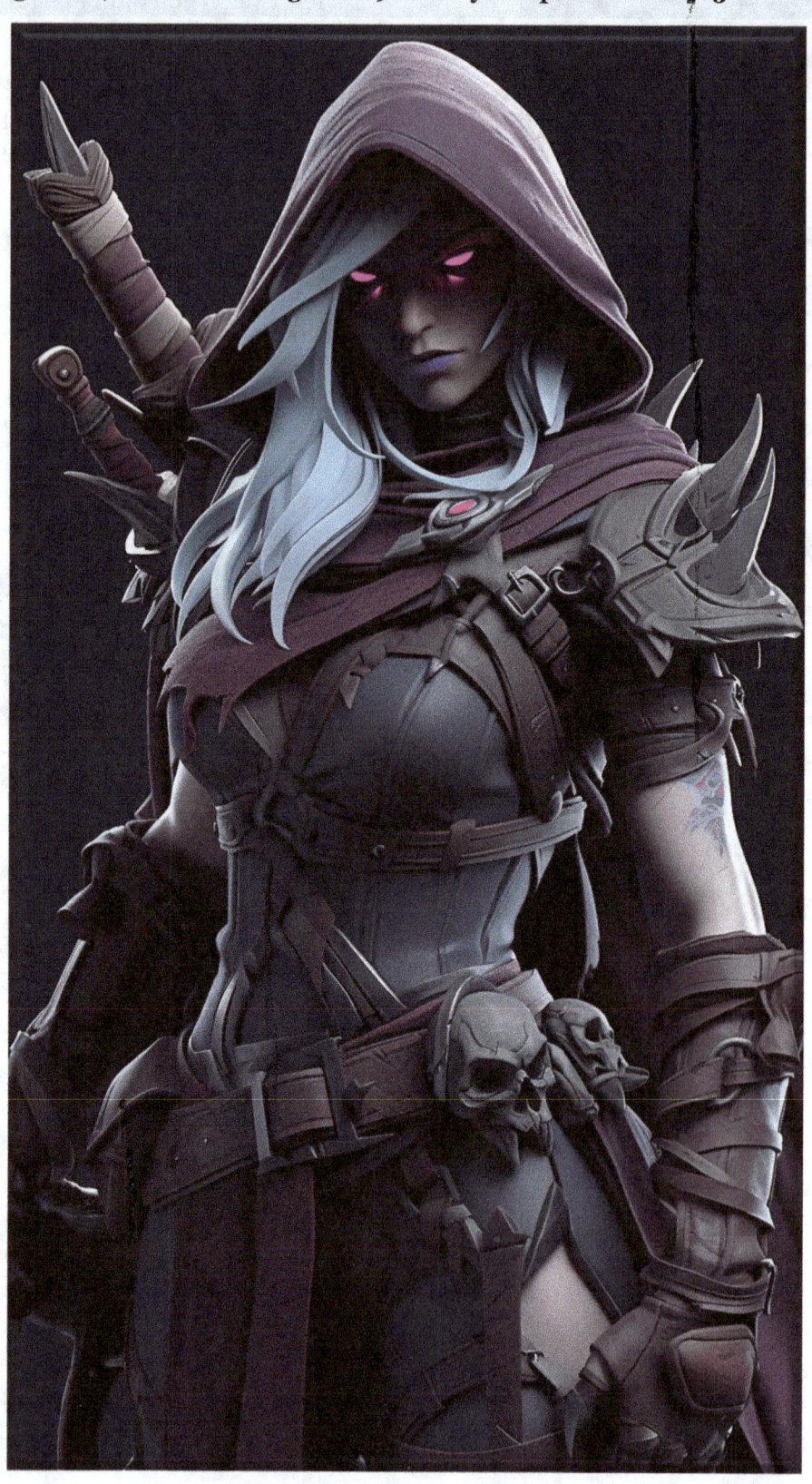

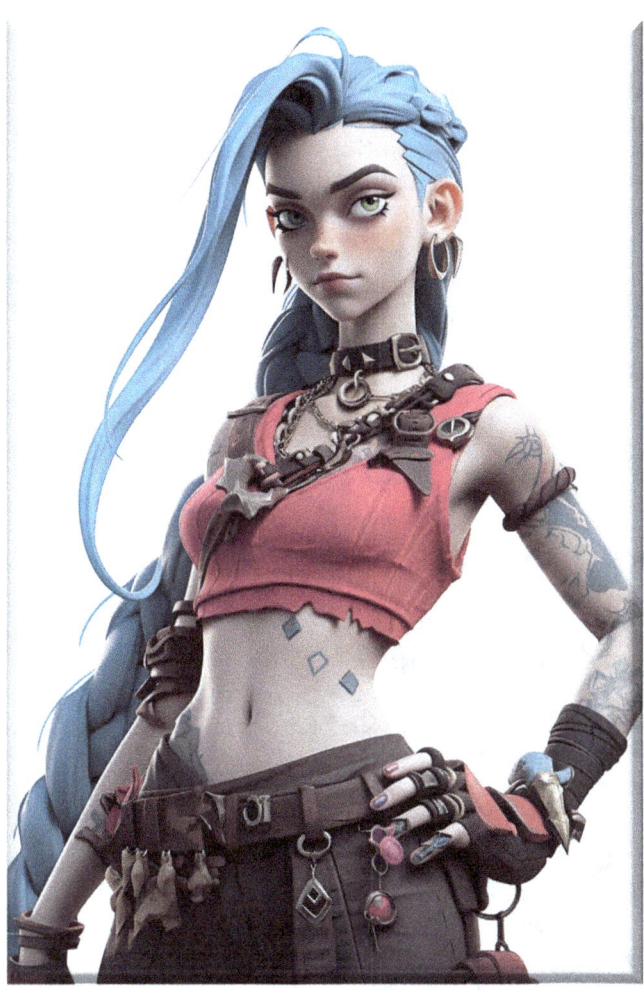

compels, and inspires people from all over the world. It brings together people from all walks of life, and even all generations, with its unique blend of creativity, storytelling, and community.

And when you combine anime with Midjourney, you'll find that you can share your own amazing anime creations with people around the world without leaving your own home. It's truly a beautiful thing.

Why Midjourney for Anime?

That's easy: Because it helps you to create stunningly beautiful digital art with ease, once you get the hang of it.

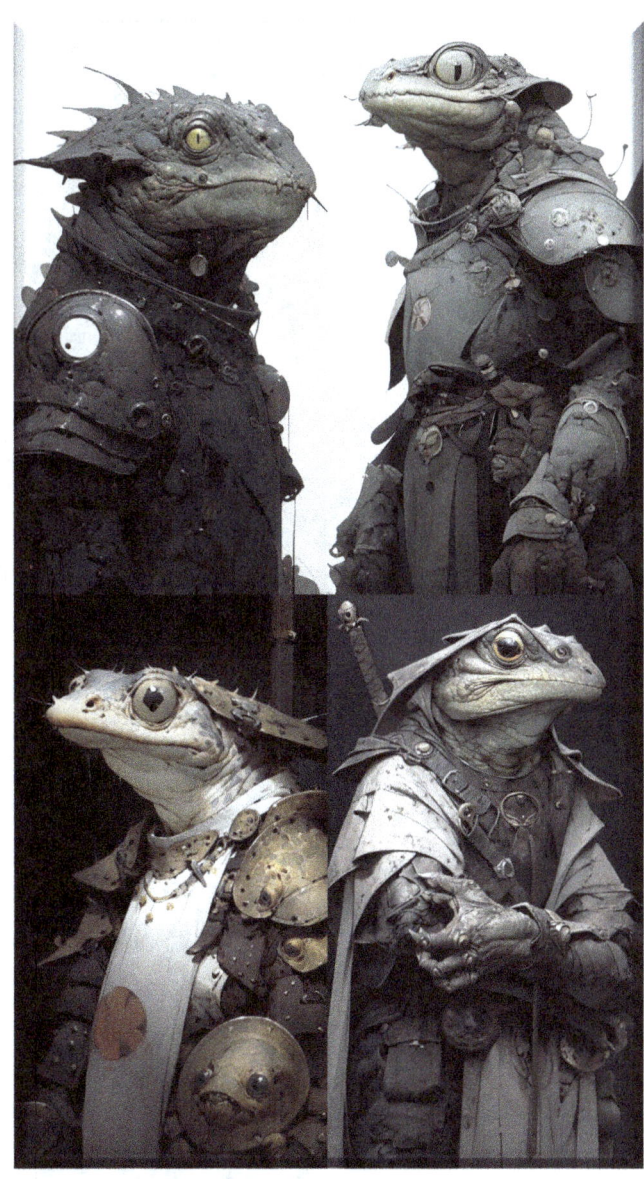

Fans of anime (sometimes self-identifying as *Otaku*) come together to celebrate their shared passion through anime cons, gaming cons, sci fi cons, cosplay, fan art, movie lines, stores, product releases, episode premiere countdowns, graphic novel release dates, bookstore events, and online discussions. To name but a few venues, of course.

More than once, I have struck up a good conversation with other anime fans just because they liked and identified the subject on my T-shirt for the day. This sense of community and camaraderie adds another layer of enjoyment and engagement to the world of anime art.

And why does all of this matter? It's because anime art is visually captivating, emotionally resonant, and a never-ending form of storytelling. It encompasses a massive range of genres – perhaps soon, even *all* genres – along with art styles and techniques.

And through Midjourney, you'll soon find that it is a digital art medium that delights,

FOLIO IMAGE 008

/imagine   **An Afropunk Samurai Warrior practicing sword fighting, in the mixed style of Moebius and Frazetta and Giancola, dynamic flowing action shot, splashes of water, night, reflections, defocused cyber city background, cinematic, with anamorphic bokeh, dramatic lighting, backlit, vibrant raking light, long shadows, boosted chromatic aberration, cyberpunk epic --ar 9:16 --style expressive --niji 5**

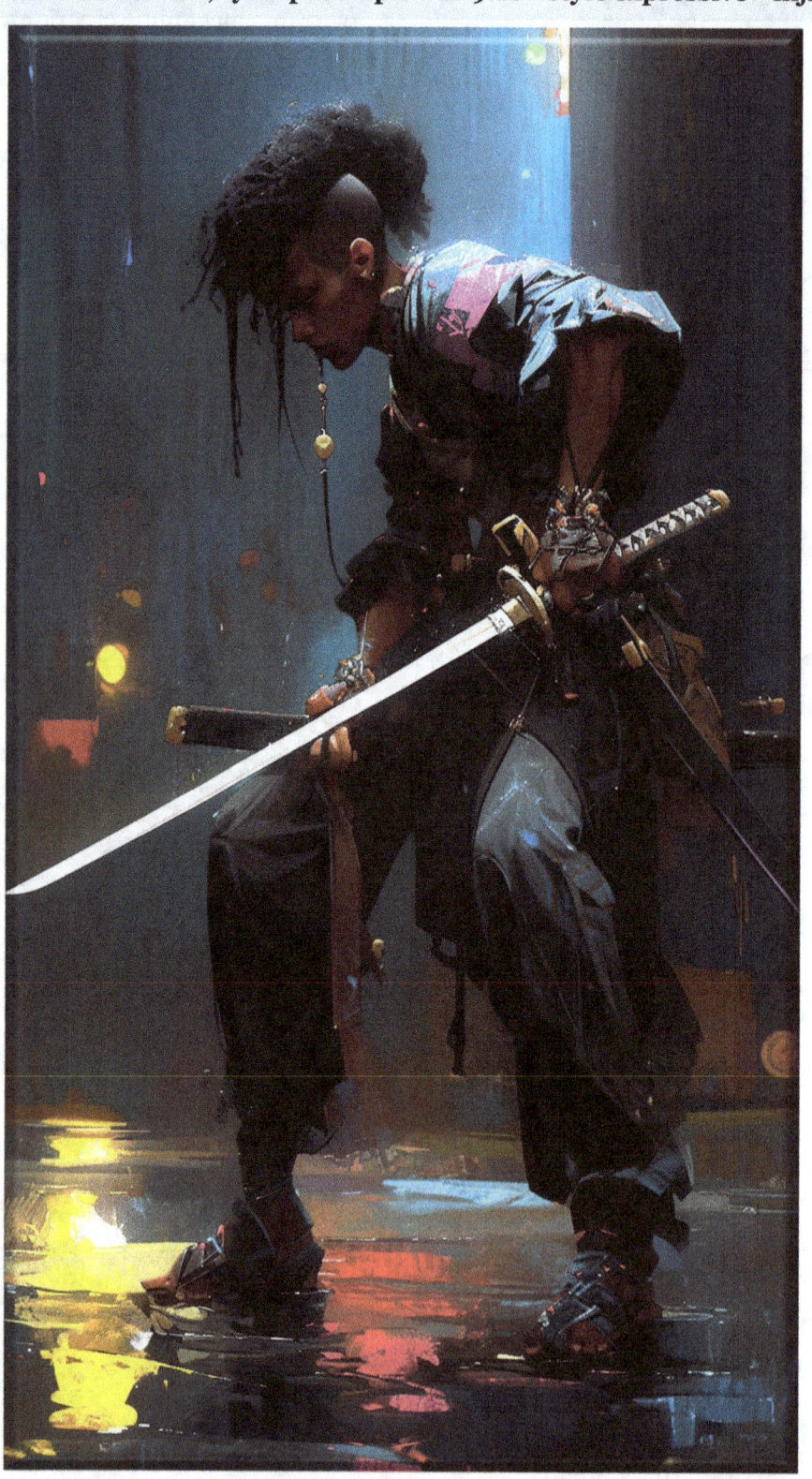

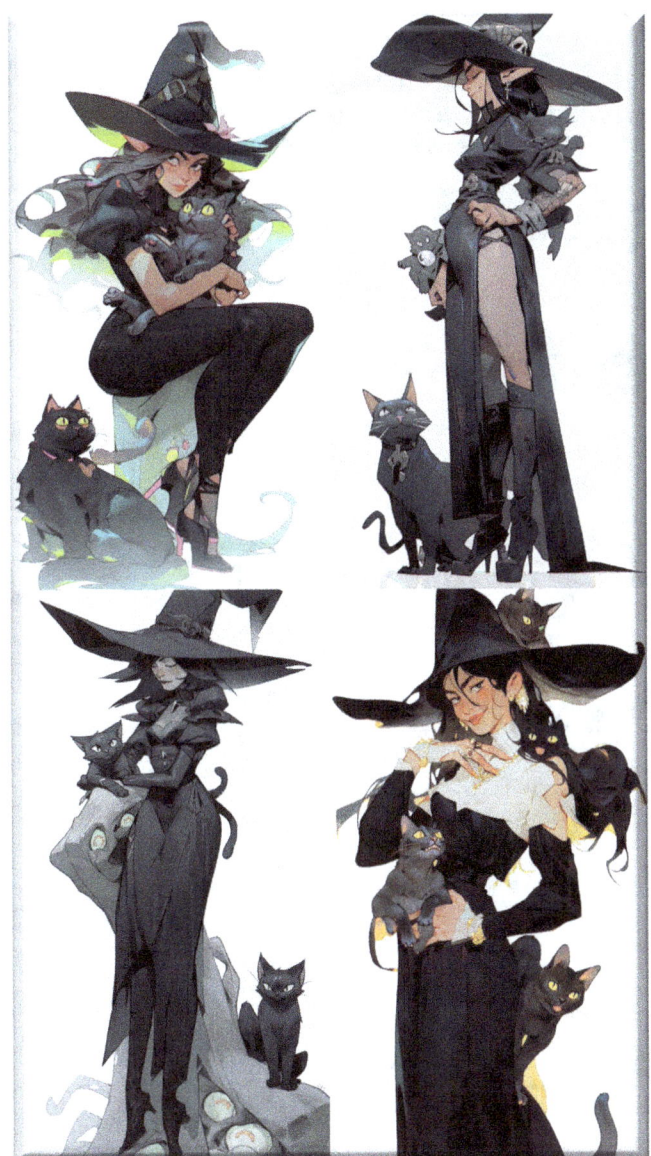

Every human is creative, even if they don't think that they are. Everyone has a vision, even if it's only in their dreams.

Midjourney levels the playing field between professionals and initiates. It gives disadvantaged or hesitant people a creative amplifier, one that they can use to voice their own convictions and to frame their own emerging aesthetic, captured in a visual form that can be shared with – and admired by – literally anyone.

Midjourney does not care how old you are, where you live, where you came from, what your initial skill level is, what your emotional challenges are, or whether or not you are differently abled.

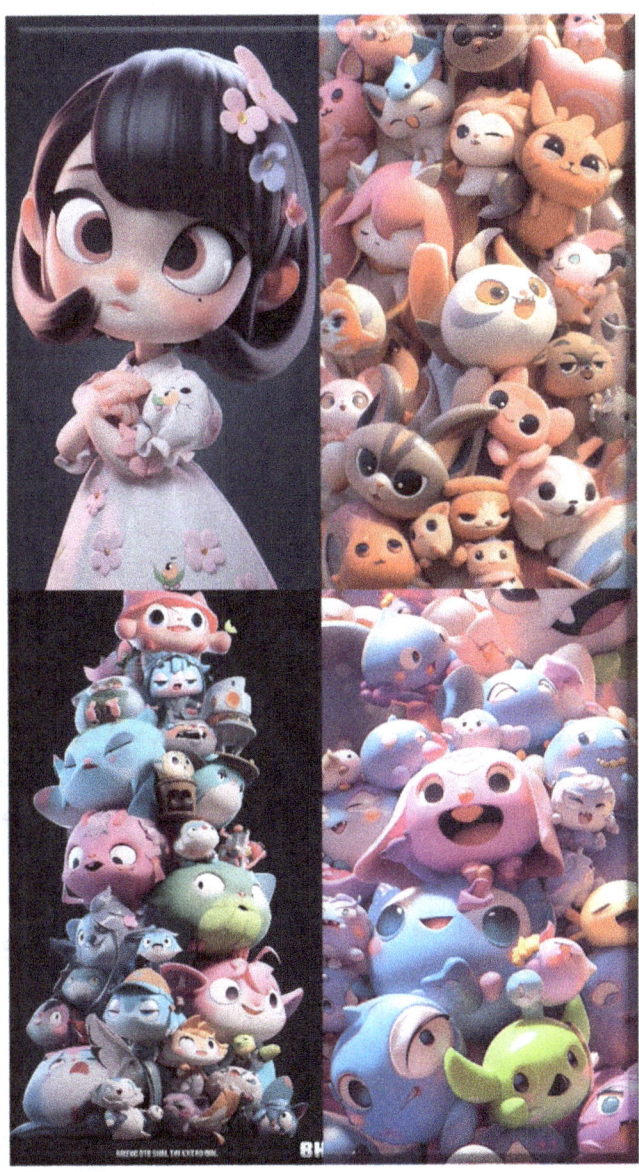

Creating anime art with Midjourney is at first very frustrating – you will bounce off of an endless array of conceptual walls that you didn't know were there – but soon, it becomes fascinating and very rewarding. You can use MJ AI to create any kind of anime art. You'll find that it's a truly exciting and genuinely immersive experience. It empowers you to unleash your creativity, to awaken your imagination, and to bring your own unique artistic vision into life.

My favorite thing about Midjourney is that it sings to people who might not be able to draw, paint, digitally create in Photoshop, or photograph professionally. Midjourney is empowering and compelling. It coaxes you to awaken your ideas, and to crystallize them into being.

FOLIO IMAGE 009

/imagine   So many characters, boys and girls, cute, Kawaii, Chibi, cartoon, colorful, adorable, playful, fun, whimsical, quirky, super cute, Japanese theme, anthropomorphic, Unreal rendering, high detail, 3D --ar 9:16 --style expressive --niji 5

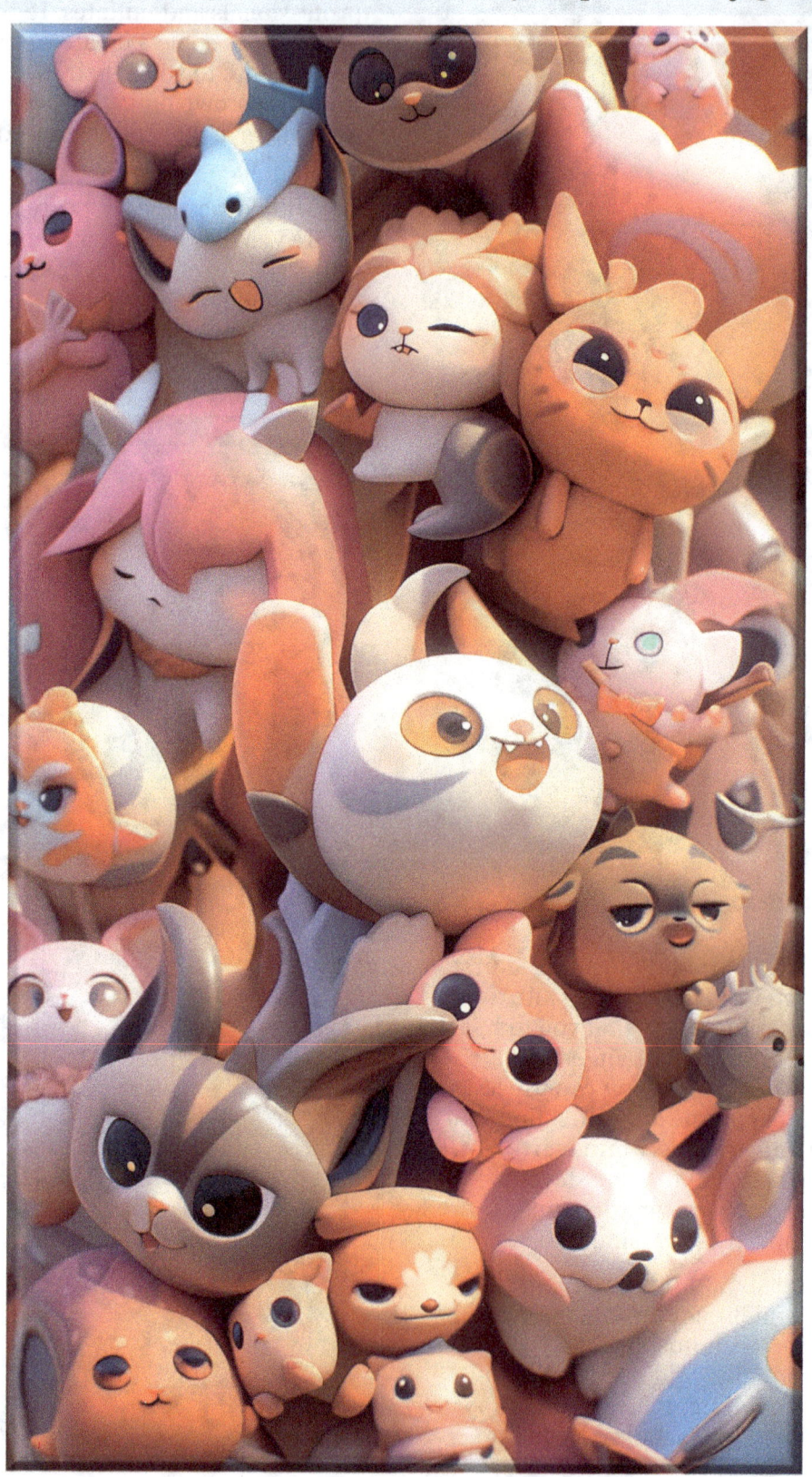

If you have arthritis, or one hand, or poor eyesight, or you can't move, or (like me) your hands hurt now when you put art pen to paper for more than a few minutes, that is perfectly fine. Because Midjourney doesn't care.

But it isn't uncaring in a malicious way. It's ambivalent toward you and your creativity in a very inviting way. I tell all of the curious people that are new to AI-empowered art – and there are a lot of them, I promise you – that Midjourney is a mansion filled floor to ceiling with unloved misfit toys. You might recognize some of the toys, but most of them will be unfamiliar and yet amazing. Once you take those toys in and make them your own, they'll immediately show you how promising and gifted they really are.

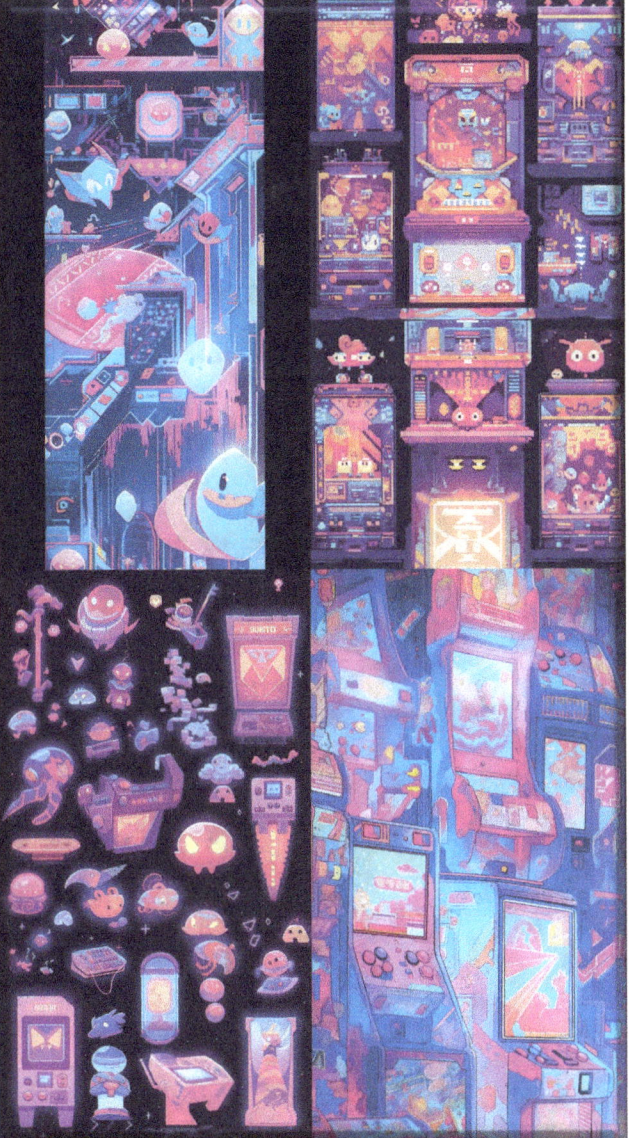

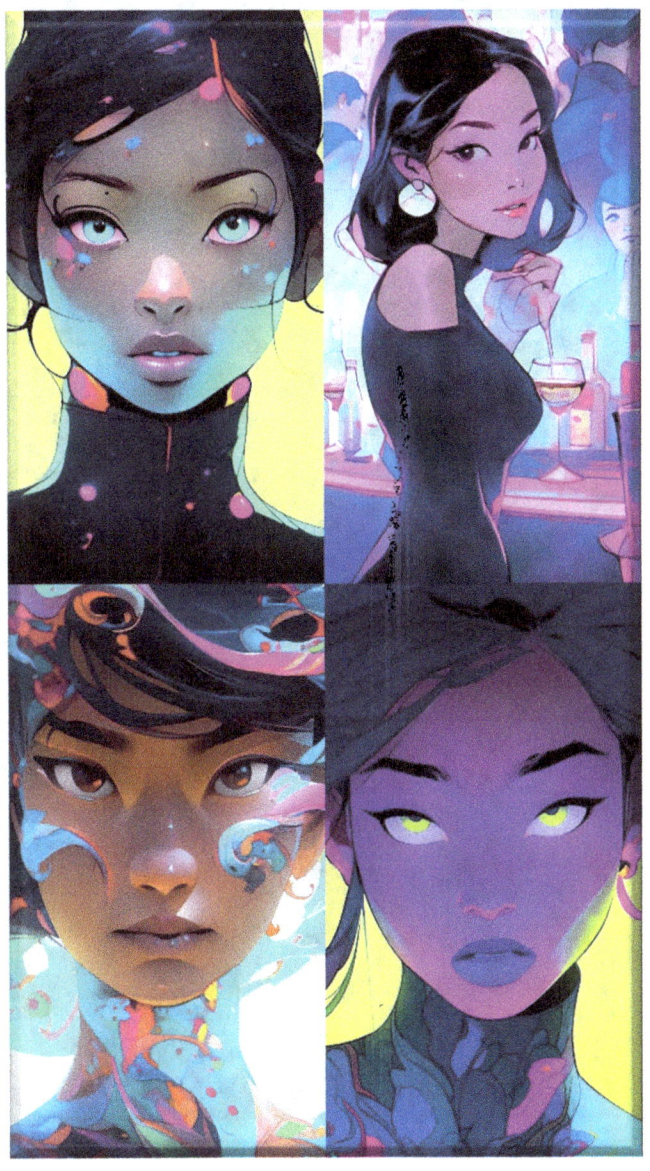

You will never be the first person to play with the toys, but you will always be the first person to play with those toys in ways that echo the scenes in your own dreams and imagination.

And you will always be the first and only person to arrange those toys in new ways that resonate with you, in ways that create new assemblages of ideas, because the number of possible arrangements is both infinite and limited only by the bounds of your own imagination.

This book serves as a guide map, if you will, to all of the best and nearest playrooms throughout the mansion that I have found (so far). But you are invited to – and in fact, you will need to – explore all of those rooms on your own.

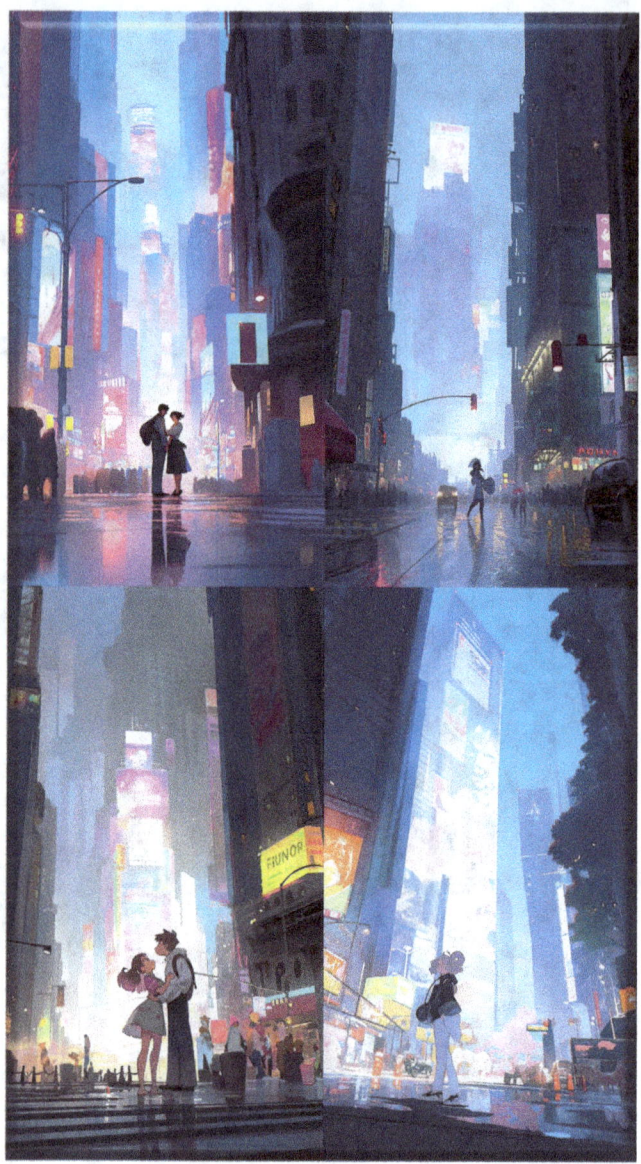

And in turn, those people will show you things that will give you more new ideas.

Such is the consensual yet individual creative potential inherent in the human spirit.

That's what Midjourney and other AI-empowered art brings to the table. And it is indeed why everyone is amazed, and afraid.

You will find that Midjourney has unique anime-specific tools that make this revolution in humanistic digital imagery even more powerful than you might otherwise expect.

I'd like to show you what that means.

Right this way, mind the owls …

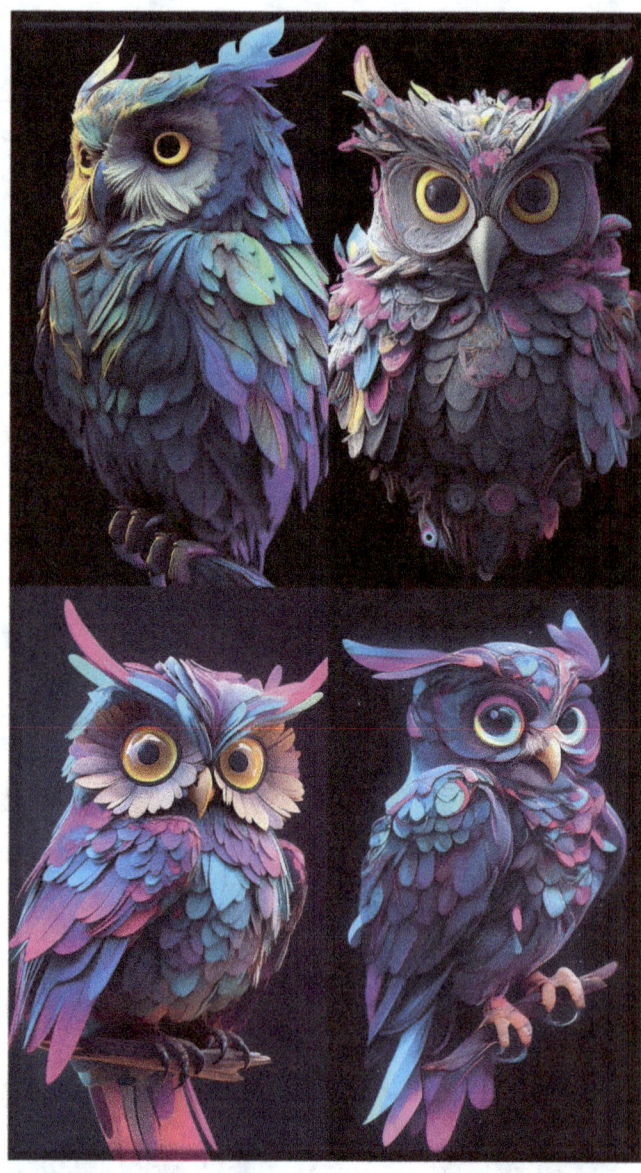

No one else can know which toys you want to pick up, and which formations you will put them in, to create your own first epic scene.

And so, you will inspire others, and they will come into the mansion too.

And you will learn new lessons from those other people's combinations – artistic decisions made by others that you want to avoid – while you're learning even more from the people that you find personally inspiring.

Because others will find in your works things that they never imagined, or – even better – things that they always imagined, but could never concretely see.

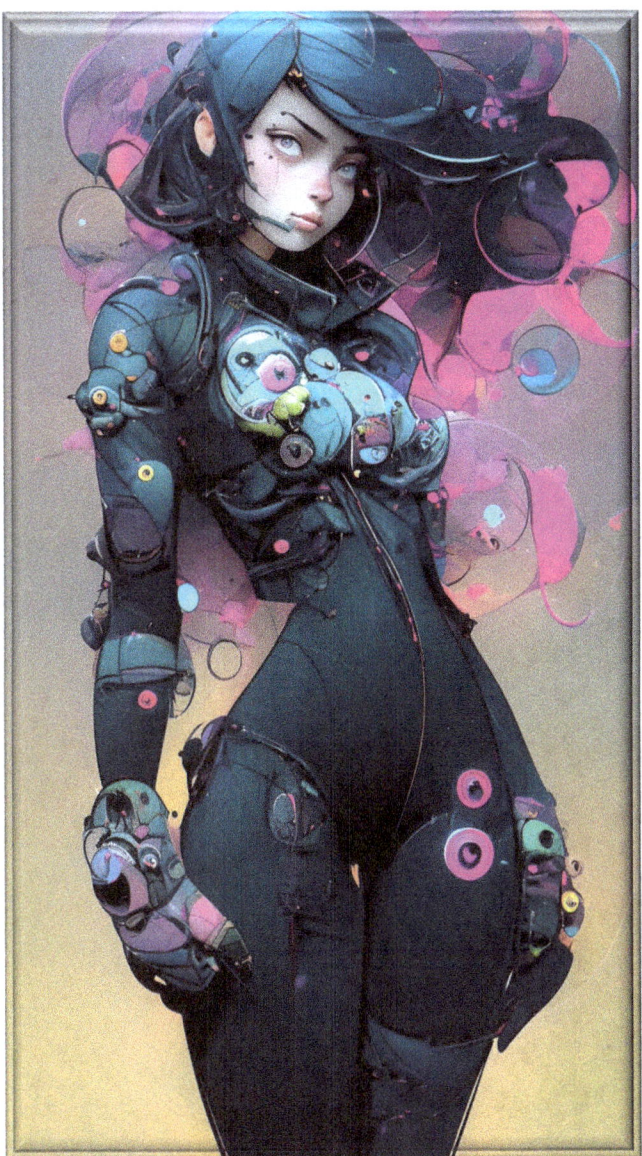

This book is here to help you if you're either bold or shy.

You'll be on your own to some extent, of course, if that is the way you choose.

But it's all up to you.

Whichever way you want to do things, the pages of this book will serve as gateways to the imaginary places that you want to get to, in order to make them real.

So let's get ready to explore!

Our first stop, right outside the mansion, is in an inspiring open place that we call Niji.

Niji, next stop, mind the gap …

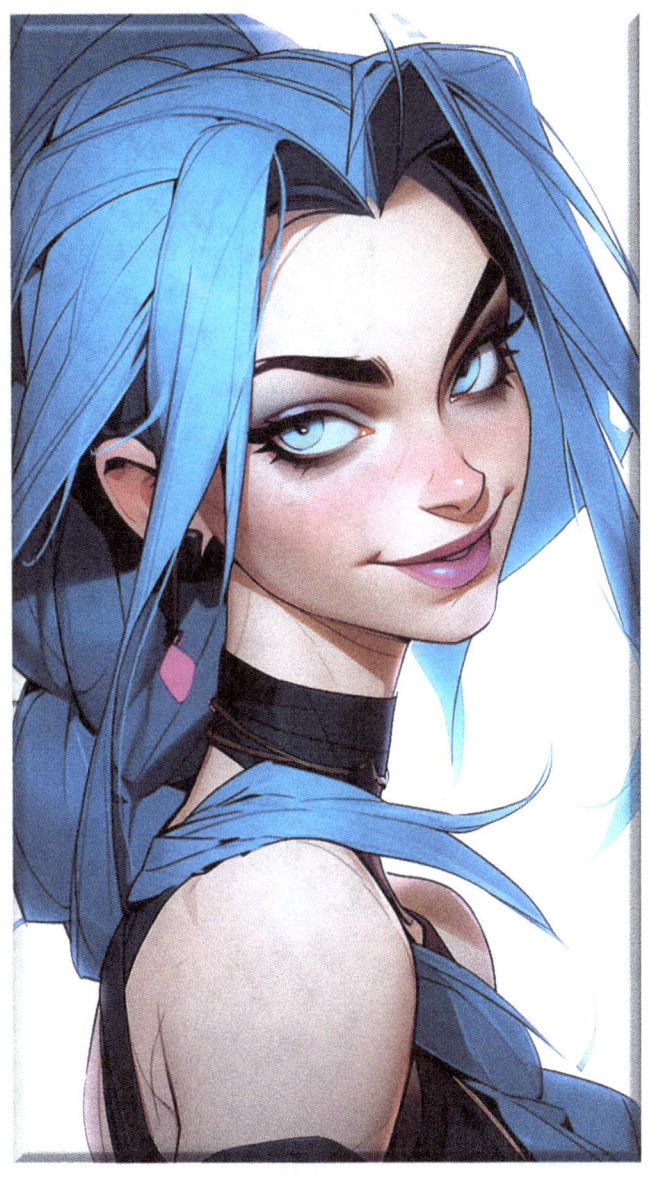

You can either read my earlier book **Beginning with Midjourney** to get started, or you can read my Jump Start guide at the beginning of this book.

If you already know what you're doing, you can use this book as a prompting guide to enhance your own codes for better image creation and improved aesthetics (not to mention many new ideas).

And on the off chance that you're the type of person who likes to dive right in and then prevent yourself from drowning, you can refer to this book's pages whenever you find yourself in a deep place that you can't quite seem to get out of.

FOLIO IMAGE 010

/imagine   **He walks in darkness, he looks to the light, attractive handsome man, tall, manly face, strong chest, strong arms, trim beard, short black haircut style, serious neutral expression, suit, walking in New York, cyberpunk street scene --ar 9:16 –style expressive --niji 5**

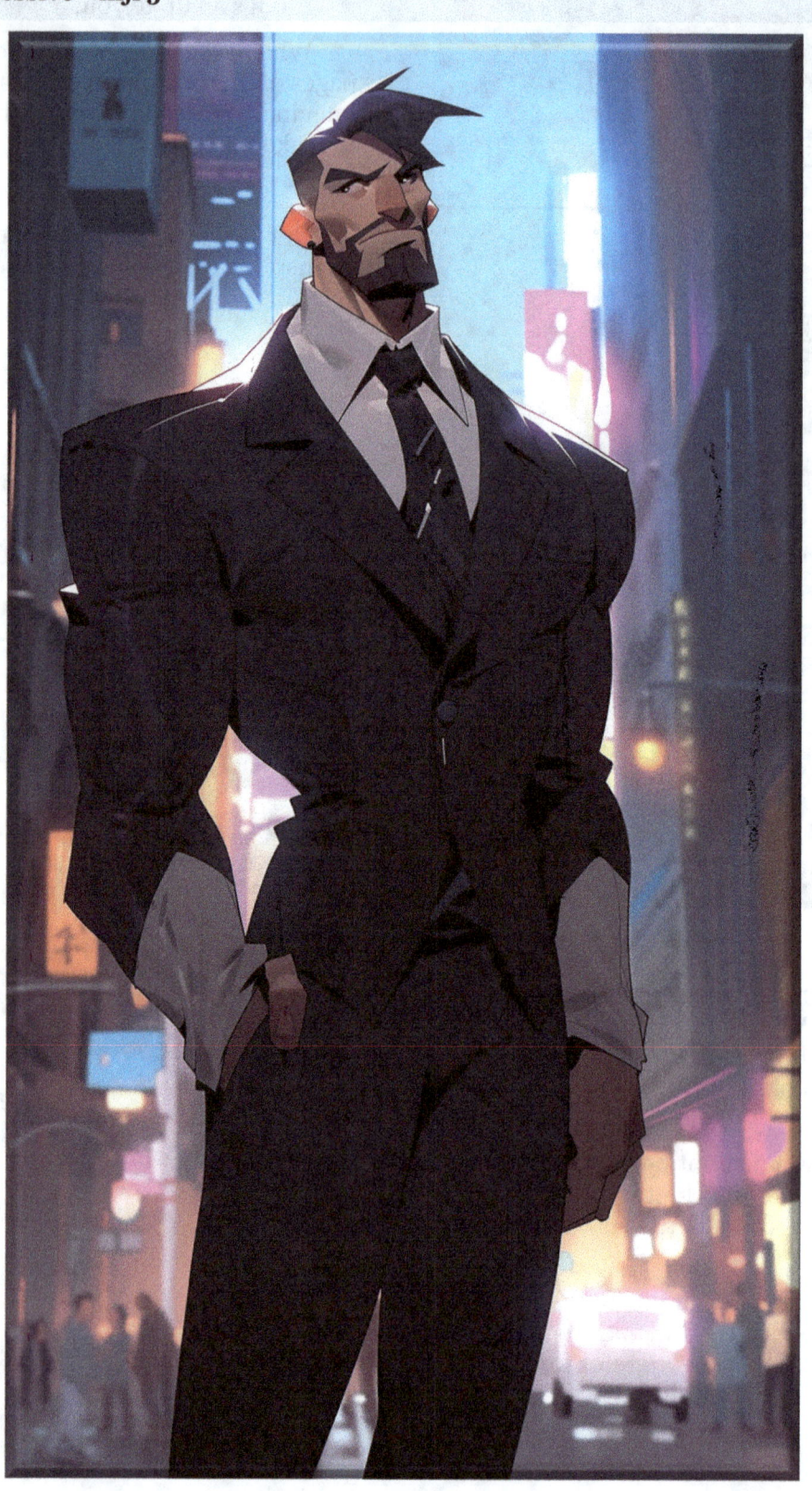

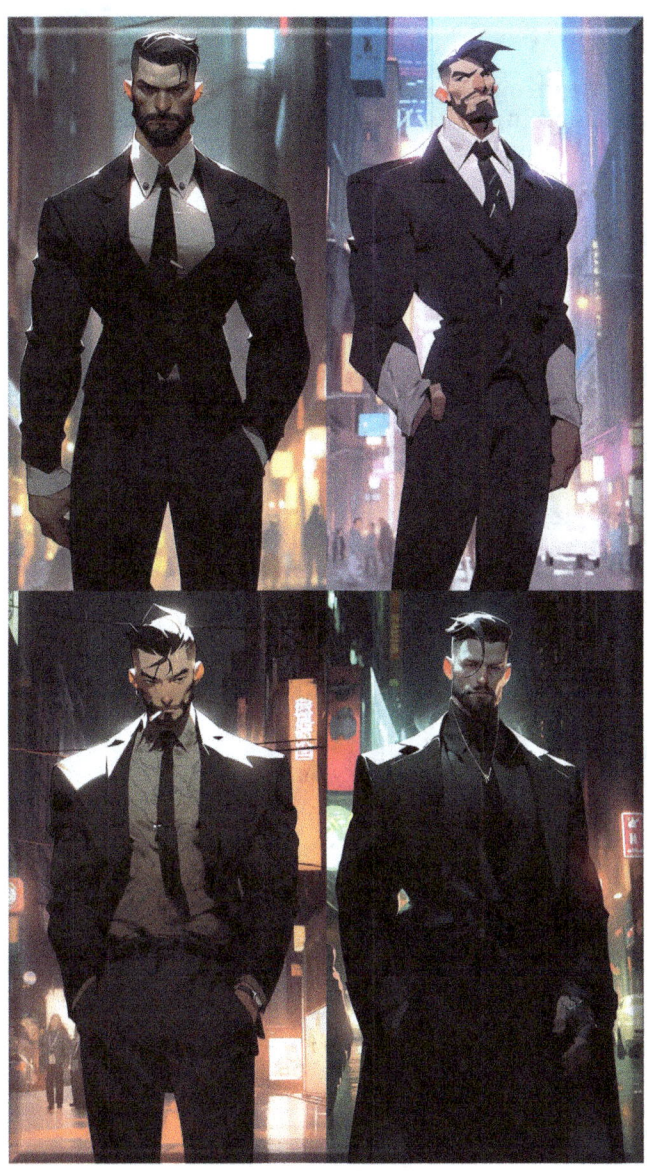

As you probably already know, a "prompt" is a descriptive code paragraph that tells Midjourney what you want to create. The additive prompt subcode **--niji** tells Midjourney that you want to craft images with a decidedly anime-driven style, look, and emotional impact.

If a prompt is an artist's box filled with paints and brushes and other tools, --niji is a very specific many-colored paintbrush that never runs out. When you tell Midjourney to use Niji, you are telling it to paint with that brush to the exclusion of others. You can see the difference by adding **--niji 5** to any MJ prompt that doesn't already include it, or by deleting it and noting how your prompt's visual output changes as a direct result.

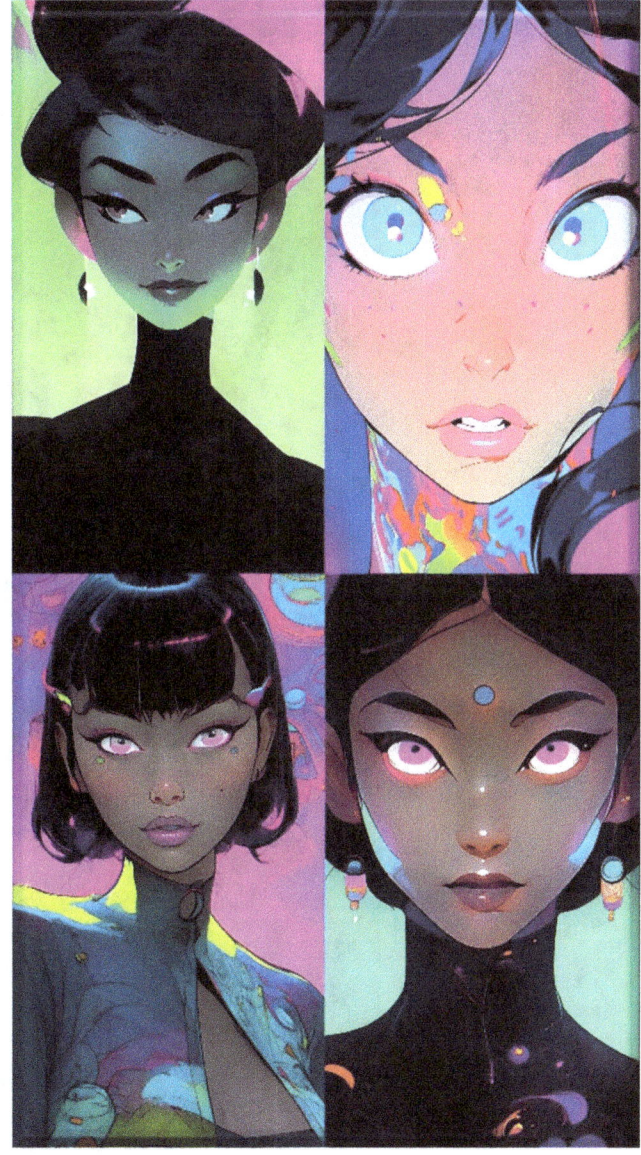

In Midjourney, What Is Niji?

Niji is an expressive space. Niji as an idea can mean "prism," "rainbow spectrum," or "two-dimensional." In Japan, Niji is a subculture that symbolizes diversity, welcomeness, free life choices, and creativity channeled through artistic expression, sharing, and storytelling.

More specifically, a bit away from counterculture and over in the world of AI-empowered art, Midjourney Niji is a groundbreaking artistic and stylistic generative model that makes anime subjects look better than ever before through the use of unique deep learning technology. And beyond the actual Niji space, it gives all non-anime subjects an anime-driven lens that we can look through to behold things in strikingly new ways.

FOLIO IMAGE 011

/imagine   **Beautiful closeup, young gorgeous stylish stunning Asian sci fi cantina bartender in the trippy galaxy cantina, penetrating mesmerizing eyes, retro futuristic 1950s space age, sci - fi beautiful pop surrealism noir art, noir pop art deco, vivid and vibrant --ar 9:16 --style expressive --niji 5**

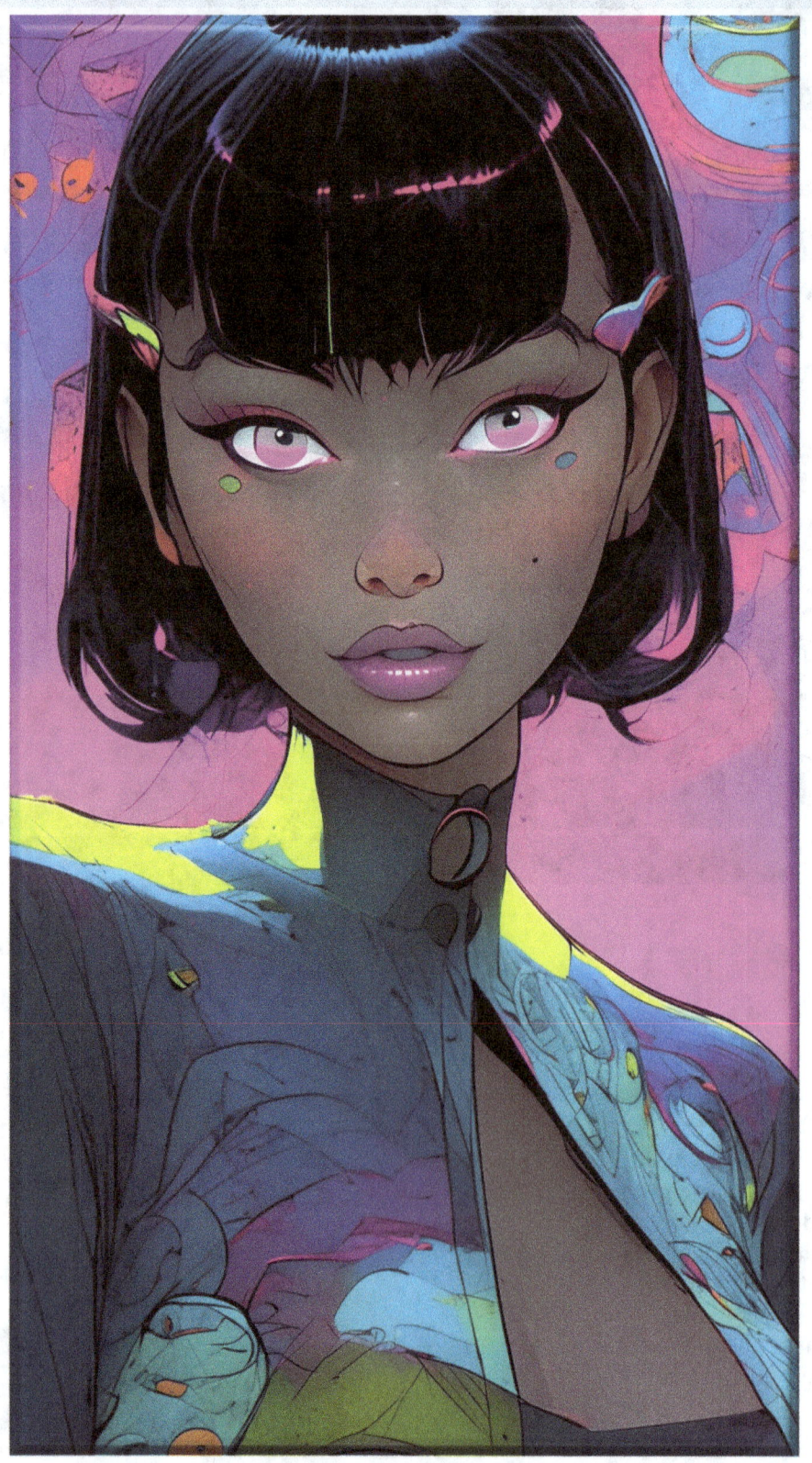

As a "mega-remixer" of AI-empowered art, there are two things that Niji excels at in particular: character portraits, and colorful dynamic scenes. And since striking characters and memorable places stand together at the very heart of the anime experience, this is a very good thing.

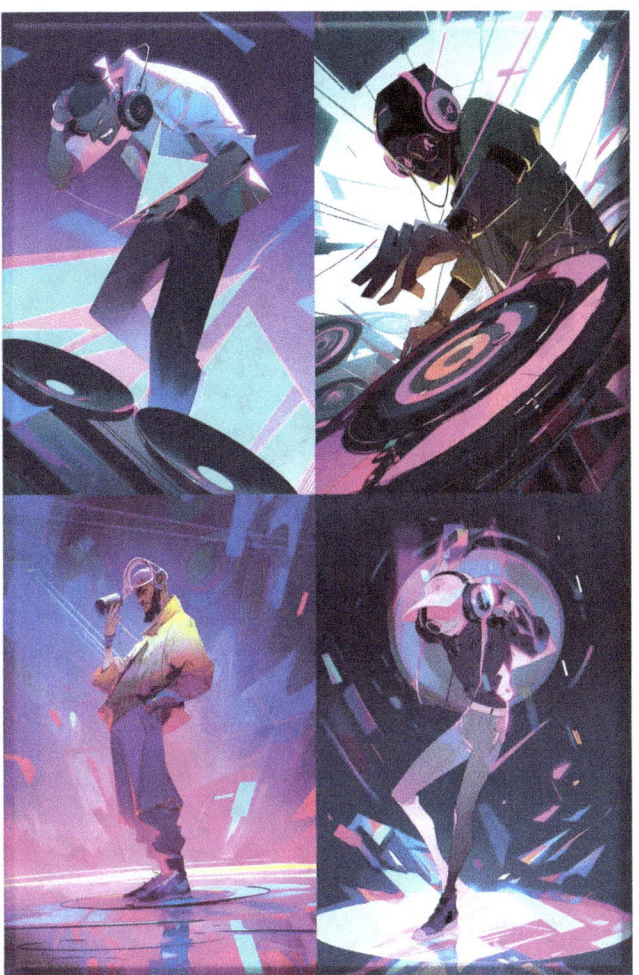

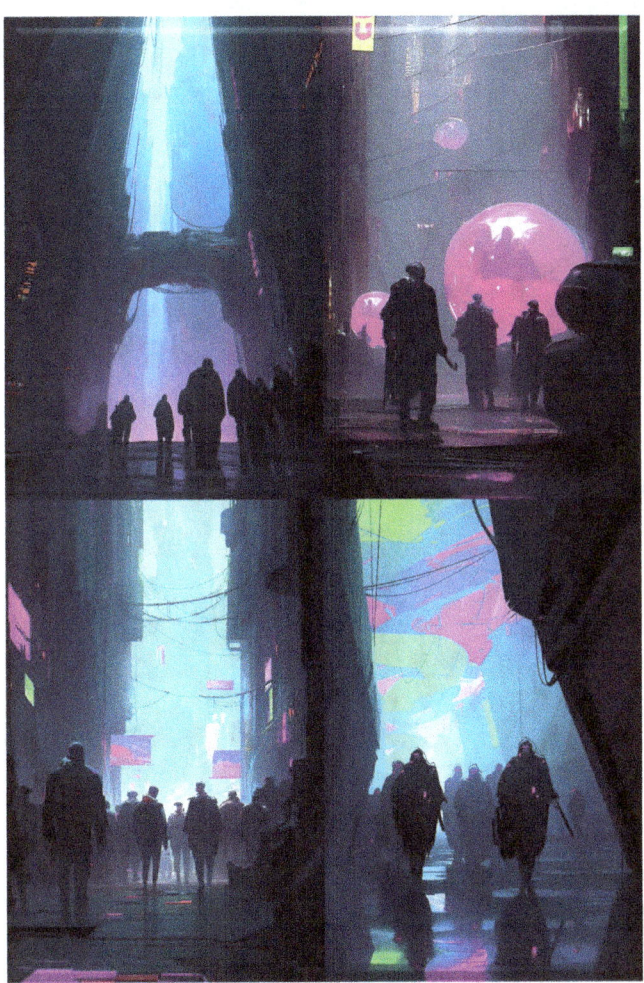

Choosing a Subject for Your Artwork

And now we know our main tool for anime in Midjourney will be Niji. But ... what if you don't know what you want to create? I know the feeling, believe me. To help, here is a quick set of ideas that you can think about. If you like a subject type, or you find someone else's idea that you can change to make iterations that are all your own, run with it. Both approaches work perfectly well and encourage your experimentation. Have fun.

Common anime art subjects include:

Action Scenes: Anime action scenes are dynamic and thrilling depictions of characters engaging in intense combat, epic battles, or adrenaline-pumping action sequences.

These scenes showcase the characters' movements, expressions, and abilities in action, with exaggerated poses and dramatic effects to create a sense of excitement and energy.

Fantasy/Supernatural: Anime fantasy and supernatural art depict magical and mystical worlds filled with fantastical creatures, supernatural powers, and enchanting settings.

These great-looking images often feature unique and imaginative character designs, intricate details, and otherworldly elements that transport viewers to a realm of wonder and awe.

Landscapes: Anime landscapes are breathtaking depictions of natural or urban environments, such as serene nature scenes, bustling cityscapes, or futuristic cityscapes.

FOLIO IMAGE 012

/imagine   **A super detailed background like Ghibli, sci fi and cinematic, flying over a psychedelic canyon, charming colorful fantasy houses clinging to the walls, like Rivendell, or Qarth, excellent lighting, epic scene --ar 9:16 --style expressive --niji 5**

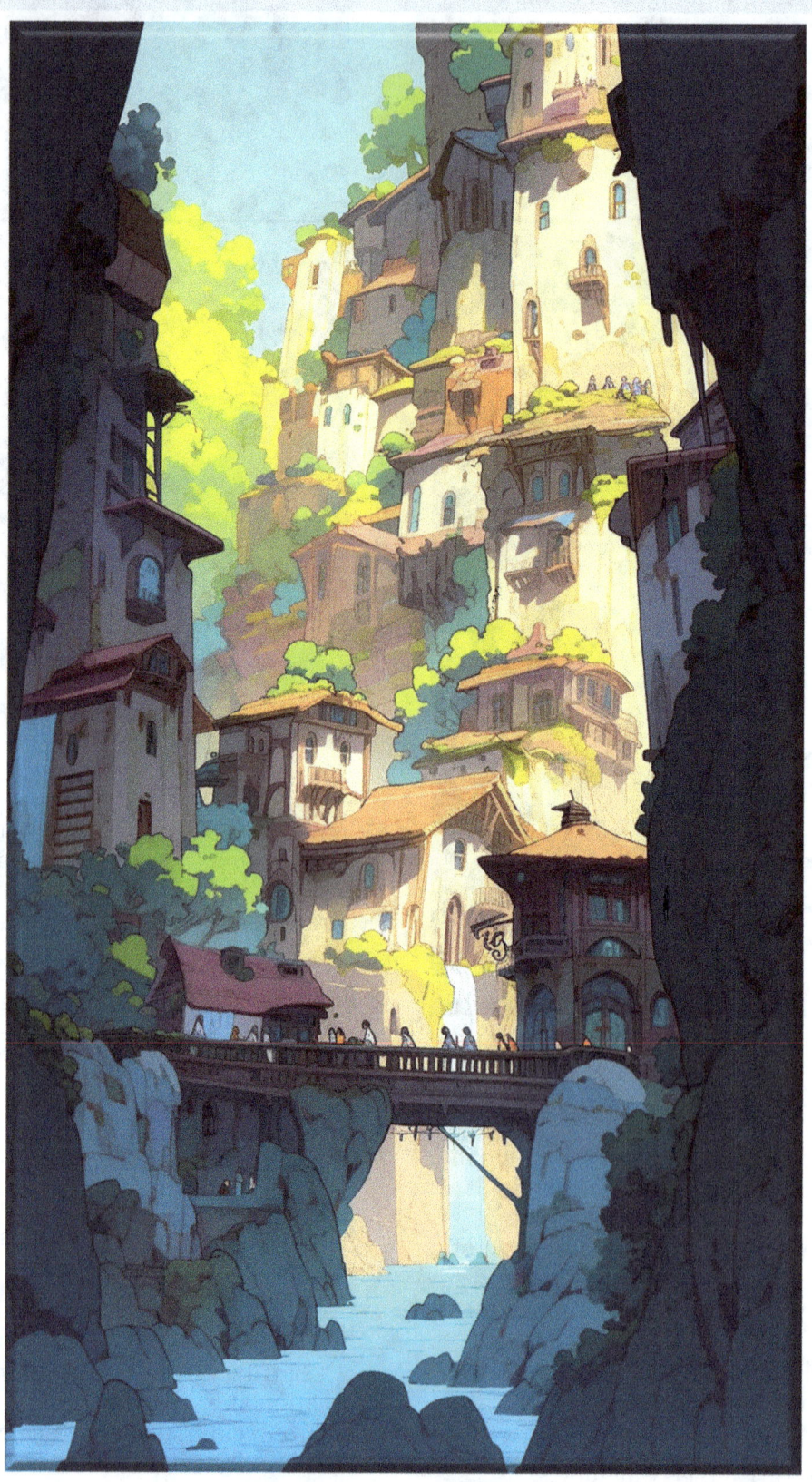

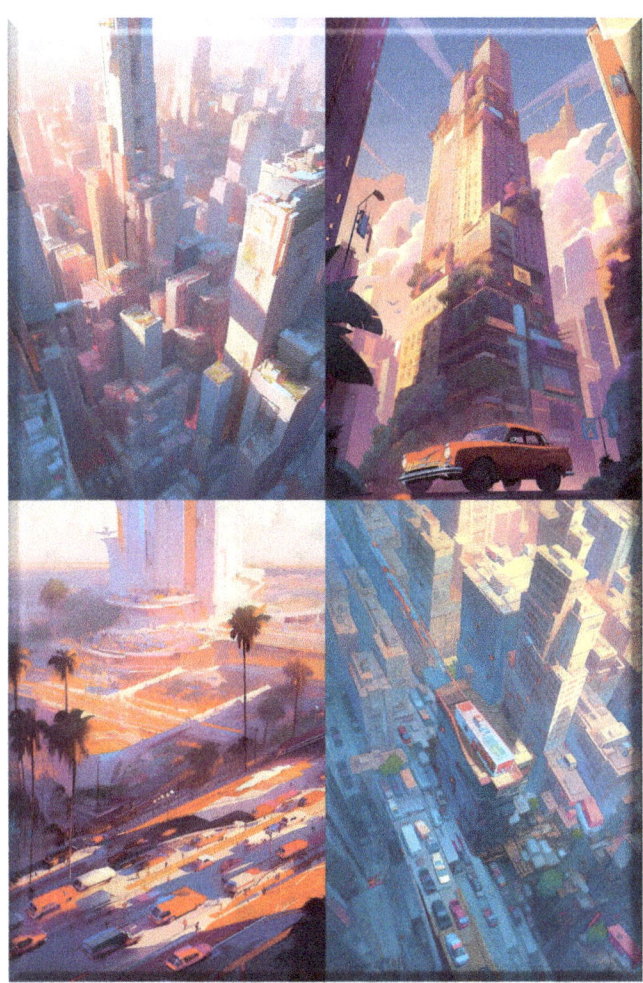

Slice of Life: Anime slice of life art portrays ordinary, everyday moments and activities of characters, often in a realistic or comedic manner.

These pieces of art focus on the characters' interactions, relationships, and daily routines, capturing the charm and humor of everyday life. Slice of life anime art can be heartwarming, funny, or relatable, and it often highlights the beauty of simple moments.

These are just a few examples of the major subjects commonly depicted in anime art. Anime is a diverse and versatile art form that covers a wide range of genres, themes, and styles, providing endless creative possibilities for artists and captivating viewers with its unique storytelling and visual aesthetics.

I personally prefer portraits, as you may have noticed, because I think the ways that people express themselves – even if they are imaginary – create stories all their own.

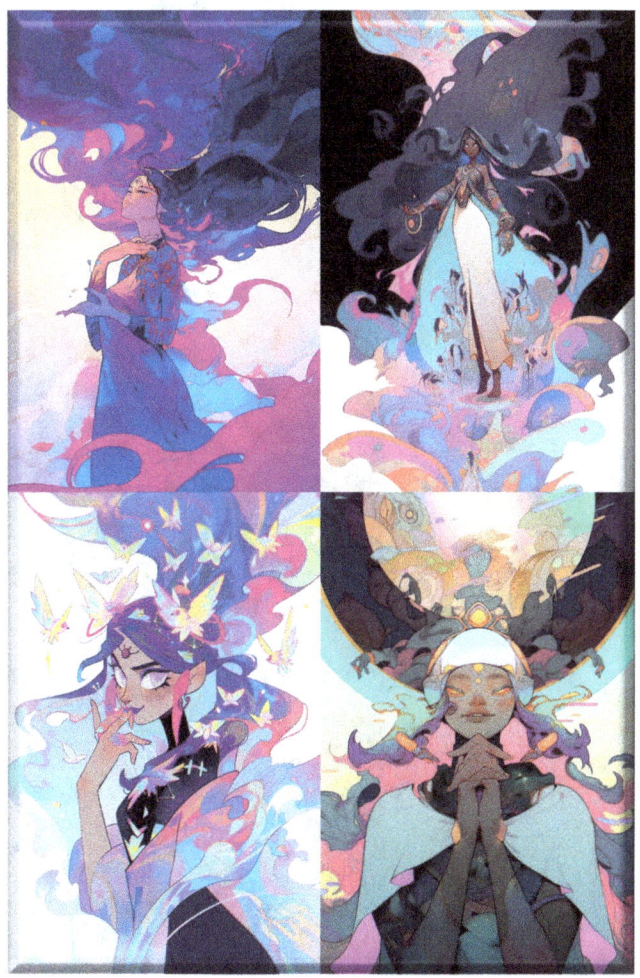

These pieces often use vibrant colors, imaginative settings, and intricate details to create visually stunning backdrops that set the mood and tone for the story or scene.

Portraits: Anime portraits are character-focused images that showcase the unique features and expressions of anime characters. These portraits often highlight the character's personality, emotions, and details such as their hairstyle, eyes, and facial expressions. Portraits can be serious or lighthearted, and they provide a window into the character's world and story.

Sci-Fi: Anime sci-fi art imagines futuristic worlds, advanced technology, and outer space adventures. These images often feature high-tech gadgets, futuristic settings, and characters in futuristic attire, showcasing the creativity and imagination of the artist. Sci-fi anime art can range from cyberpunk aesthetics to space opera adventures, and it often sparks the imagination with its futuristic possibilities.

FOLIO IMAGE 013

/imagine   Super detailed cinematic still, like Pixar or DreamWorks, wonderful carefree days of childhood visualized, beautiful emotional scene, inspirational, adored, nostalgia incarnate --ar 9:16 --style expressive --niji 5

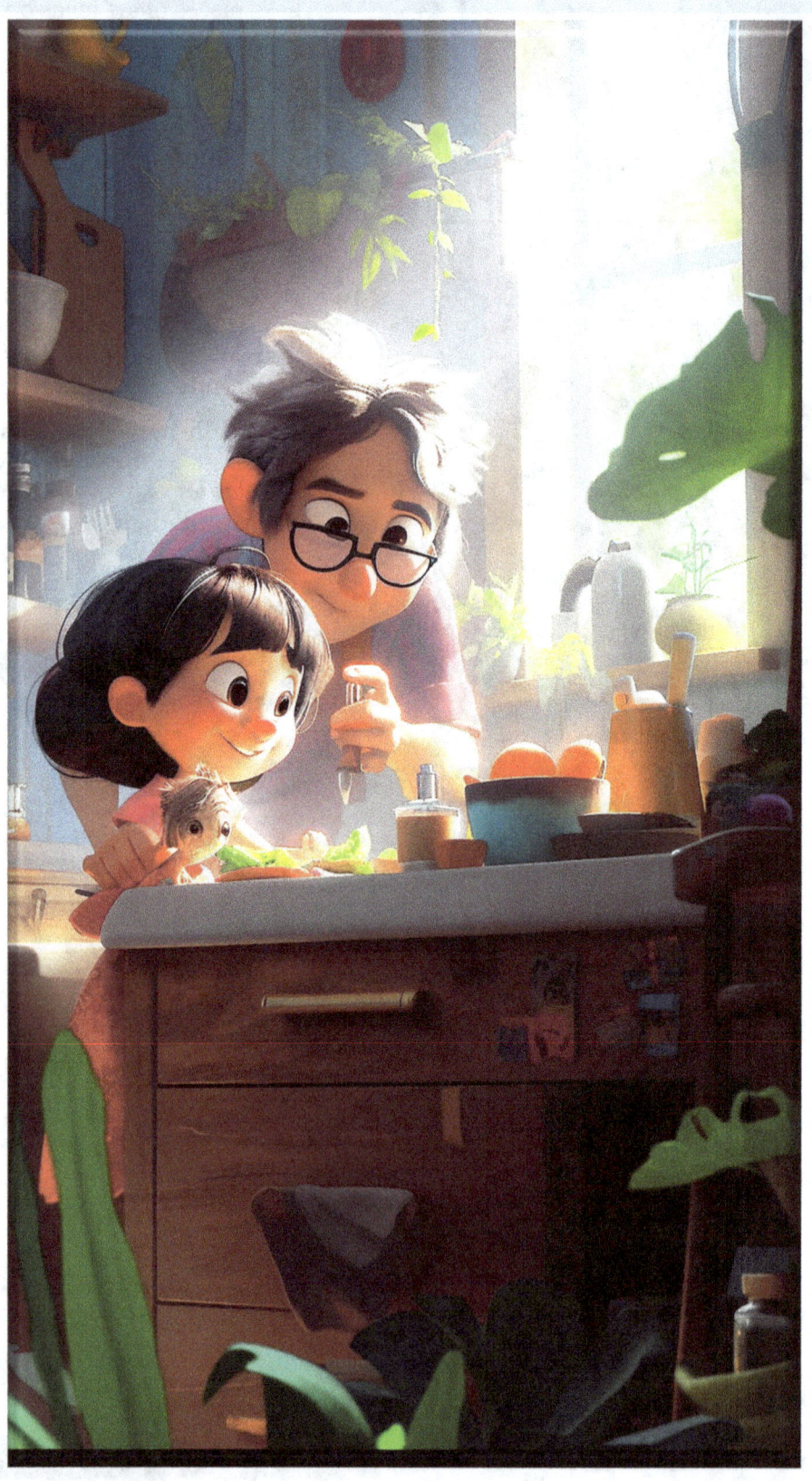

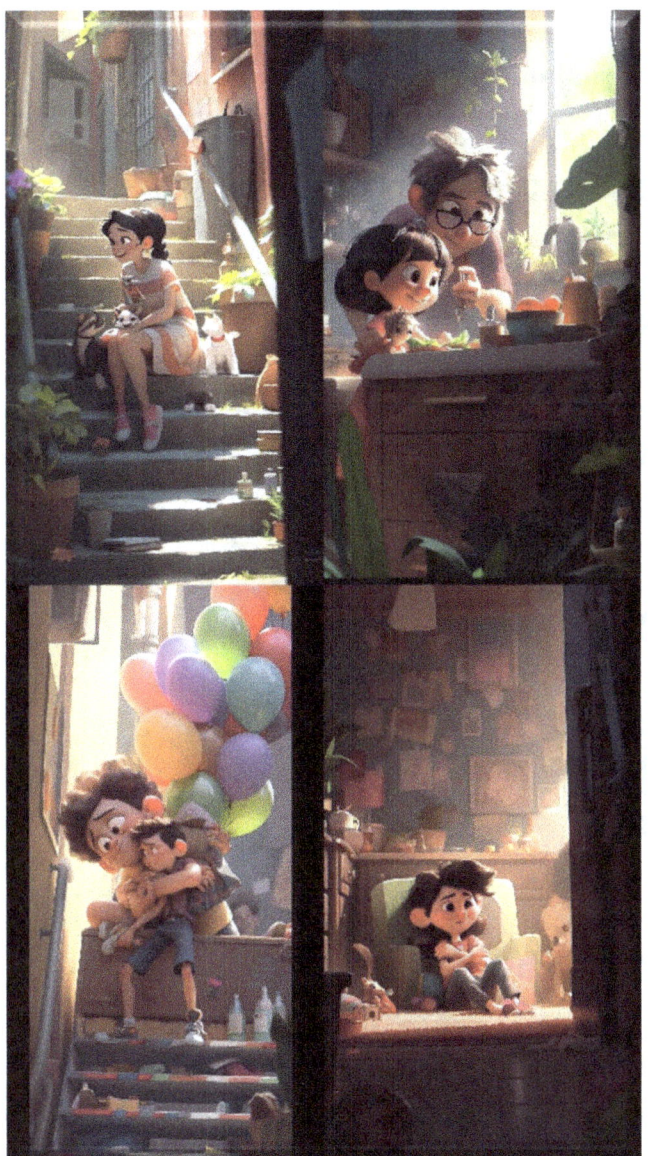

It is impossible to choose just a few anime-influenced artists to make a "greatest hits" role call to list them here, simply because there are so many gifted people working in the field that any attempt at a list would be incomplete.

Nevertheless, here is a starter list of some of the most famous anime artists who have made significant contributions to the world of anime and have garnered widespread recognition.

These are some of my personal favorites over the years.

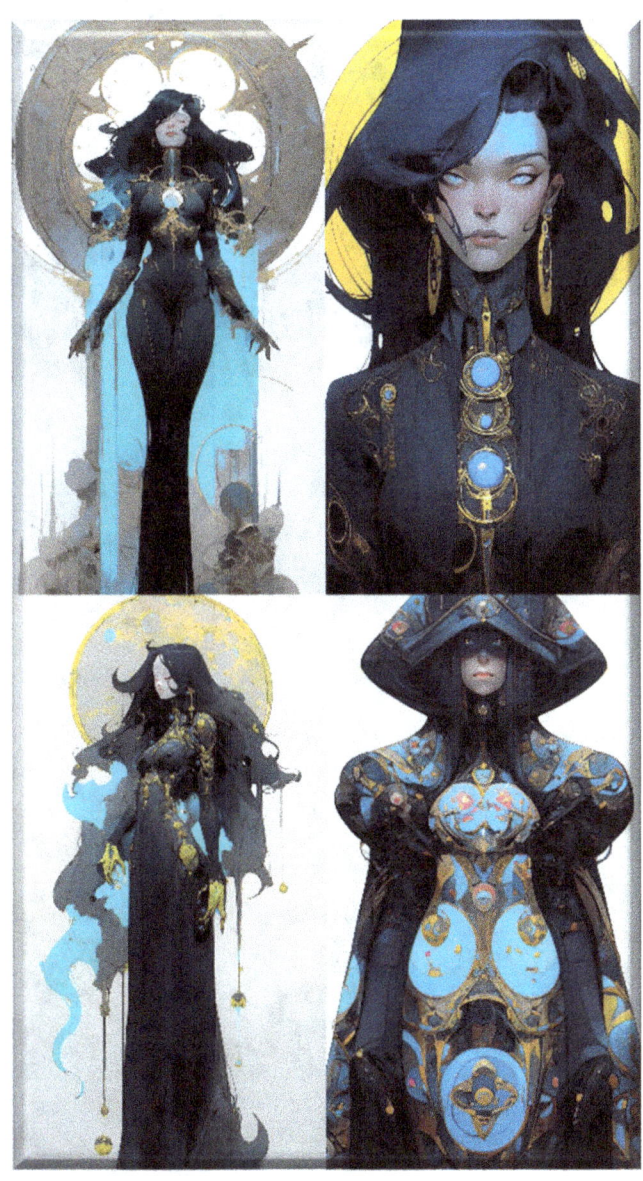

Legendary Artists in Anime

Sometimes, you will want to evoke the style of a particular artist just to see what it looks like, or to see if the tone changes have a dramatic effect on your own art series for a few images.

I recommend that you should usually be using more than one artist as respectful inspiration, so that you can blend styles without borrowing someone's signature look wholesale.

For example, I would recommend combining Hideaki Anno with Alphonse Mucha (new and retro), or blending the styles of Akira Toriyama and Leonardo da Vinci (classic and *way* retro all at once). And the more research of artists that you do, the more that you will learn, too.

Akira Toriyama: Toriyama is a manga artist and character designer best known for creating the popular manga series *Dragon Ball*.

FOLIO IMAGE 014

/imagine　**Beautiful interior, an interior of a historic building with stained glass windows, in the style of saturated pigment pools, moody tonalism, luxurious geometry, intricate cut - outs, classical architecture, beloved scene --ar 9:16 --style expressive --niji 5**

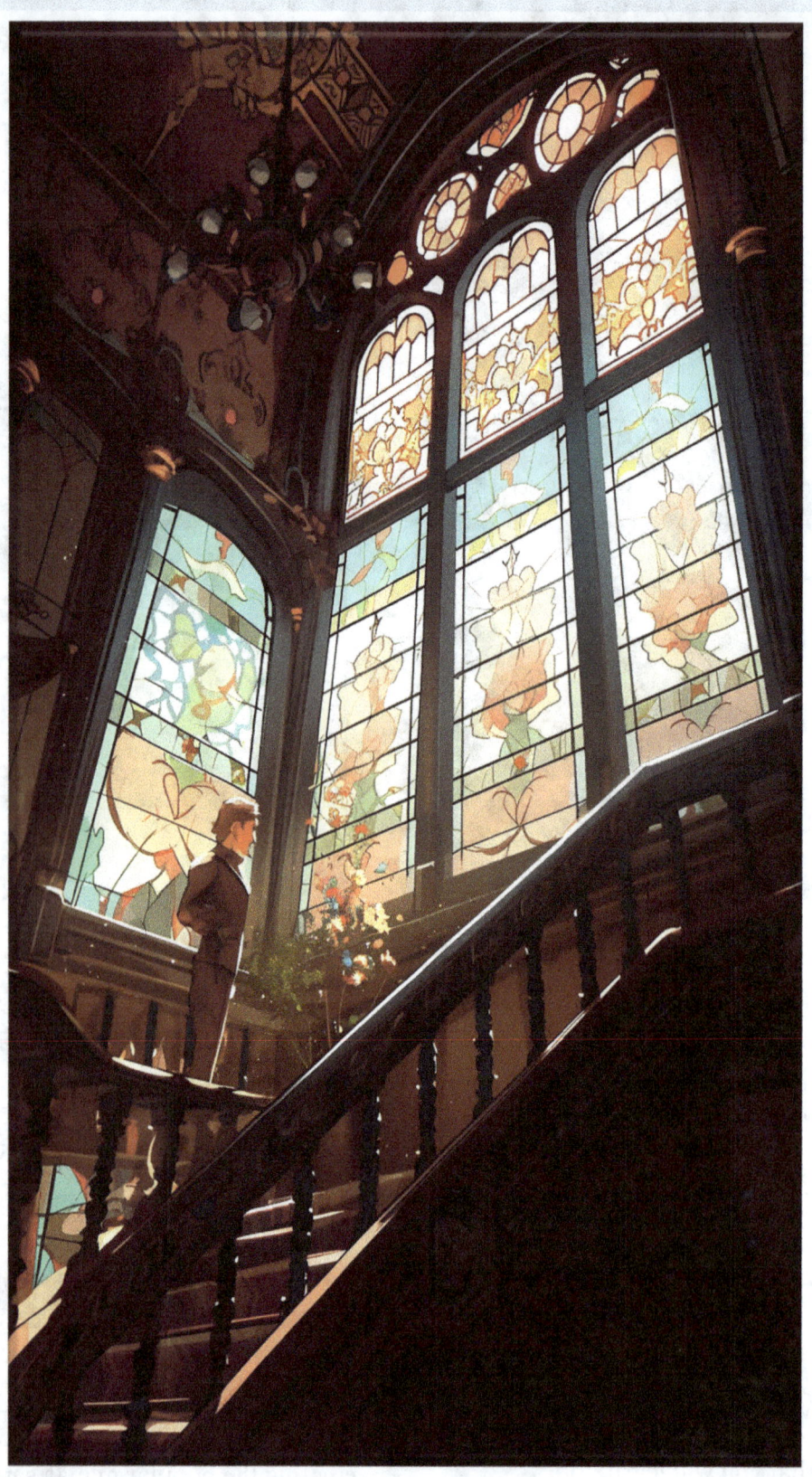

His dynamic art style and imaginative character designs have made *Dragon Ball* a global phenomenon, inspiring numerous anime adaptations, movies, and merchandise.

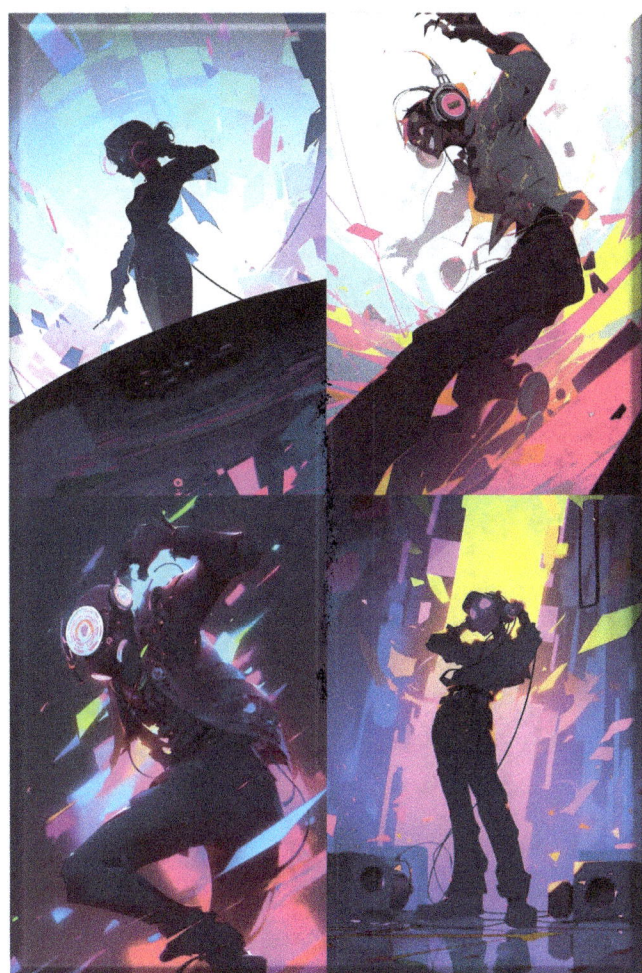

CLAMP: CLAMP is a female manga artist group consisting of four talented artists: Nanase Ohkawa, Mokona, Tsubaki Nekoi, and Satsuki Igarashi. They are known for their diverse range of works, including *Cardcaptor Sakura*, *Tsubasa: RESERVoir CHRoNiCLE*, and *xxxHOLiC*, and are acclaimed for their intricate character designs and compelling storytelling.

Hayao Miyazaki: Renowned for his captivating storytelling and breathtaking visuals, Miyazaki is a legendary anime artist and director. He co-founded Studio Ghibli and has created beloved films such as *Spirited Away* (my personal favorite), *My Neighbor Totoro*, and *Princess Mononoke*.

Hideaki Anno: Anno is a renowned anime director, writer, and animator known for his groundbreaking work on the critically acclaimed anime series *Neon Genesis Evangelion*. He is known for his distinct visual style, thought-provoking storytelling, and innovative use of symbolism and psychology in his works.

Makoto Shinkai: Shinkai is a celebrated anime director, writer, and animator known for his visually stunning films such as *Your Name* and *Weathering With You*. His works are known for their breathtaking animation, compelling characters, and heartfelt storytelling that often explores themes of love, longing, and human connection.

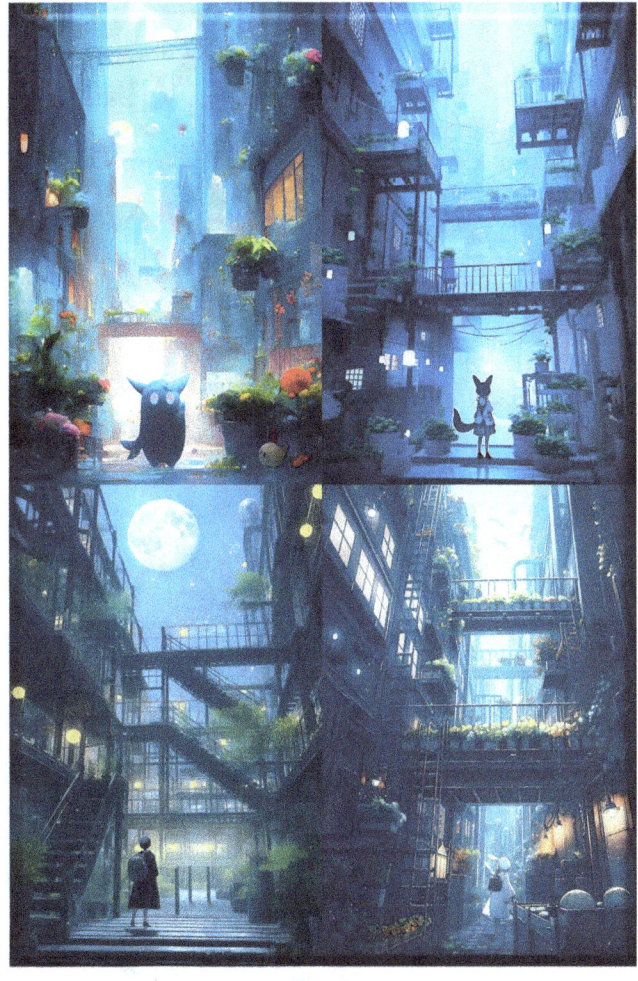

Mamoru Hosoda: Hosoda is a renowned anime director and screenwriter known for his heartfelt and visually stunning films such as *Wolf Children*, *The Girl Who Leapt Through Time*, and *Summer Wars*.

FOLIO IMAGE 015

/imagine   **Surreal infographic, technical drawing, poster illustration of the full body and detailed exploded breakaway head of a stunningly beautiful young woman android, constructed of all kinds of circuits and wiring and robotics and cyborg technology, androidcore, with laser light, LED lights, AI, ultra - realistic. ultra - detailed, sharpened details, beautiful, otherwordly, futuristic, unsettling blazewave --ar 9:16 -- style expressive --niji 5**

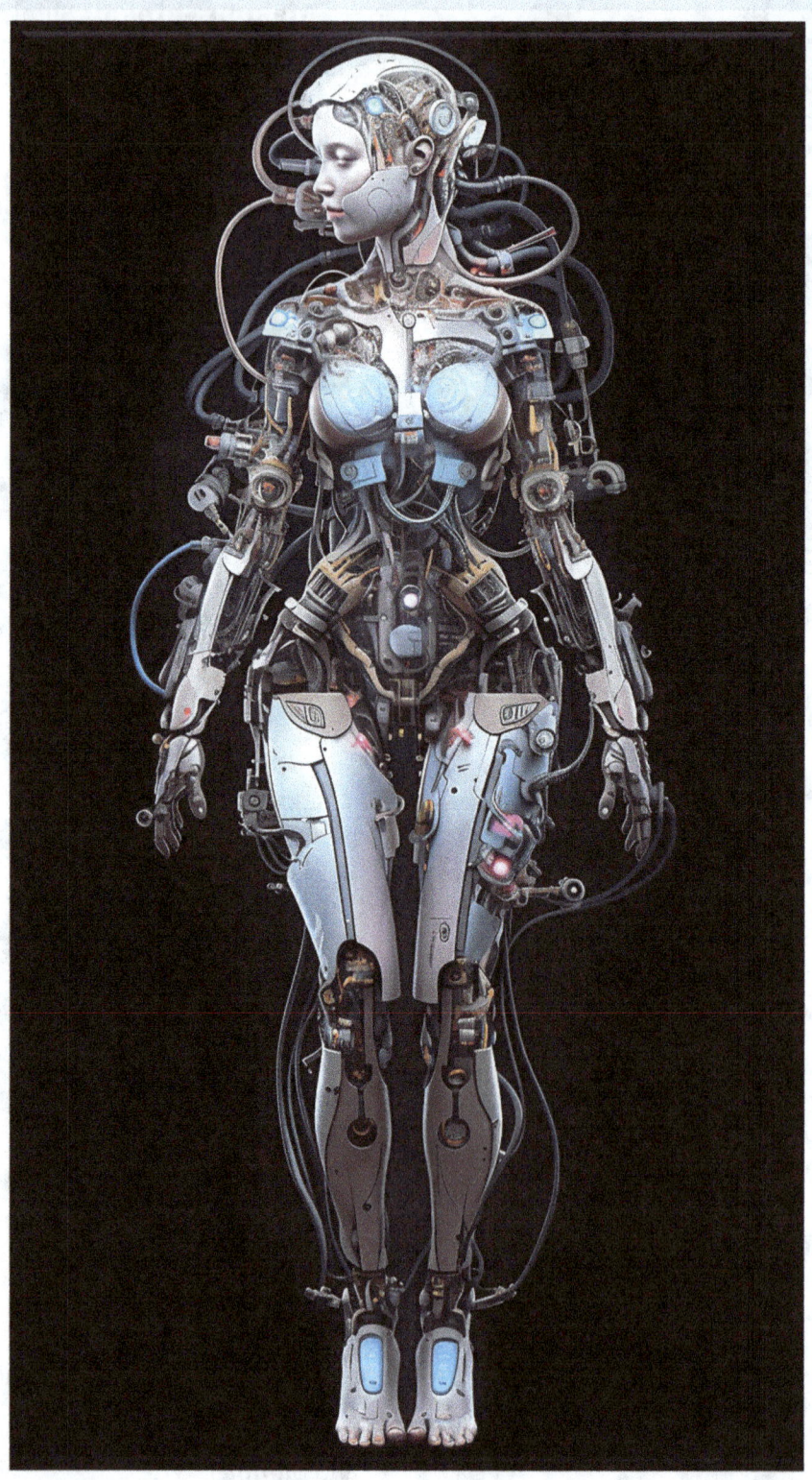

His works often blend fantasy, drama, and slice of life elements, and are known for their emotional depth and relatable characters.

Naoko Takeuchi: Takeuchi is a manga artist best known for creating the popular manga series *Sailor Moon*.

Her iconic art style and memorable character designs have made *Sailor Moon* a cultural phenomenon, influencing numerous other anime and manga series and inspiring a devoted fanbase worldwide.

Yoshitaka Amano: Amano is a renowned Japanese illustrator and character designer known for his distinct and intricate artwork.

He has worked on iconic anime series like *Final Fantasy*, *Vampire Hunter D*, and *Gatchaman*, and is known for his unique blend of fantasy, surrealism, and fine art influences.

If I have offended anyone by leaving their sincerest favorite off this list, my apologies.

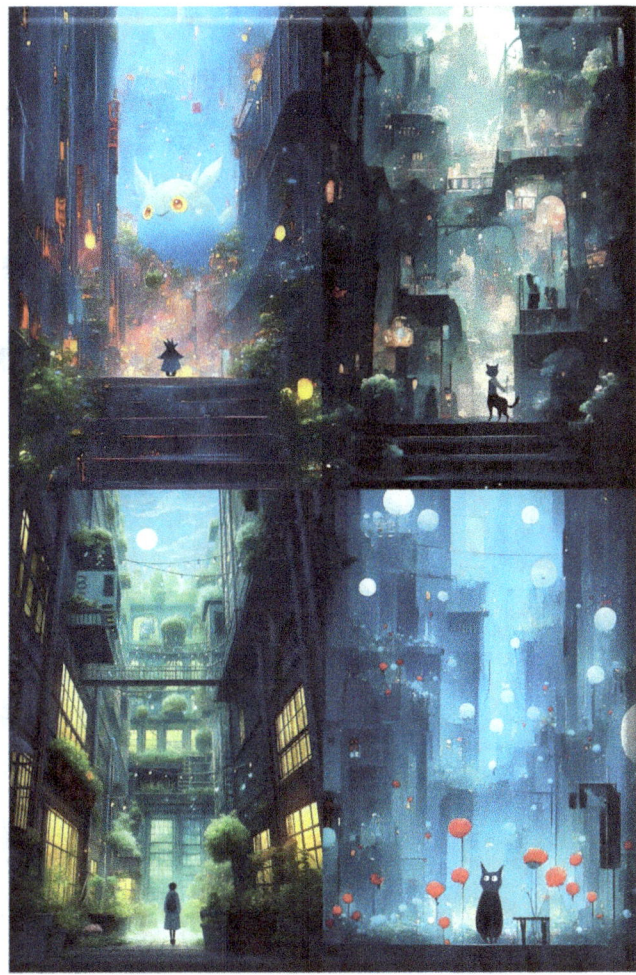

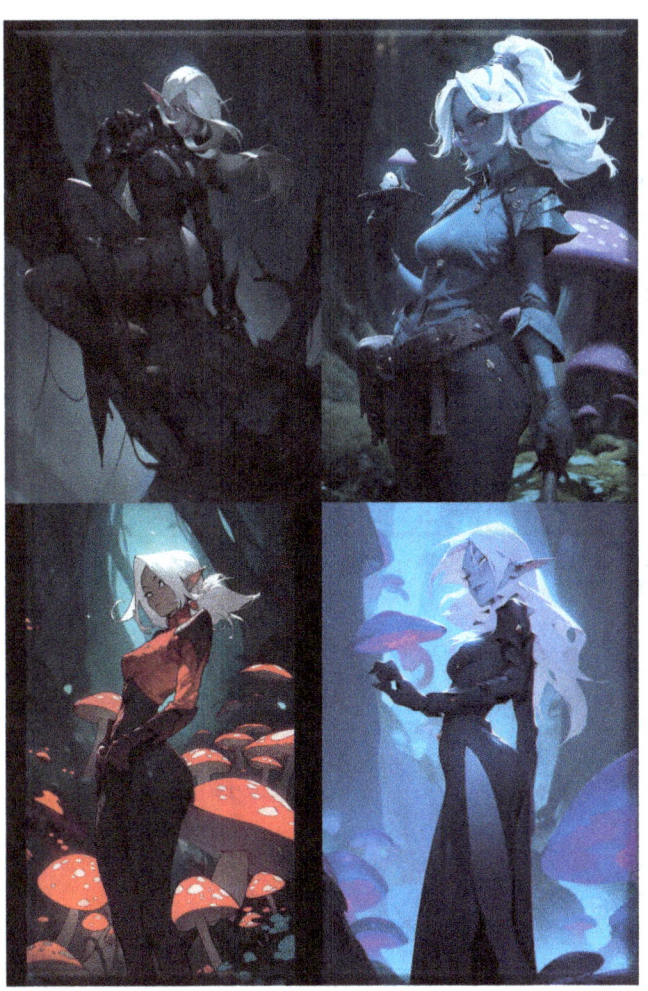

Listing and saving the best for last, Amano might be my personal favorite.

I fondly remember spending my last food money for the day in Japantown, San Francisco on one of his new deluxe full-color print books filled with *Final Fantasy* works and other splash pages of unapologetic majesty.

Way, way too much money for the full glorious import version from Japan. Didn't matter. Price was not a matter of concern. It was mine. That was it, and that was everything.

Fortunately, another nice person fed me that evening. San Francisco can be a little expensive.

Long story ...

FOLIO IMAGE 016

/imagine   Femme, catwoman empire style, detailed, illustration by Adam Hughes, or Stanley Artgerm, or Ilya Kuvshinov, so beautiful, haunting, retro --ar 9:16 --style expressive --niji 5

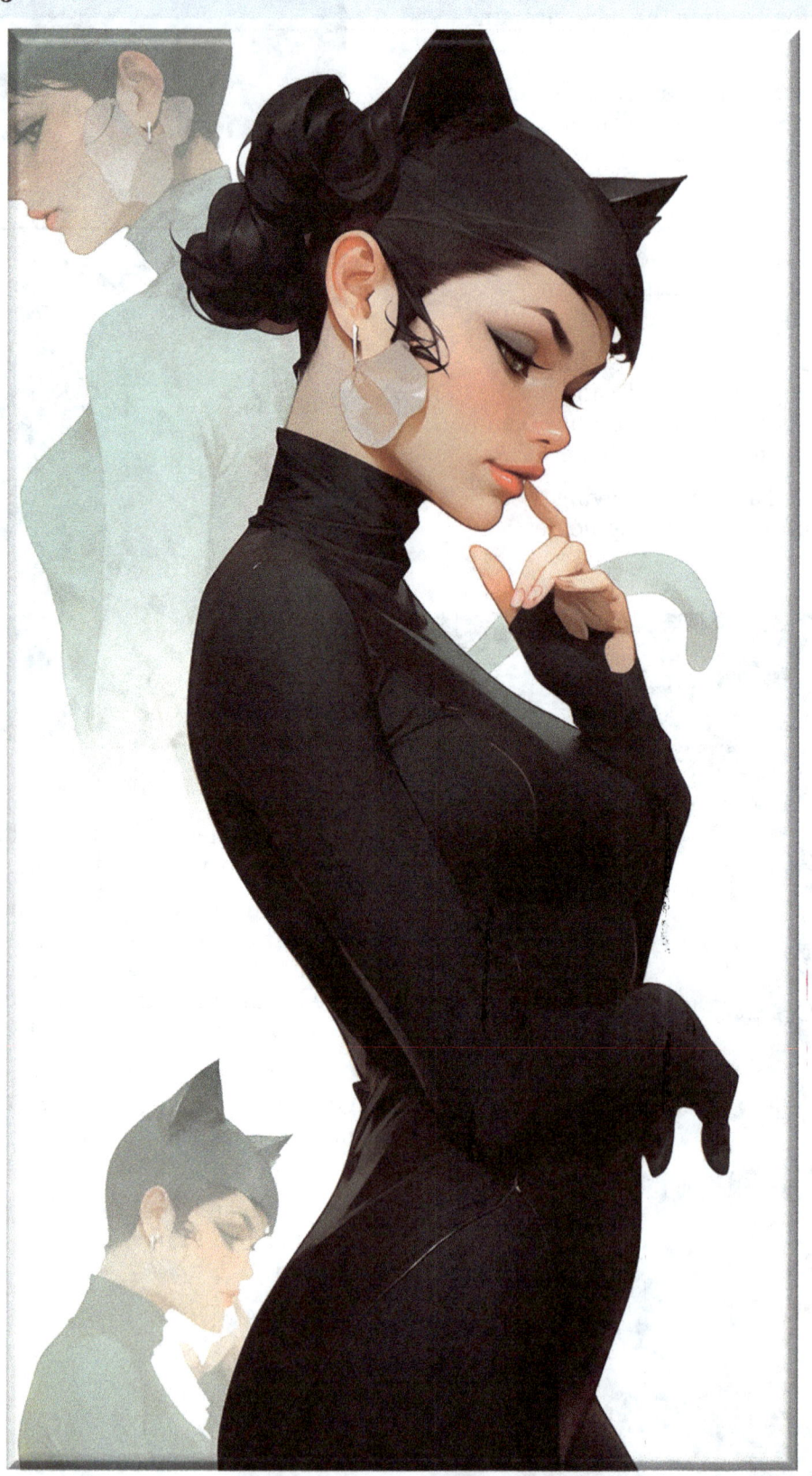

THREE:
ART CRAFTING

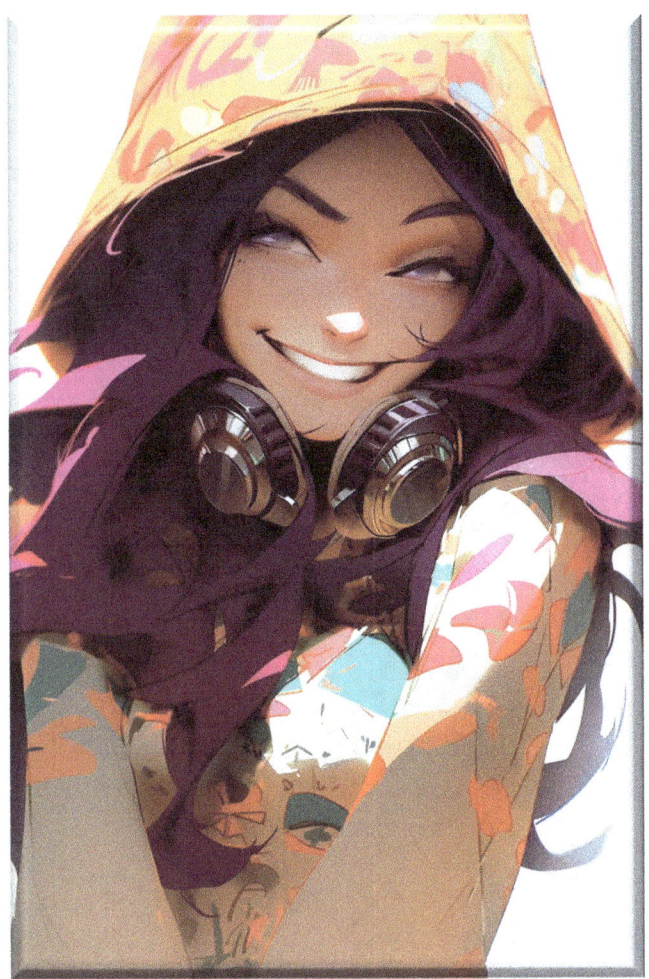

If you want to get serious about creating anime art in Midjourney, it helps to be honest with yourself about your goals and ambitions.

If you just want to create images for yourself, then celebrate the fact that you have freedoms. You don't need to worry about other people or the outside world too much if it's all for you.

You can admire your images, change them up in Photoshop, draw text on them with Paint, mash them together to create new works, or use the images as guides for your own drawing, painting, and story writing. The possibilities are endless.

But if you want to share your imaginative creations with others, you need to think about the real world that we live in and the businesses that reside there. And if you want to make an income with your images, or use them for marketing or promotion, you need to make sure that you're safe and won't get yourself into legal trouble.

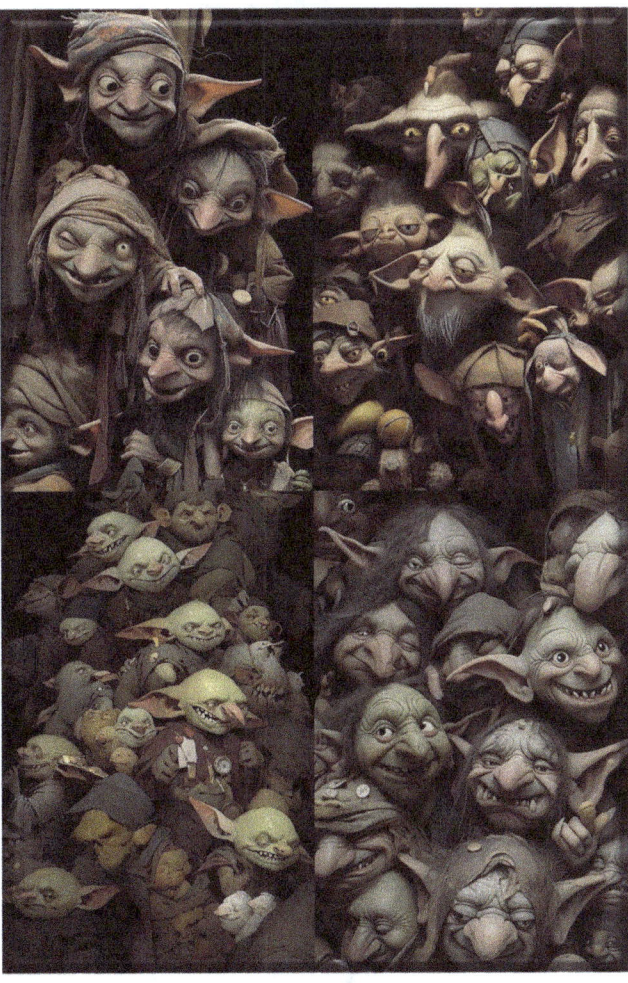

What Kind of Creator Will You Be?

If you just want to see what Midjourney can do, page through this book and enter in the /imagine prompts for the images that you like. Change whatever words you want, and see what is possible. All of the images you create are yours to keep. Be mindful, of course, that others can see your created images and they can borrow your prompts to make their own art too. And you can do the same, if you see something on Midjourney that you like from someone else.

It's all AI art in the public domain, until somebody customizes an image with a human hand. You can copy any prompt you see and customize it for yourself.

FOLIO IMAGE 017

/imagine   **Super fine detailed digital Manga street art, of a beautiful tantalizing 25 year old woman wearing a sheer garment with midriff showing, beautiful eyes, vivid colors, fantasy, soft glow, beautiful, high angle shot, 8k --ar 9:16 --style expressive --niji 5**

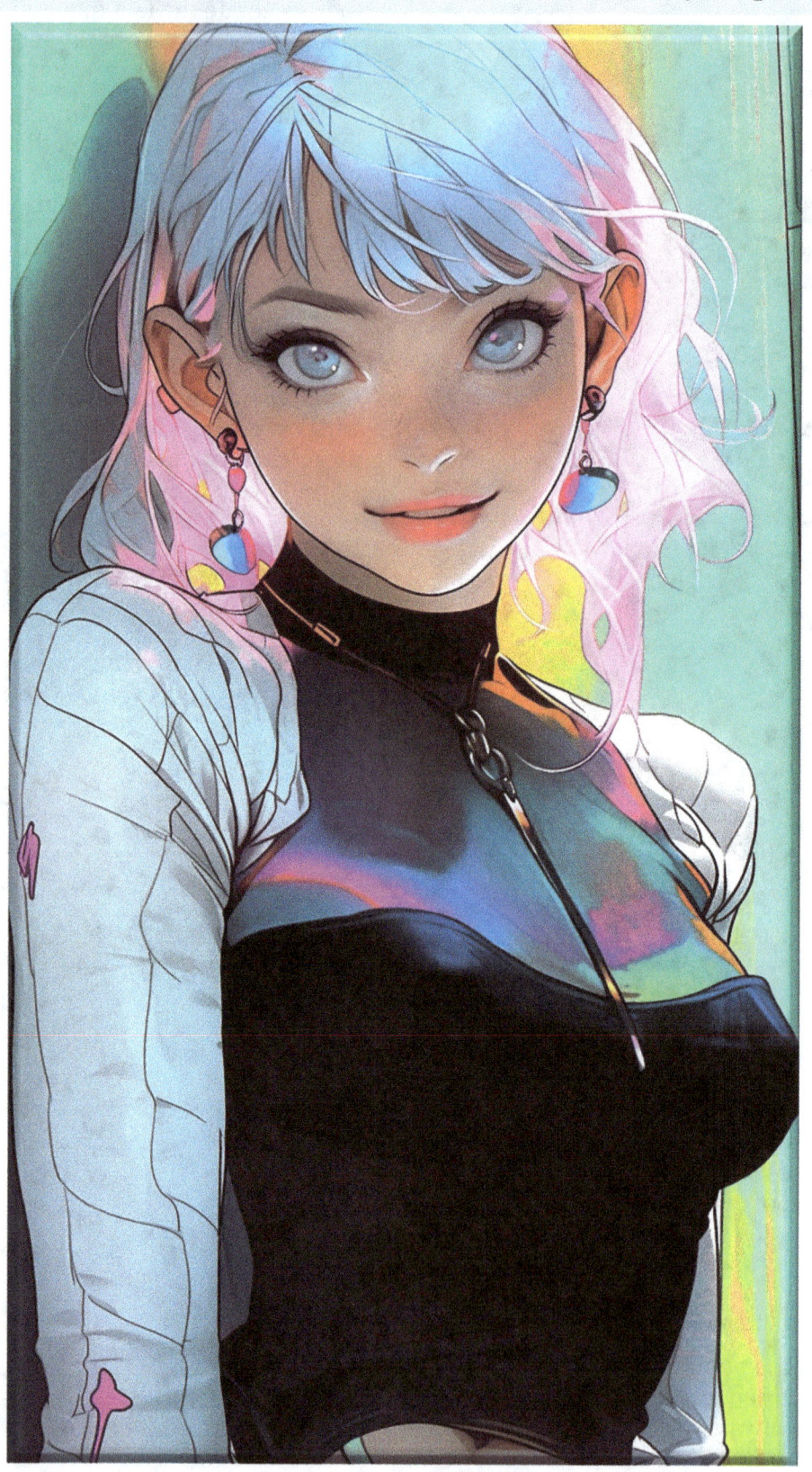

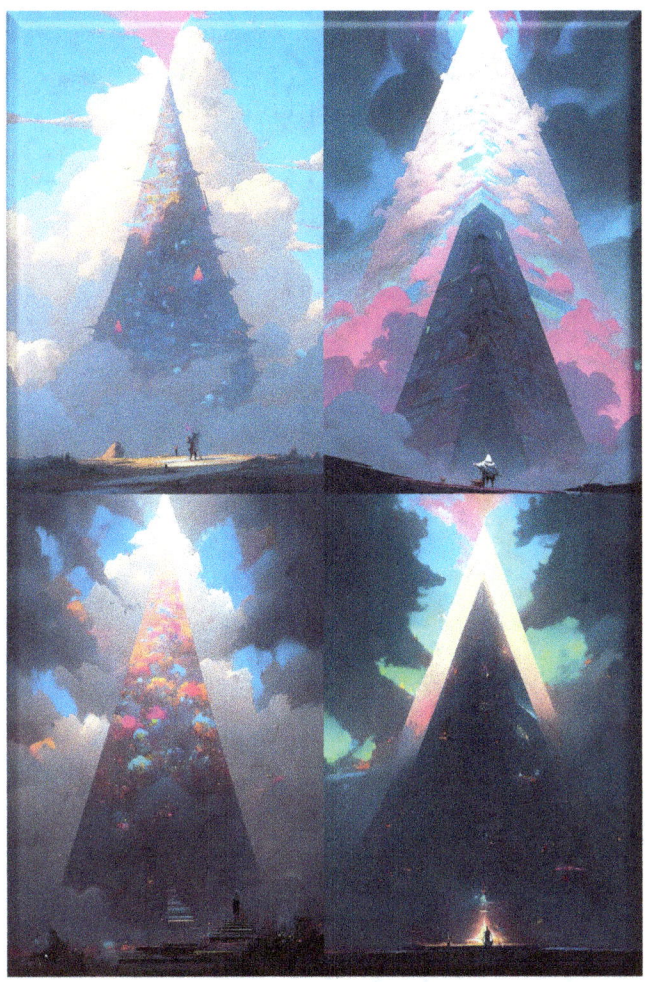

Creating for Yourself

Be free. Have fun, and don't violate the Midjourney or Discord terms of service, keep it kind toward others, and PG-13 in the art. Your saved images are your own. That's really it.

Creating to Share

Be mindful. If you are designing images to share without a profit motive, you are creating fan art. A lot of fan art is not technically legally permitted, and if you are creating art using other companies' intellectual property (the characters, game environments, stories, and images that they make money with), you're relying on that company's good graces to keep creating your shared fan art without any concerns.

Some very established companies are complete buttheads about copyright and infringement, and will warn you to take your shared images down. Most companies will

tolerate what you do, so long as you don't claim their property as your own or try to make a lot of money off of it. Some companies are very cool to their fan art communities, and will encourage you to keep going. But every company is different, and some companies even feel two different ways about two different properties that they own.

I as the author of this book cannot give you any legal advice, as I don't know where you live or what the laws are, whenever and wherever you happen to be. But I can give you friendly advice, and tell you that you should probably get a "feel" for a company and its fandom before you start making and sharing huge amounts fan art starring their intellectual property.

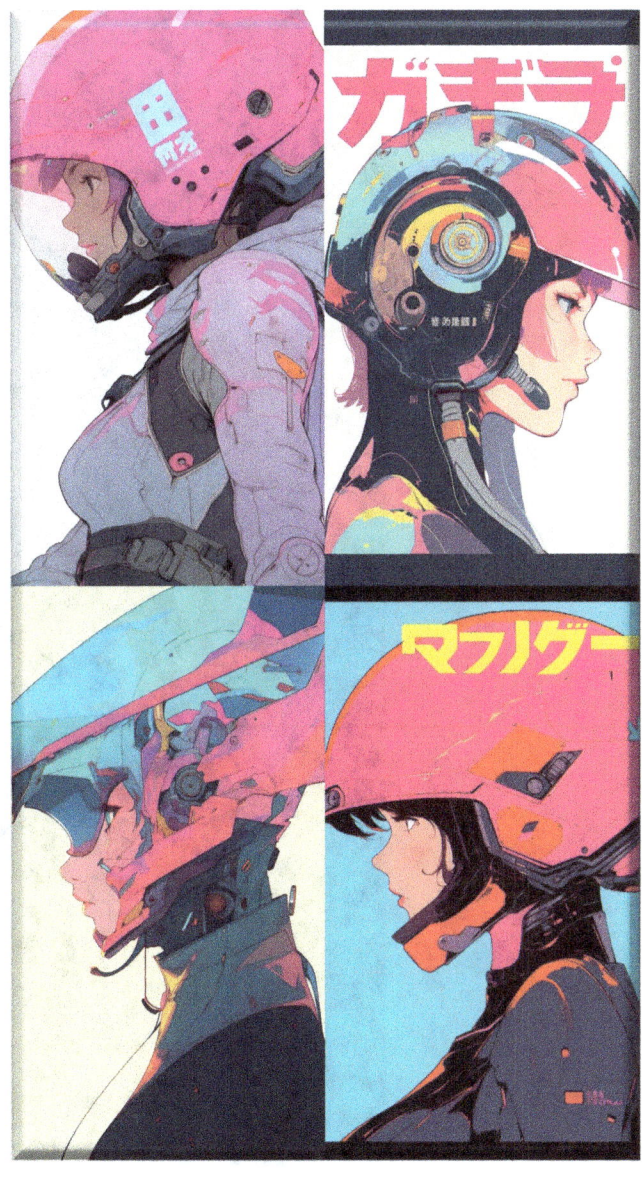

FOLIO IMAGE 018

/imagine   **Psytrance, fantasy girl, standing in a busy club, in a sci fi theme, colorful, in the style of Artgerm or videogames, dark themes, sharp brushwork, clockpunk, Kathrin Longhurst, bold palette --ar 9:16 --style expressive --niji 5**

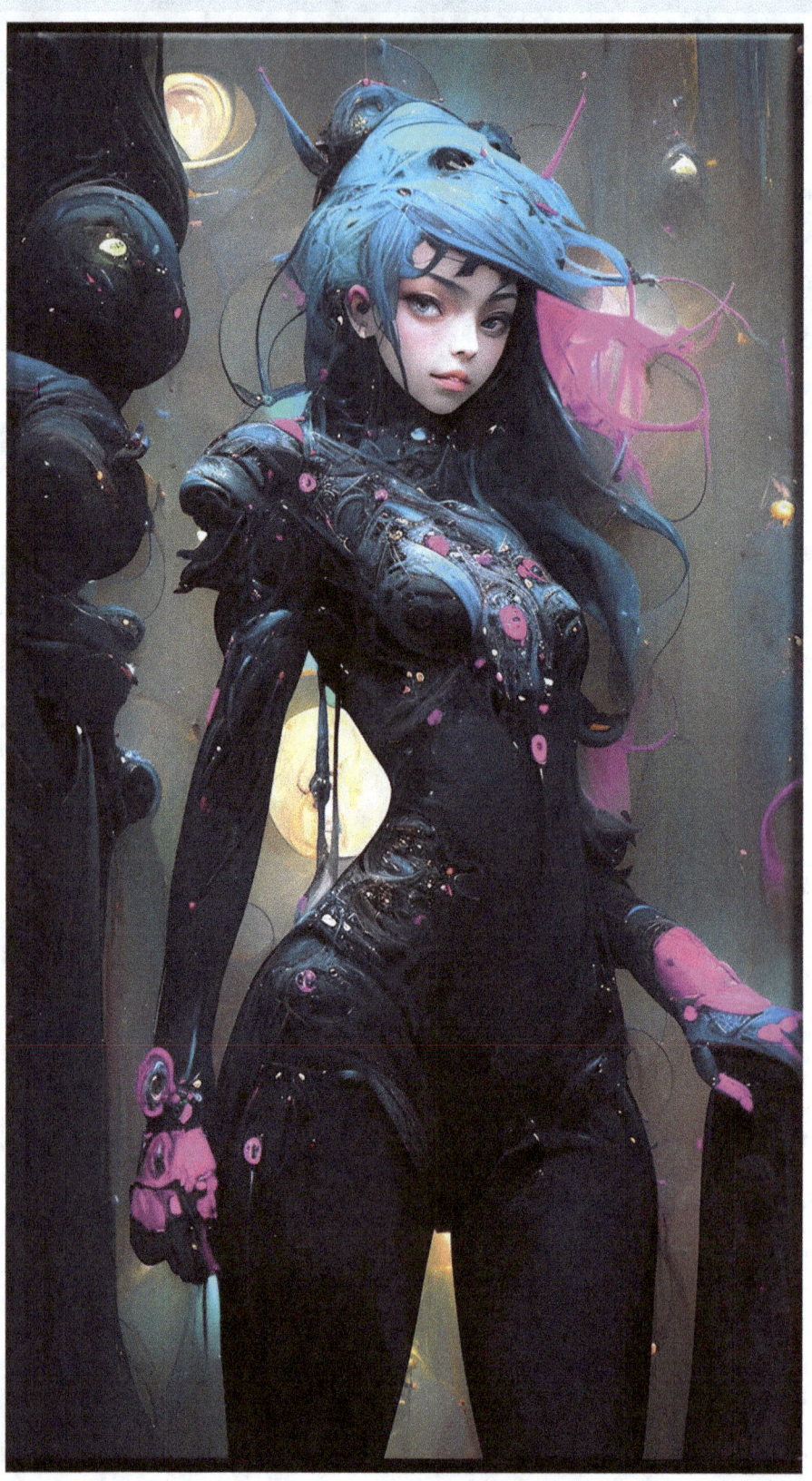

On the other hand, if you want to create your own anime on Midjourney that is totally original with no references to other companies' characters or commercial products or IP, more power to you. There is no one that can stop you.

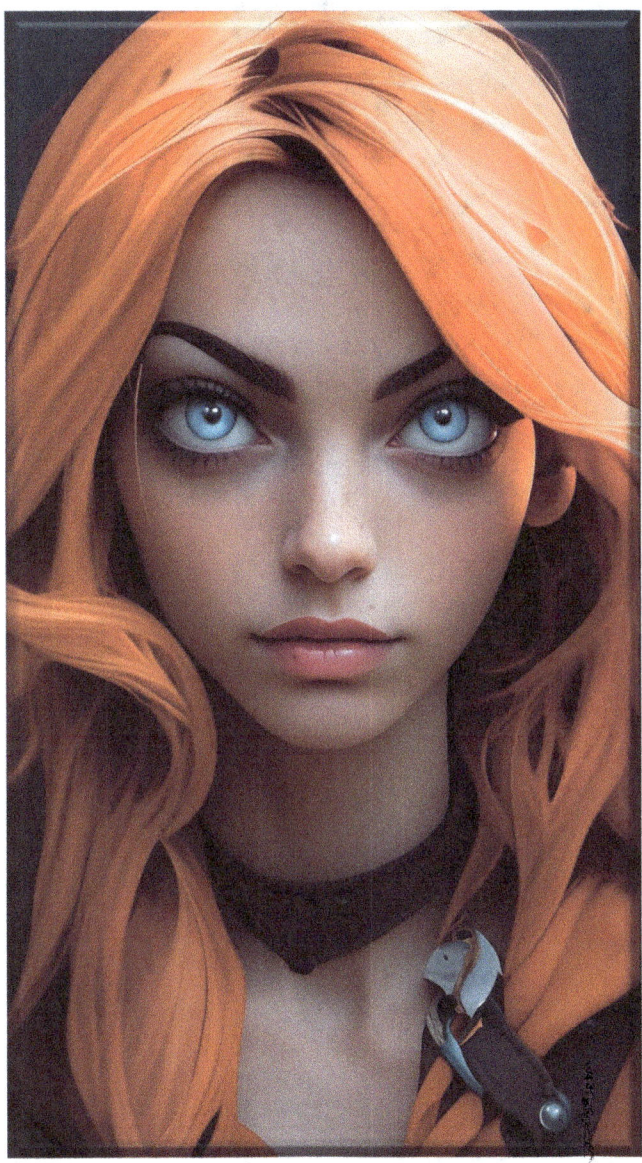

Creating to Profit

Be careful.

I don't recommend that you do this. Midjourney Niji trains on a lot of different pieces of contemporary art, and you might not want to use Niji for big commercial projects such as graphic novels or movies.

The AI field can be perilous from a legal perspective because things are changing so quickly, and I do not want to lead you astray.

Technically you can do it, if you're vigilant and savvy, but I don't want to give any advice that will age badly.

You might note that I have not signed or modified or finished any of the images in this book, and there is a good reason for that.

It's because I made no changes to these images, outside of contrast, brightness, and color correction. All of the generative flaws are still there if you want to look for them.

It's also because I do not claim any ownership of these images, which were made using the --niji 5 command. You can feel free to copy and modify any of them for your own use.

But please don't use them as your own art! The unchanged images throughout this book belong to Midjourney and the community.

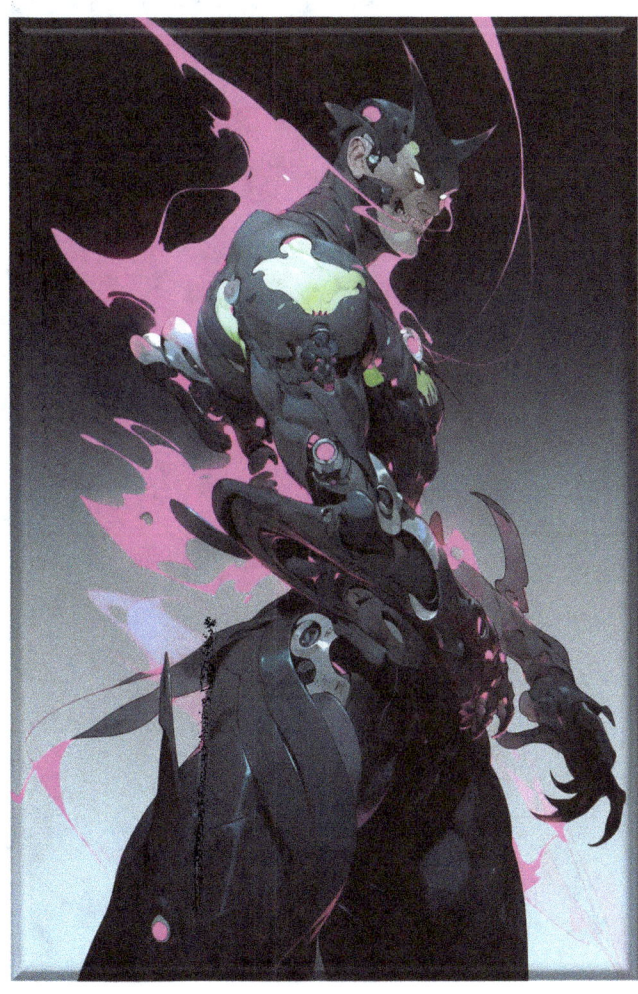

FOLIO IMAGE 019

/imagine   Glossy and smooth shaded Felidae, manifesting in the form of a tiger tax, black and gold swirling colors, abstract, surreal epic, elegant luxury, mysterious and mystical, cinematic light --ar 9:16 --style expressive --niji 5

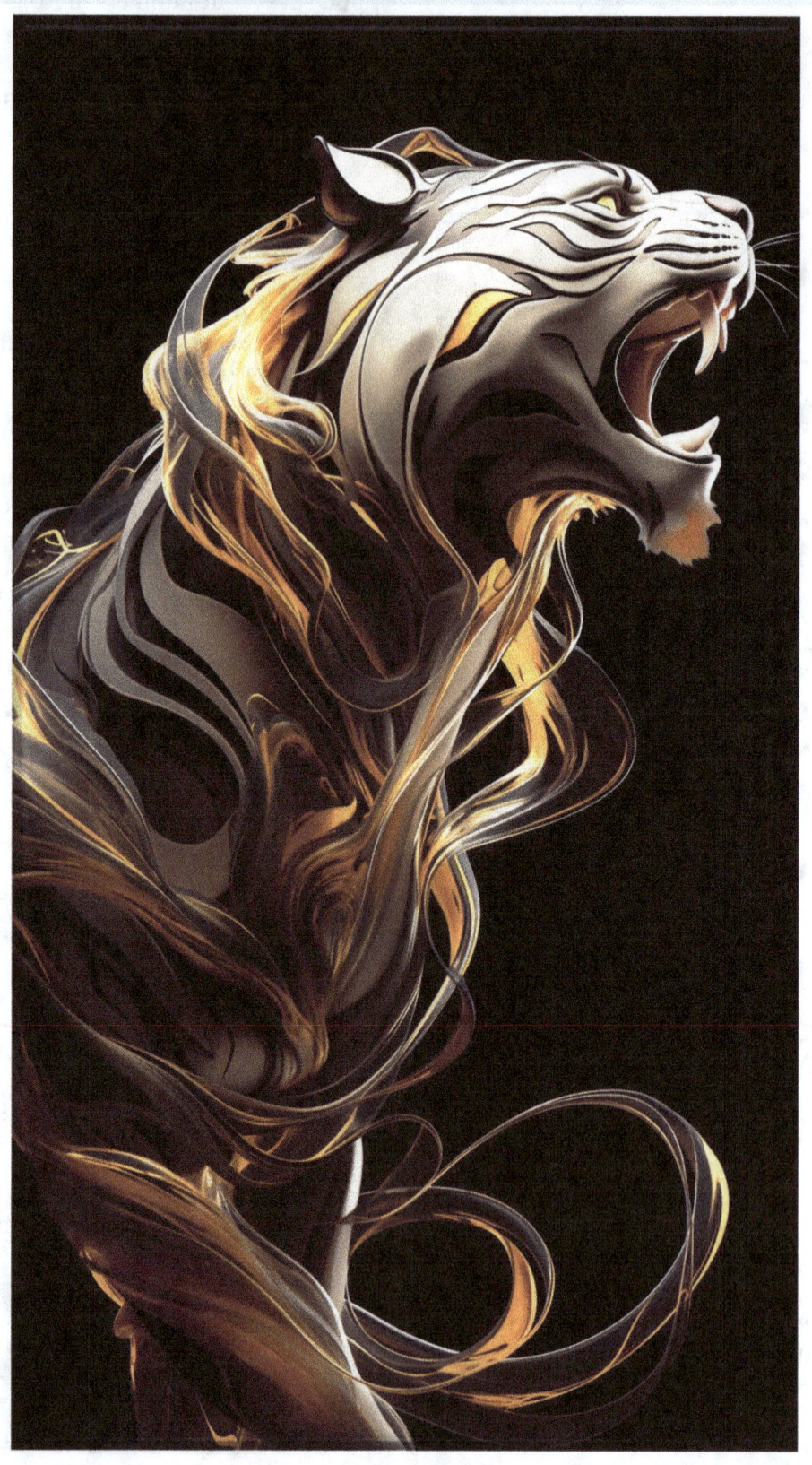

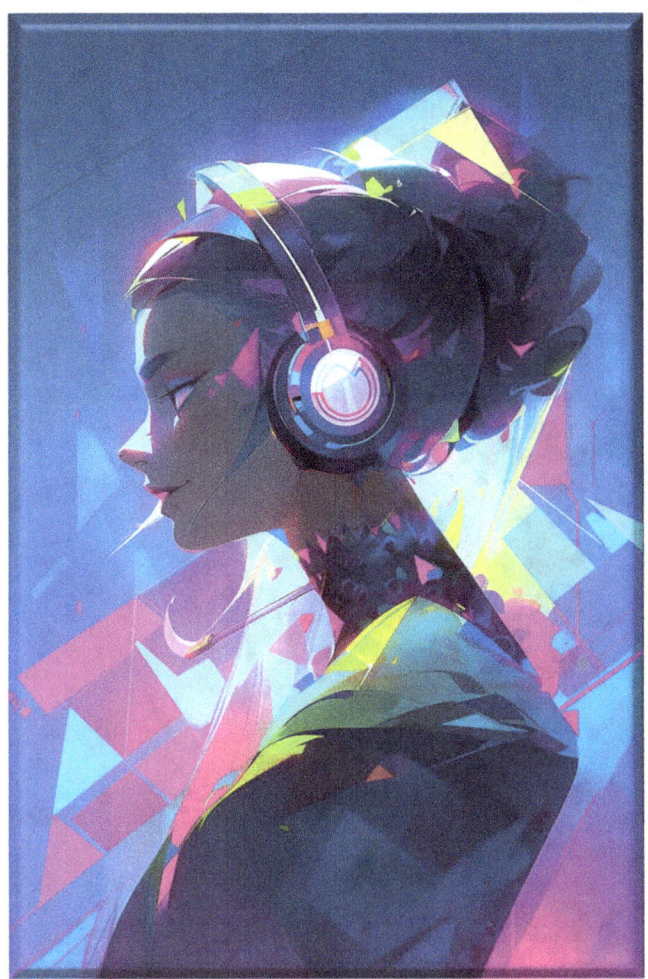

nation's legalities, while simultaneously being free and practical and creative and enjoying yourself. You should do what humans have always done:

As an expression of joy and freedom and humanity, be inspired by the world around you, and things that you see and feel. Your thoughts in engaging with such things are uniquely your own. Then, create your own art and expressions that reflect the world back at the world, in your own unique way.

In acting upon your inspirations, do it in such a way that you are creating something blended, considered, personalized, and new, rather than just reiterating what others have already created and controlled.

In doing so, you are acting as any other artist in the world. You are assimilating your experiences and reactions to stimuli in a unique way, in order to create things that have never before existed.

These images that I generated are not copyrighted, in accordance with current USA law (spring 2023) as it pertains to AI-empowered imagery without a significant human-driven modification component.

My AI Art Technique: DNA Mixing

Considering all of the above, you might want to know how I personally recommend that you approach Midjourney-driven anime art – and the reality of intellectual property – in a corporate world. This world is filled to overflowing with wonderful shows, games, books, celebrities, and infinite opportunities to create your own AI-empowered art.

And fortunately, looking at, thinking about, and enjoying all of these things while you create is not a crime!

My general recommendation is that you should always be mindful of AI and IP and your

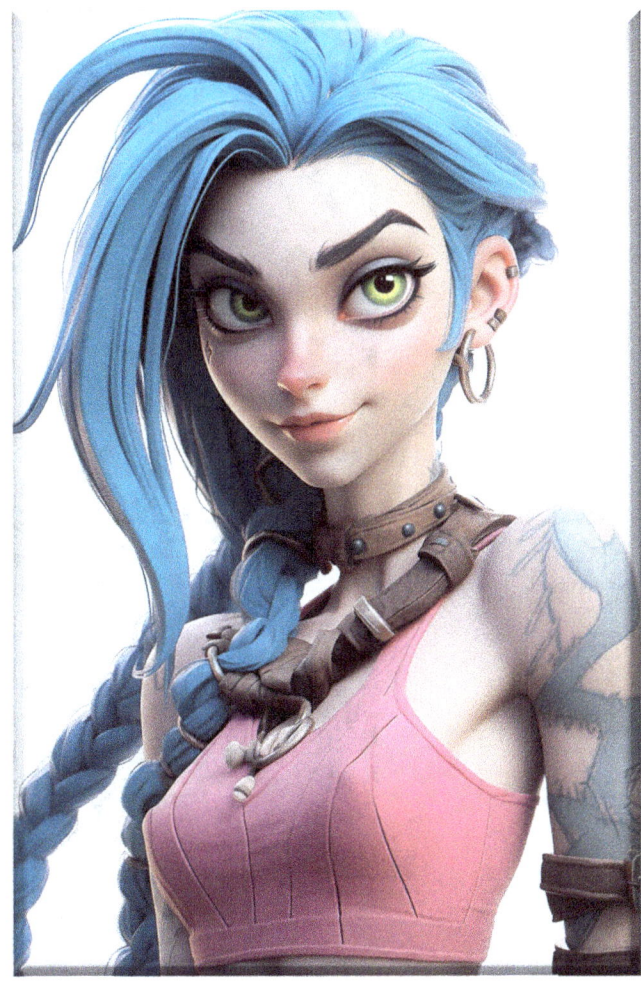

FOLIO IMAGE 020

/imagine   **Anime star fighter pilot, in polished mech suit in cockpit of ship, holographic HUD, glass displays give readout of ship's status, cyberpunk, like Mandalorian Gundam Battlestar Galactica, hyper - realistic, intricate fine details, Hasselblad photography, 32k, UHD, HDRI --ar 9:16 --style expressive --niji 5**

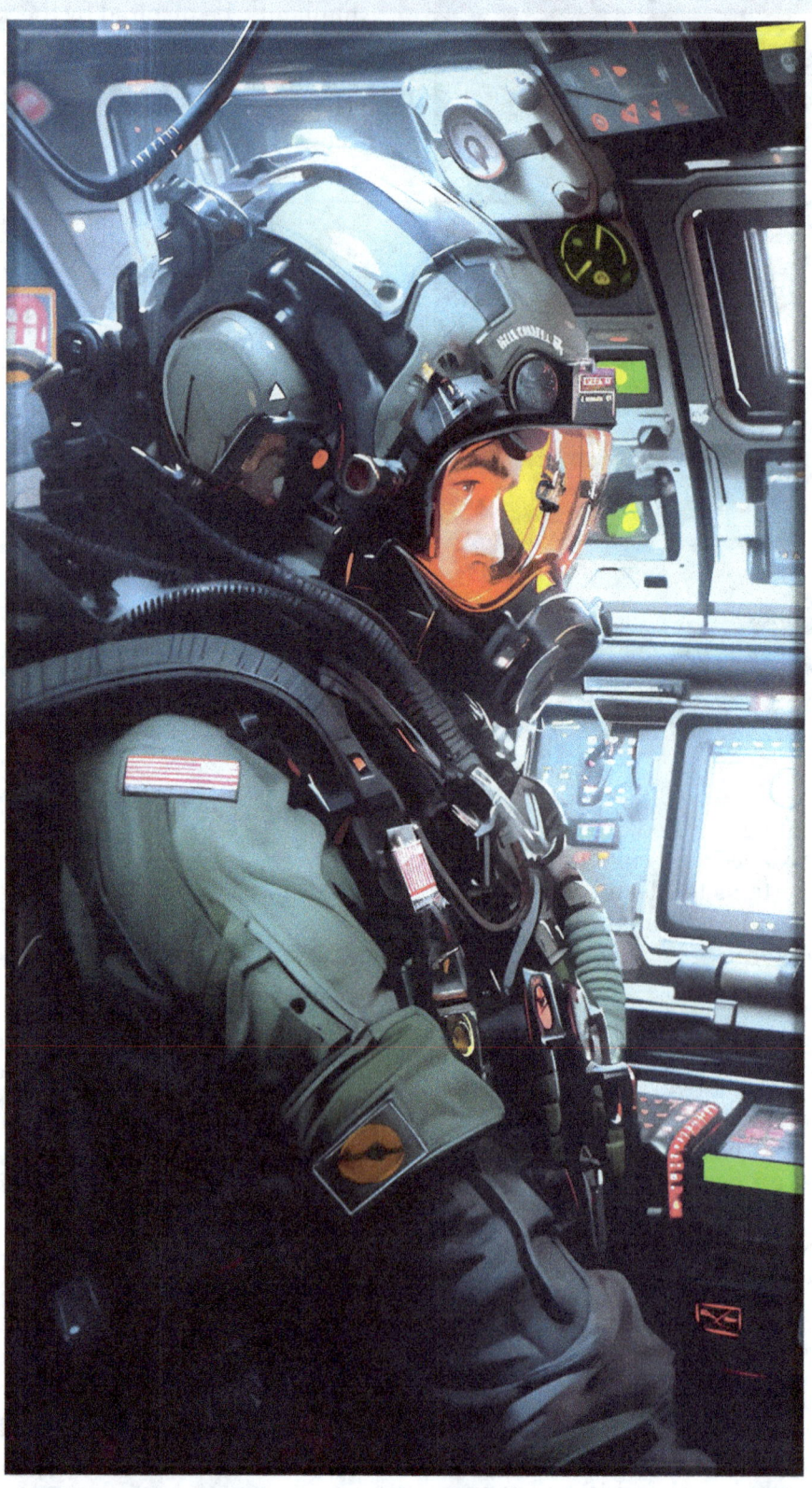

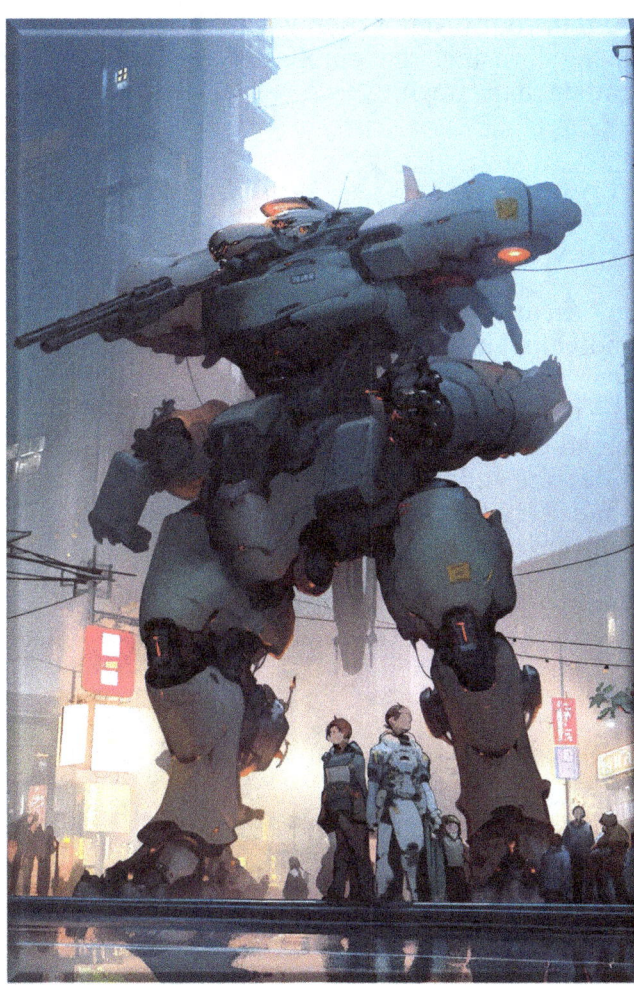

combine them to make purple, even though the purple is 50% red and 50% blue, it is still something absolutely different. Everyone can see the elements that created purple, from the coolness of blue and the warmth of red. But everyone can also see that purple is not blue, and purple is not red. Purple is its own thing.

Then, when you create sub-shades of purple (amethyst, lavender, royal purple, violet, wine, and so on into infinity) and splash them near other colors that you have blended, you are so far beyond blue and red that no one can truthfully say that your new creation is only the embodiment of its original DNA strands.

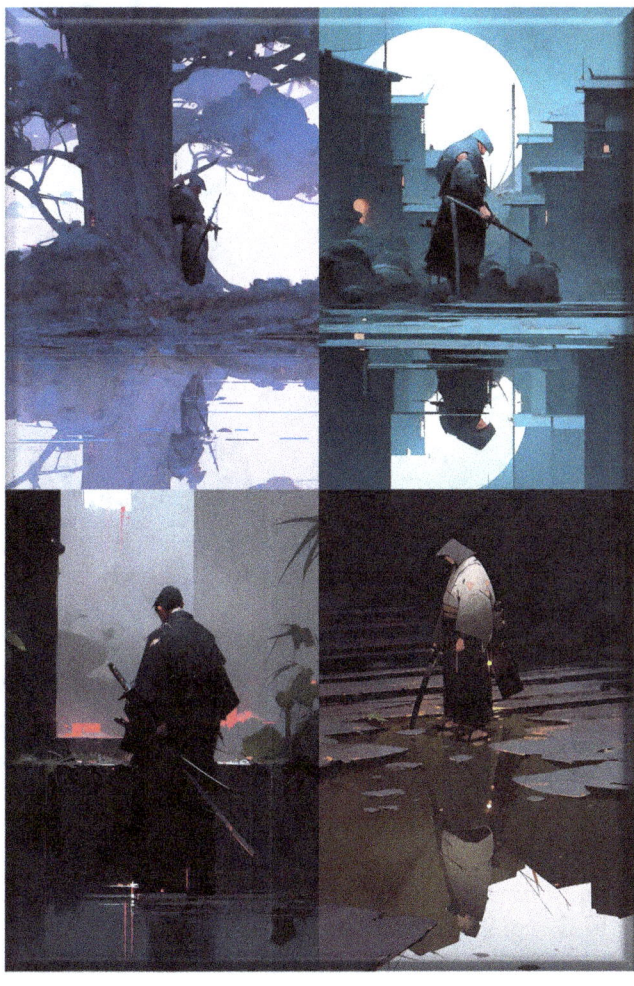

Other works of prior art might look like yours, to a certain degree. But when you combine many considered ideas into a new mix, your new creations are nevertheless unique.

You have the same right to create art as anyone else. In fact, you have *more* right to create art than anyone who would move to forbid or suppress you, because you are seeking to create free expression, while they are seeking to destroy it.

To ensure that you are drawing from past influences and blending their best elements to create something new, I recommend the art technique that I call **DNA Mixing**. This means that you are taking two or more different strains of some type of thing, and blending them to create something that shares the nature of those strains, while also becoming its own thing. Two parents create a baby who is a uniquely growing individual, as it were.

As a simple essential example, red and blue are both very distinct primary colors. When you

Rather, it is a new piece of manifested expression, which we call art. *Your* art. The fact that your art tools were datasets and code, where others might use a paintbrush, or a pencil, or a digital tablet, is irrelevant to the core truth. All of these art tools are merely implements, used to channel human creativity into crafted artwork via the *prompting* of an inspiration-engendering idea.

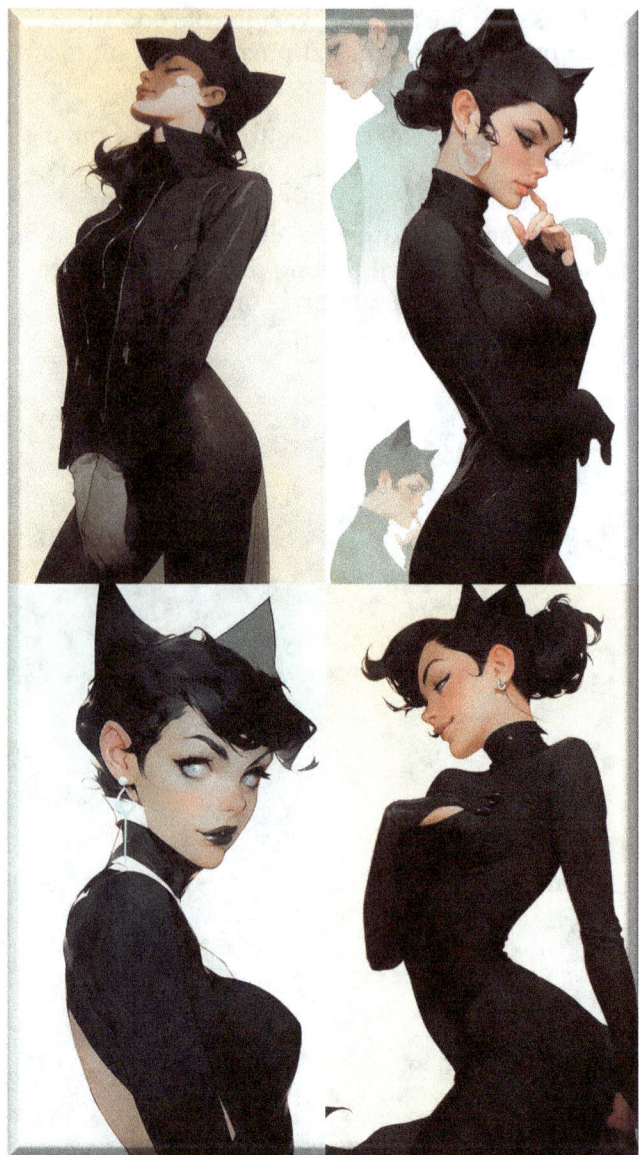

To be brief: Use multiple DNA strands to create new things, that only somewhat look like old things. Whatever happens legally, politically, or culturally in the future, being forward-looking, mindful, and quietly sensible will always be the best approach.

I recommend that you consider the following DNA pools at a minimum: art styles, living artists, deceased artists, established characters, public domain characters, anime products (books, games, shows, etc.), public domain products, core aesthetics, and punk aesthetics.

And in your prompt coding, you should consider using phrasings that emphasize inspiration, rather than copying.

[DNA I]

Art Style DNA Strands

An art style cannot be copyrighted. An individual artist, however, holds the copyright over their own creations. Works do not fall into the public domain until long after the artist or creator has been deceased. This is because we celebrate and improve living humanity, rather than stagnating and solely dwelling upon those who are already gone.

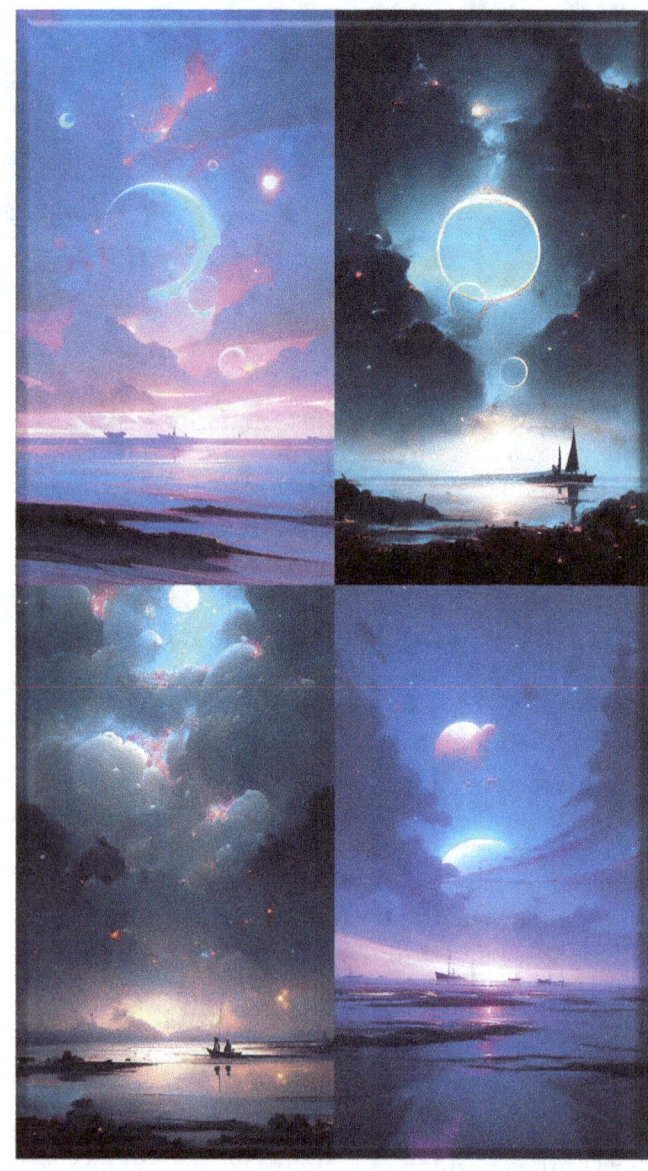

FOLIO IMAGE 021

/imagine   **Close up, a gecko anthropomorphic commander, wearing heraldic designed plate armor, Warhammer vibes, in the styles of Moebius or Takato Yamamoto or Sergio Toppi or Russ Mills or Aaron Horkey, very detailed, moody, cinematic lighting, ethereal, volumetric fog, Rembrandt lighting, glowing volumetric atmosphere, long shadows, vibrant raking light, boosted chromatic aberration, subsurface scattering -- ar 9:16 --style expressive --niji 5**

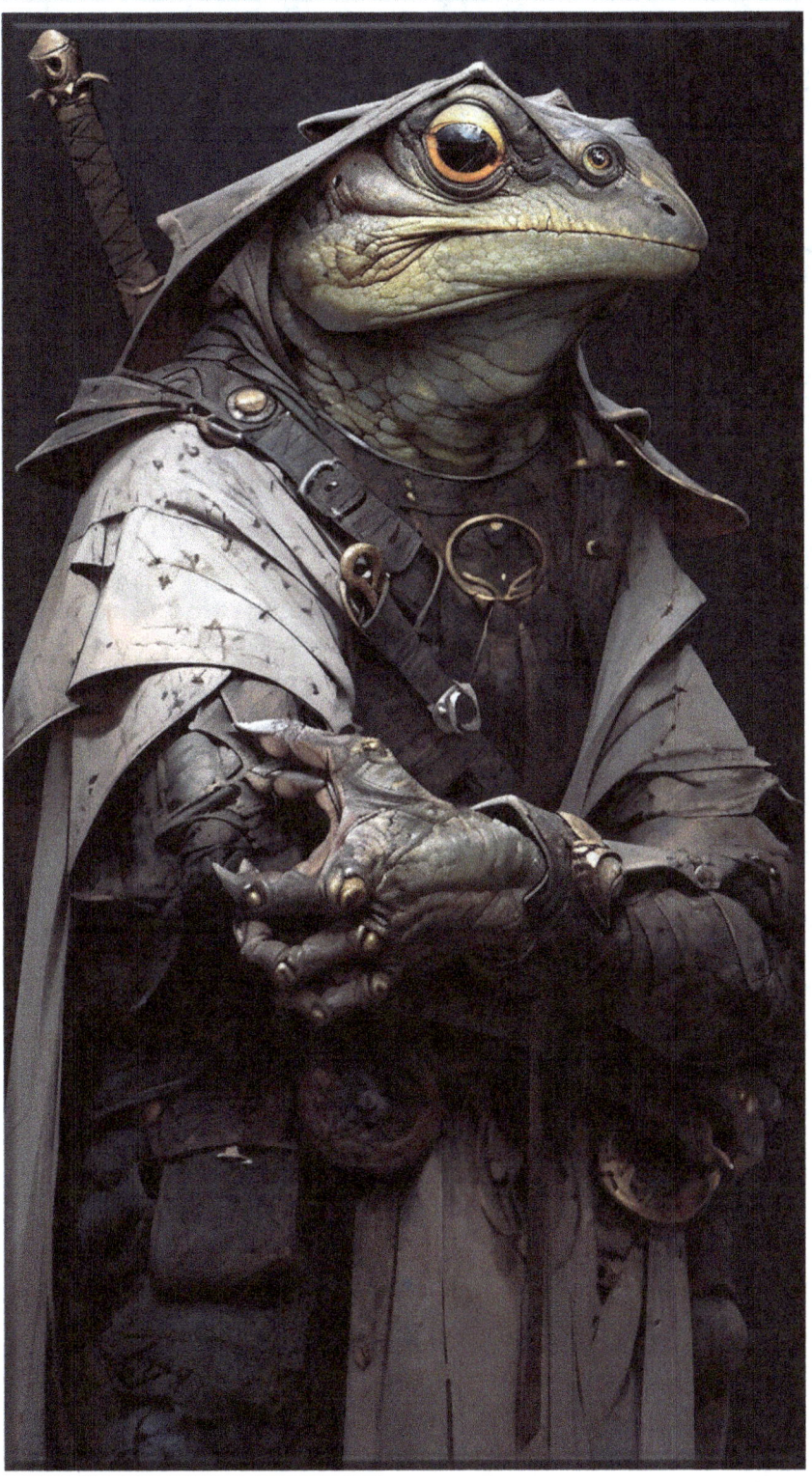

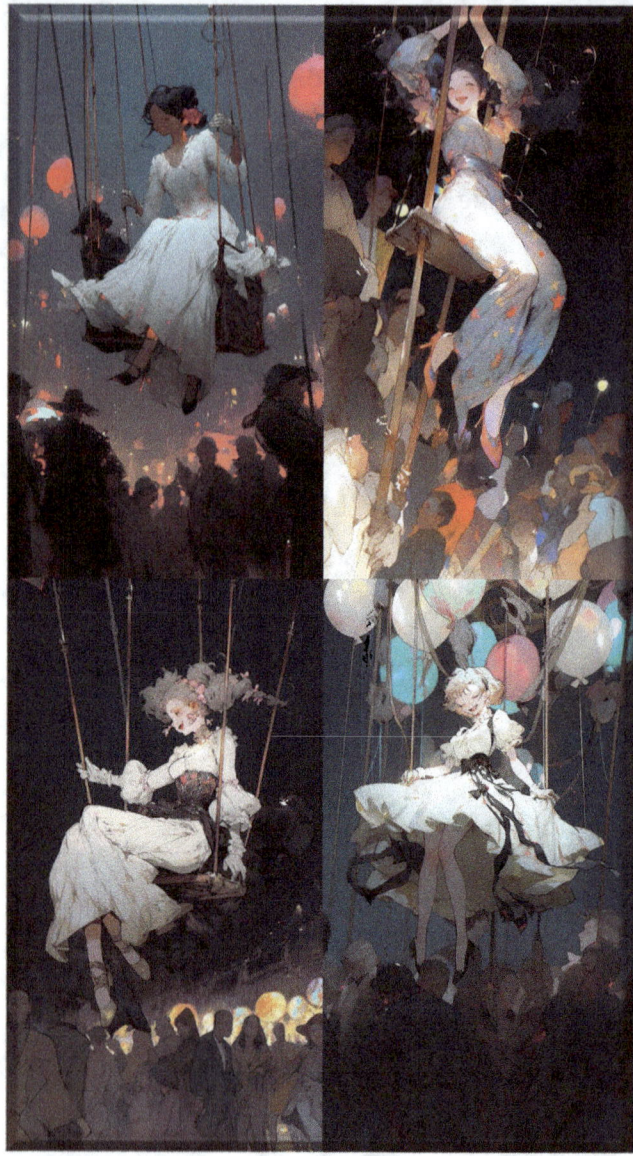

In creating anime art, this is a bit trickly to consider because anime is already an art style. But there are sub-styles and related style keywords, such as:

~

[1] Action Figure (anime art made to look like a collectible toy figure);

[2] American (USA art inspired by Japanese anime influences and originals);

[3] Beautiful (anime designed to be nice to look at);

[4] Bioarchitecture (scenes of incredible sprawling builds that are alive and technical);

[5] Bishojo (anime featuring cute girls and young women);

[6] Bishonen (anime features cute boys and young men, sometimes androgynous);

[7] Cartoonish (anime that is deliberately less realistic looking);

[8] CGI (art that looks like digital movie special effects);

[9] Chibi (cute or humorous disproportion);

[10] Gakuen (school drama storylines);

[11] Gekiga (anime with dark and realistic themes);

[12] Ghibli (a famous studio, known for its colorful and evocative cinematic imagery);

[13] J Horror (supernatural, eerie, or scary art);

[14] Jidaimono (historical drama, particular of events that are interest to Japanese culture);

[15] Josei (anime for a mature female or feminine-minded audience);

[16] Kawaii (cute and innocent young characters known for their happiness);

[17] Kemonomimi (characters with cute animal features, such as eyes, ears, or tails);

[18] Kodomomuke (entertaining childlike characters in stories for young audiences);

[19] Maho Shojo (anime about girls who have magical powers and alter-egos);

[20] Manga (comics or graphic novels with a powerful Japanese aesthetic);

[21] Mecha (giant robot-like armored vehicles);

[22] Moe (anime that maxes out the cute, appealing, and empathic qualities of characters);

[23] Niji (as already described);

[24] Realistic (anime that is deliberately more real looking);

[25] Seinen (anime for a mature male or masculine-minded audience);

[26] Shojo (feminine anime with coming of age stories and character growth);

[27] Shonen (masculine anime with coming of age stories and character growth);

FOLIO IMAGE 022

/imagine   **Mood piece, oil painting of a vibrant street scene in a bustling, multicultural city, in the style of Dan Mumford, Chris Samnee, Kilian Eng, a great new topographics poster, highly detailed --ar 9:16 --style expressive --niji 5**

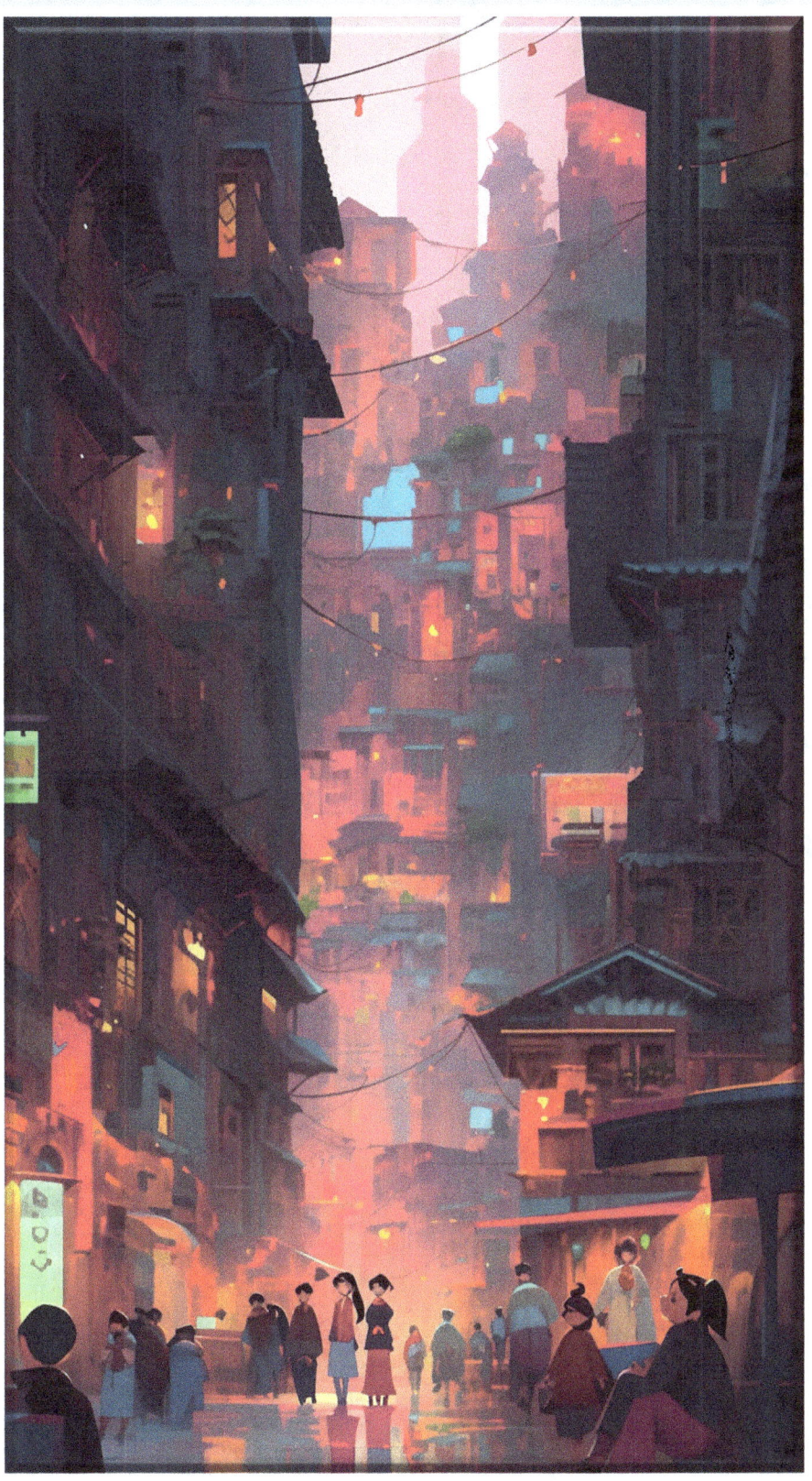

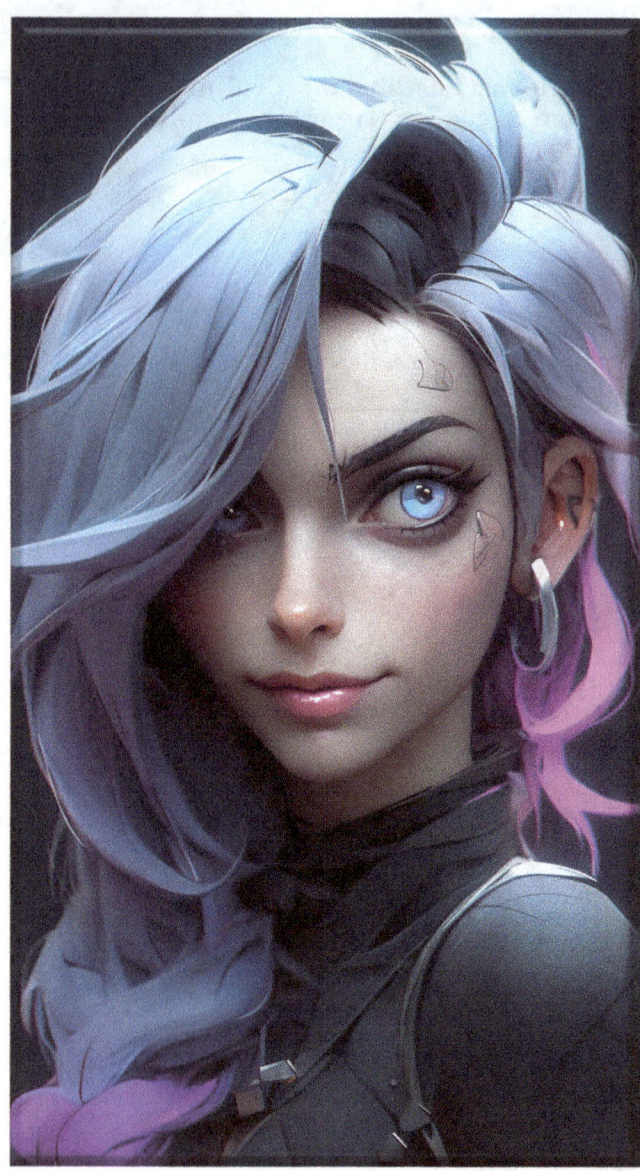

believe will never work together, and then challenging yourself in prompt crafting until you break through with something amazing. That is the personal style that I go for in every project. Remember that art styles cannot be copyrighted, and nobody owns the above sub-genres or terms.

You can use them whenever you want without too much concern. So that's one of the safest DNA strands. And what other types of strands of DNA should you choose from? That is entirely up to you, but I would recommend considering some of the following strands that I use all the time (as these are the exact types of thematic choices that millions of others are making throughout the world, as they create their own art, which is theirs).

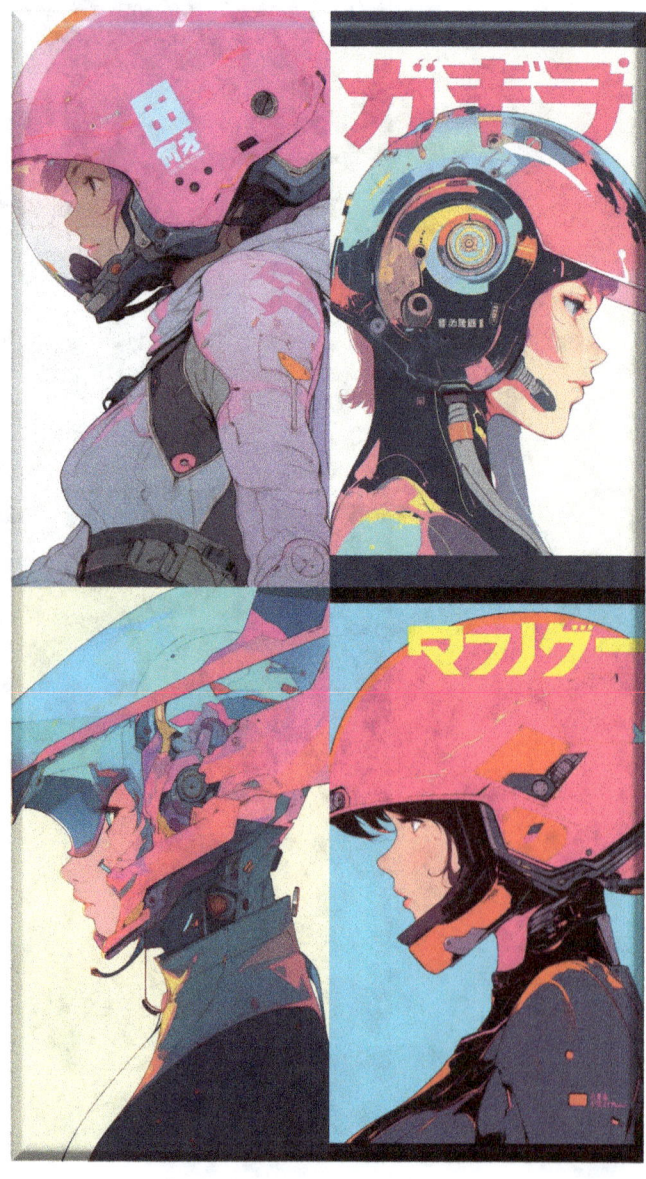

[28] Videogame (anime that features game character concepts or 3D models);

And **[29] Weird** (self-explanatory, but sometimes in the aesthetic of Lovecraft).

~

(I leave finer distinctions to others; here, we are discussing Midjourney prompt codes, mixing, remixing, and creative opportunities.)

Whereas a purist would tell you to keep each style type to itself, I will here gleefully tell you to mix at least two of these styles into the DNA of your prompts.

Some of the best discoveries in Midjourney come from mashing up styles that other people

FOLIO IMAGE 023

/imagine **Cityscape painting, Manhattan skyline by Elaine Moore, or in the style of Kurt Wenner or Carl Barksor Hiroshi Nagai or Syd Mead or Dan Mumford, puzzle - like pieces, subtle lighting contrasts, ai, trompe - l'œil and illusionistic detail, 32k UHD --ar 9:16 -- style expressive --niji 5**

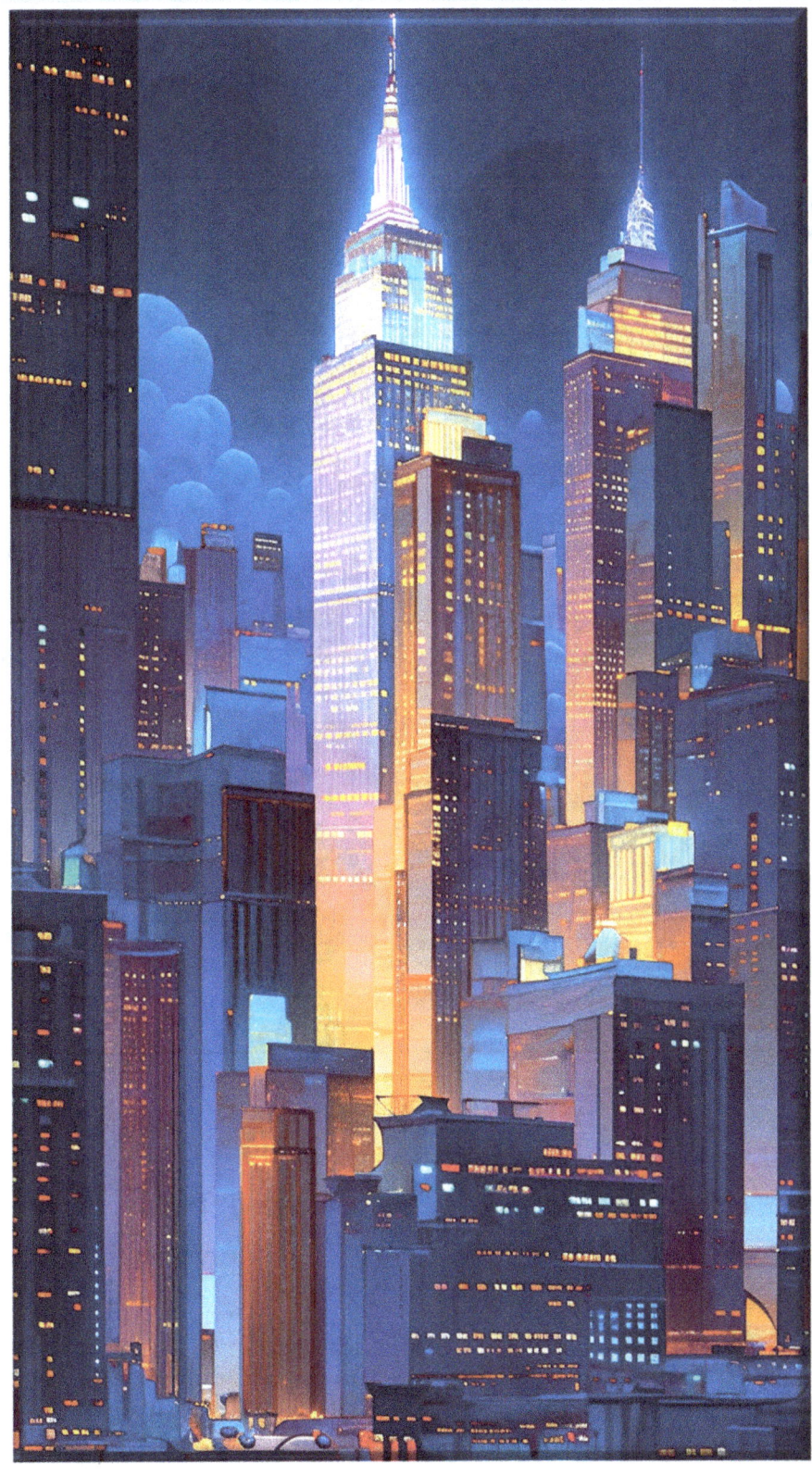

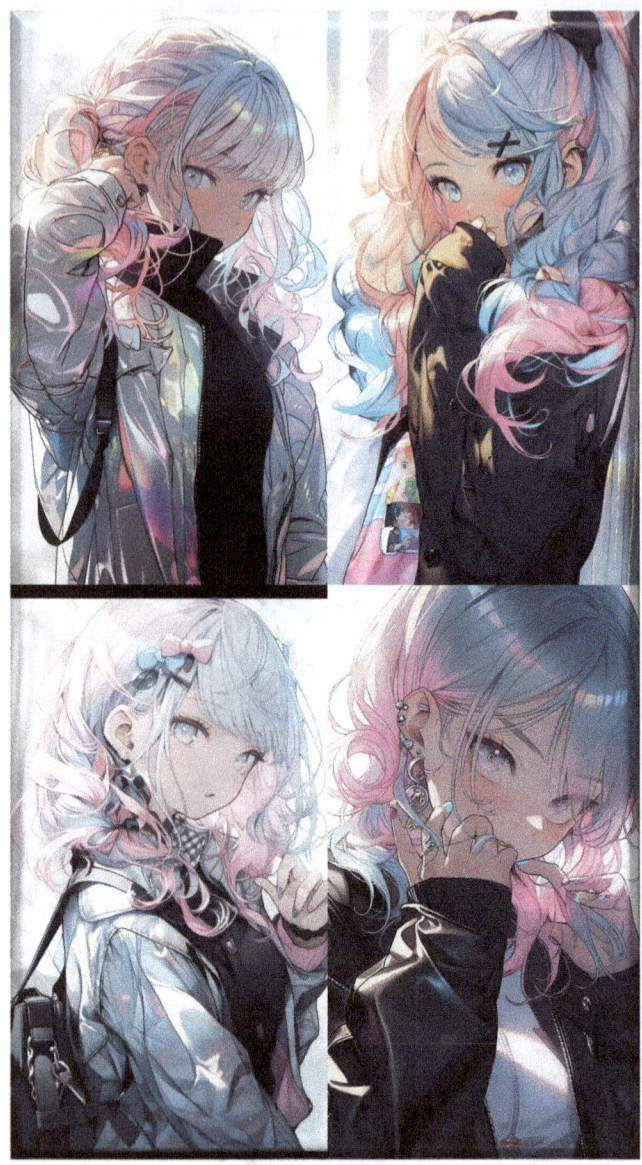

reminder that art styles cannot be copyrighted. I would also encourage you to list either no living artists at all, or more than one living artist, but never just one. Therefore, you would be wise to use the prompt language "in a blended style of Yoshitaka Amano, Hayao Miyazaki, and Akira Toriyama," rather than "art by Yoshitaka Amano." Remember, blending creates new things, while copying creates derivative things.

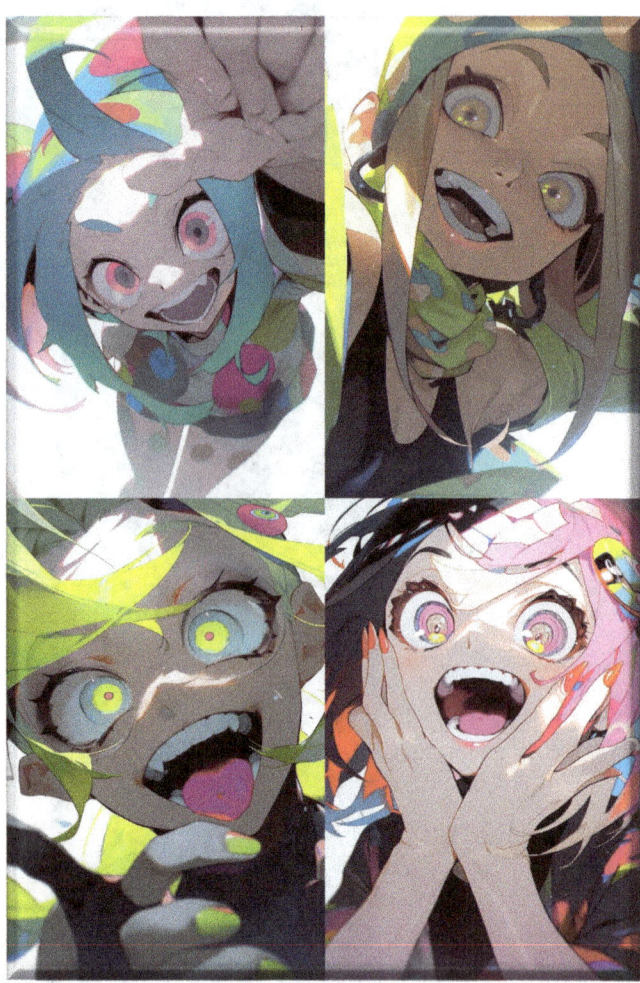

[DNA II]

Living Artist DNA Strands

There are many fine living artists who create anime or anime-adjacent artwork.

The Comfortable Approach: If you are not worried about future infringement issues, you can use one artist's style at a time and really explore it in nuance and various subjects. I've seen people using a single artist's style in a prompt many thousands of times.

The Careful Approach: In considering their influence on your own creations, I would encourage you to always use the term "in a blended style of" rather than "by" with the

[DNA III]

Deceased Artist DNA Strands

The Comfortable Approach: If an artist is no longer with us, and their estate is not looking to make hundreds of millions of dollars, and you don't see any bad news in searches, you can continue their legacy and use their style (although I recommend at least considering the information in The Careful Approach, below).

FOLIO IMAGE 024

/imagine   A detailed full body witch with black cat illustration, wetcore, traincore, storybook illustration, edgy caricatures, deconstructive rough clusters, hard - edge painting, mechanical realism, Art Nouveau inspired illustrations, speedpainting --ar 9:16 --style expressive --niji 5

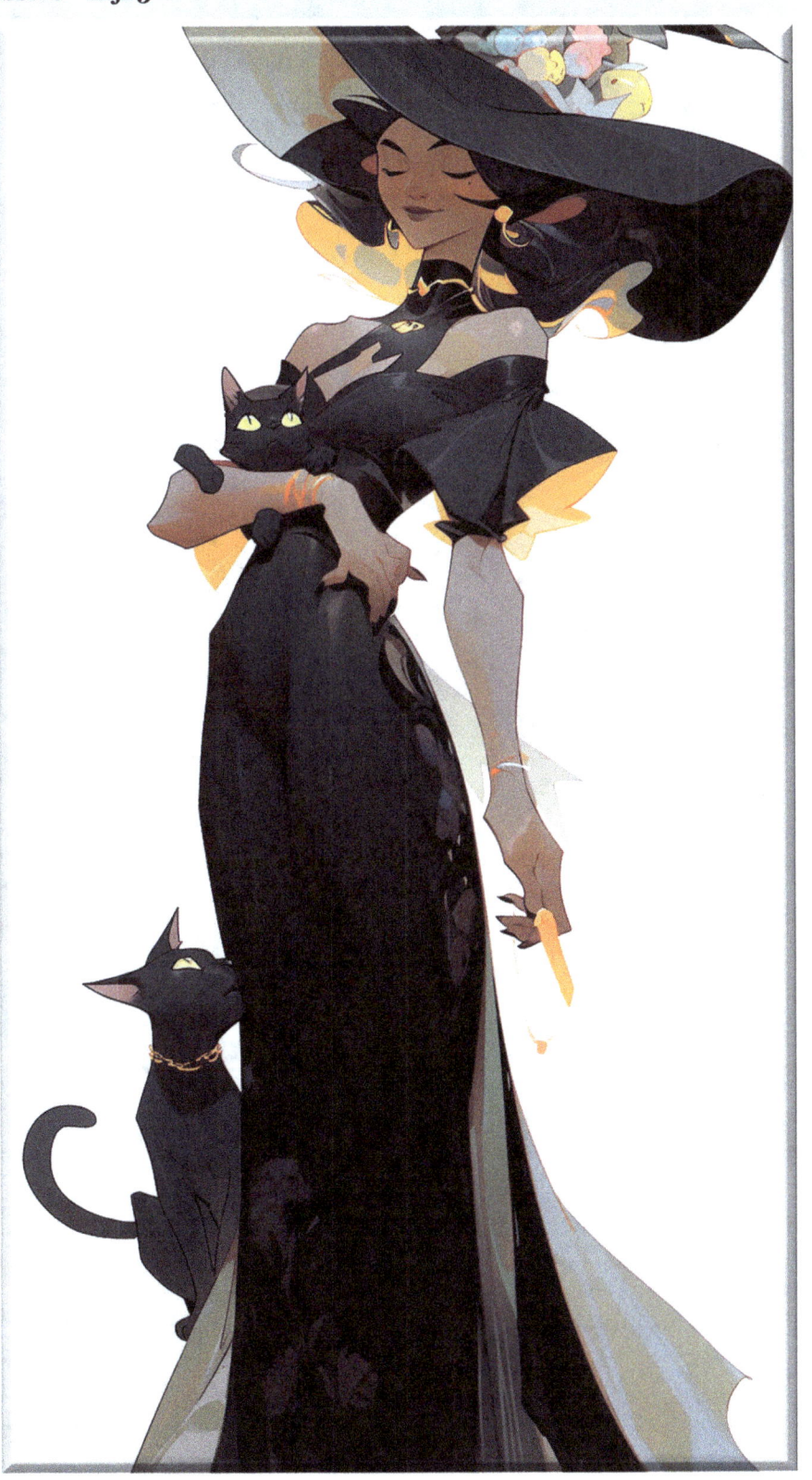

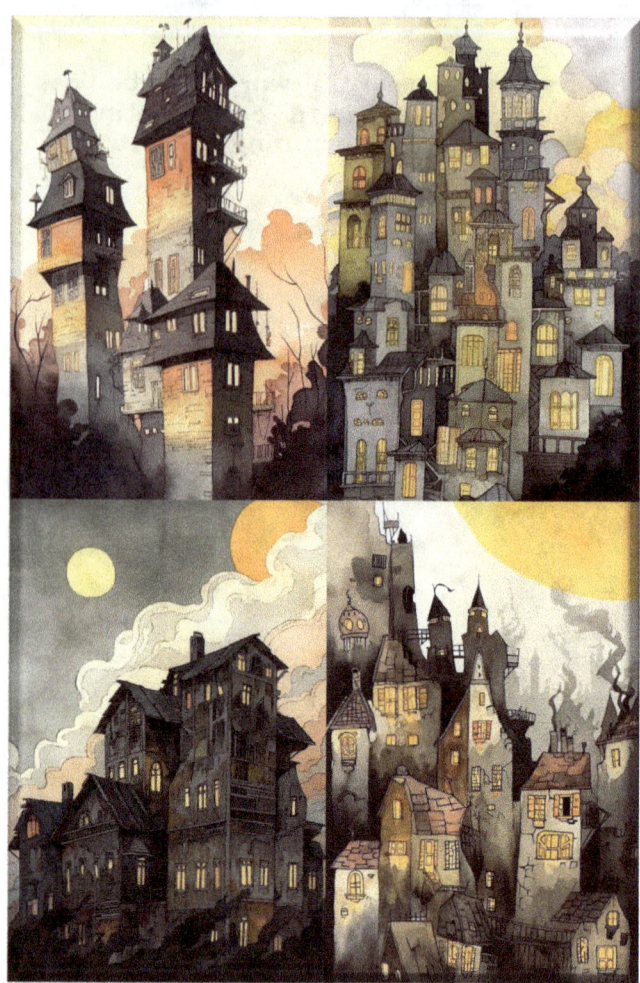

(We are again thinking about new creative opportunities, rather than established directives and genres.)

I have gotten interesting results using one or more of the following favorite artists. You are more than welcome to include your own.

Edgar Degas, Leonardo da Vinci, Michelangelo, Claude Monet, Alphonse Mucha, Vincent Van Gogh, John William Waterhouse, and more.

You might also want to look into the vast collection of art held by the Metropolitan Museum of Art, and other organizations who have released millions of images and representational art into the public domain.

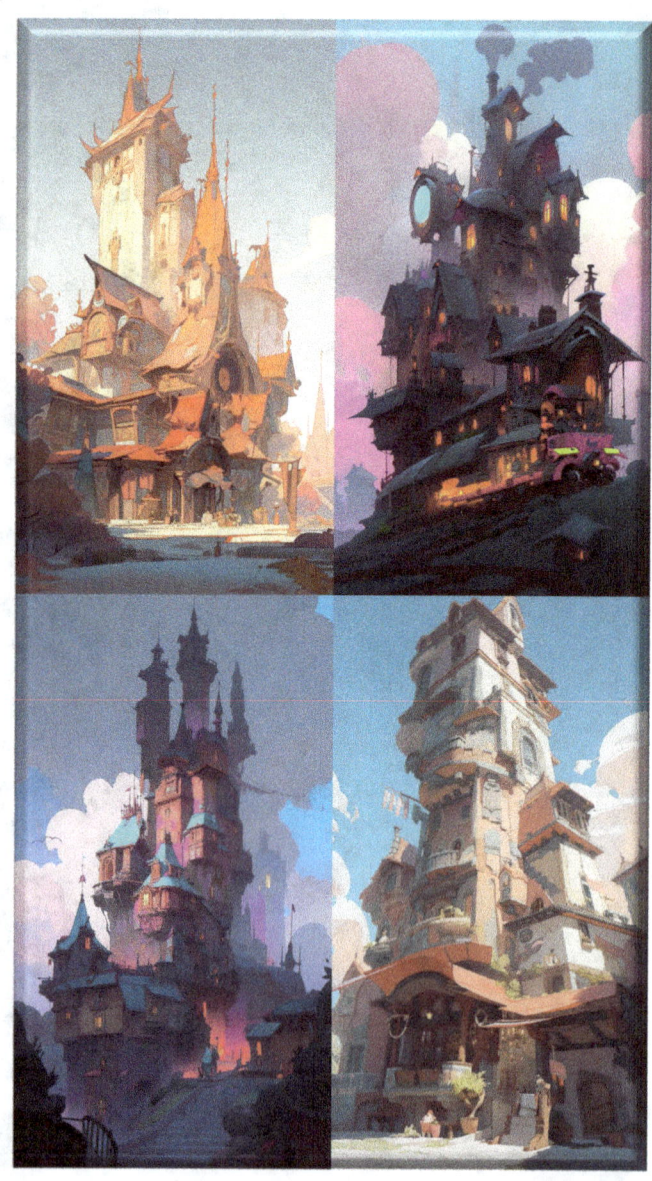

The Careful Approach: Stick to artists from long ago who are in the public domain. Anime is a relatively new art form, dating back to the early 1900s, the 1950s, or the 1960s depending on who you ask and how far you want to go back into its roots.

Therefore, when you consider the great deceased artists of the field, you will note that very few of them are yet in the public domain. But we want to go into the public domain, because it greatly lessens the amount of DNA in your works that could be claimed as someone's copyright.

Therefore, even if you don't use any Living Artist DNA Strands in your prompts, I always encourage you to use one or more Deceased Artist DNA Strands that go back into the public domain.

This necessarily involves digging deeper into the past than anime itself.

FOLIO IMAGE 025

/imagine   **Concept art, inspired by retro - arcade games, like Pac Man, Galaga, Space Invaders, Tron, geometric pixelation, fluorescent, illusionary, iridescent, prismatic, translucent, ethereal, vibrant, luminescent, radiant, phosphorescent fluidity --ar 9:16 --style expressive --niji 5**

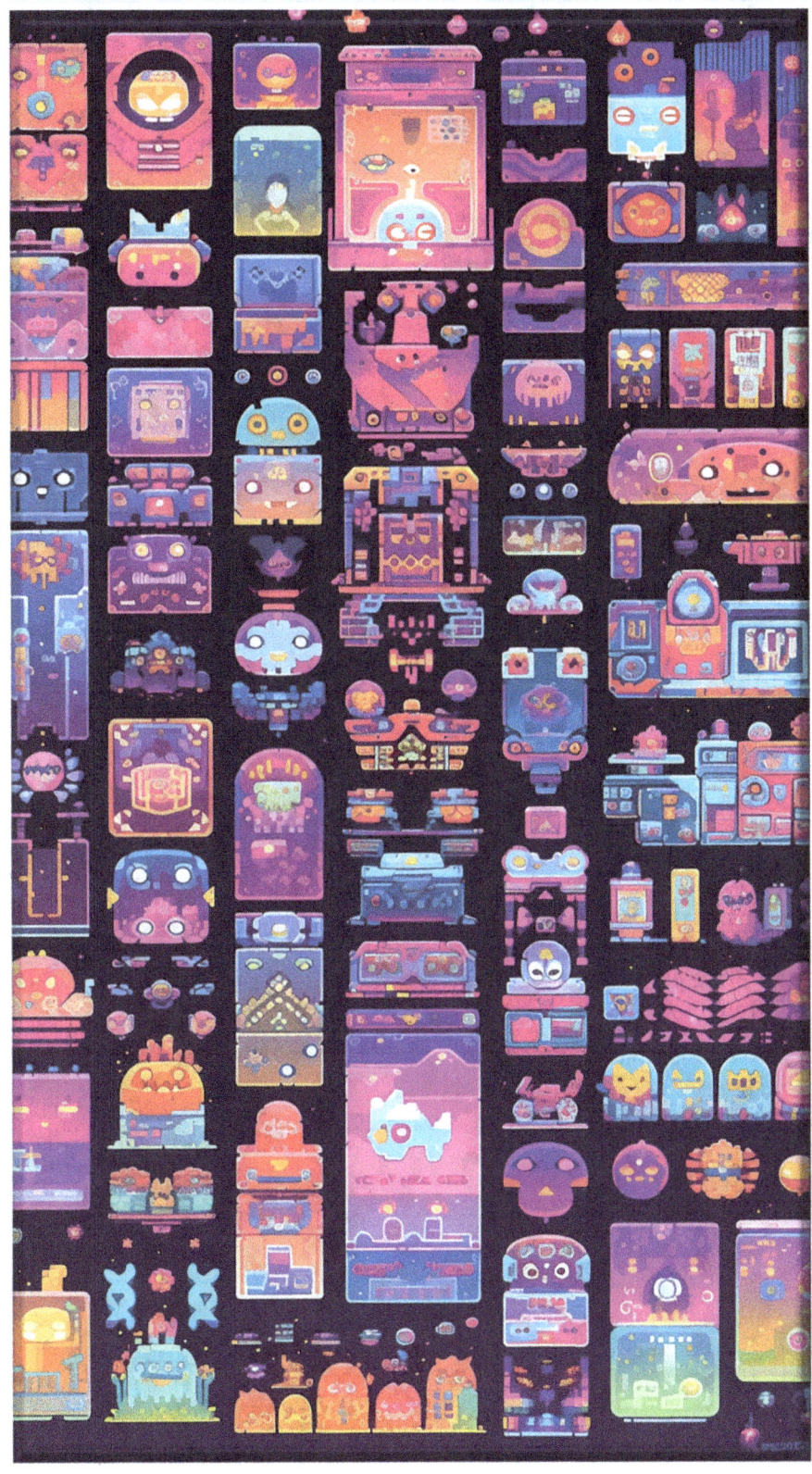

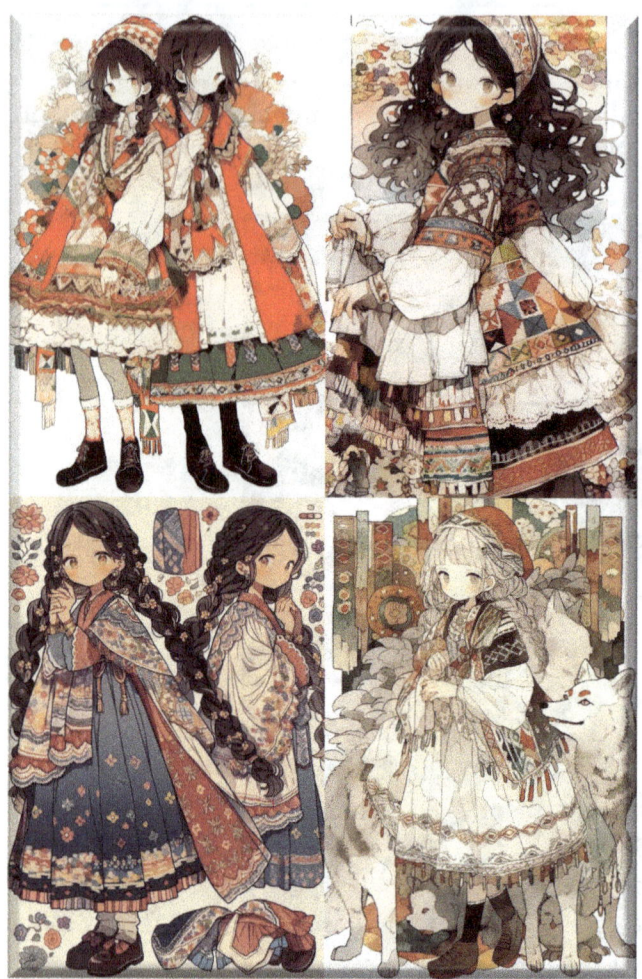

[DNA V]

Public Domain Character DNA Strands

The Comfortable Approach: Use any public domain character in your non-profit fan art. Even if your subject is trademarked, you're too little for anyone to go after, 99.9% of the time.

The Careful Approach: You must be careful in using characters that are in the public domain, because of trademark law and the fact that some estates prey upon the fact that their ancestors created a character.

Therefore, I would caution against using the prompt term "Disney's Alice," but you can certainly use "Alice in Wonderland" (created in the 1860s by Lewis Carroll).

In a similar vein, instead of using Sherlock, prompt "a Victorian consulting detective wearing a deerstalker cap." (And even there, be careful.)

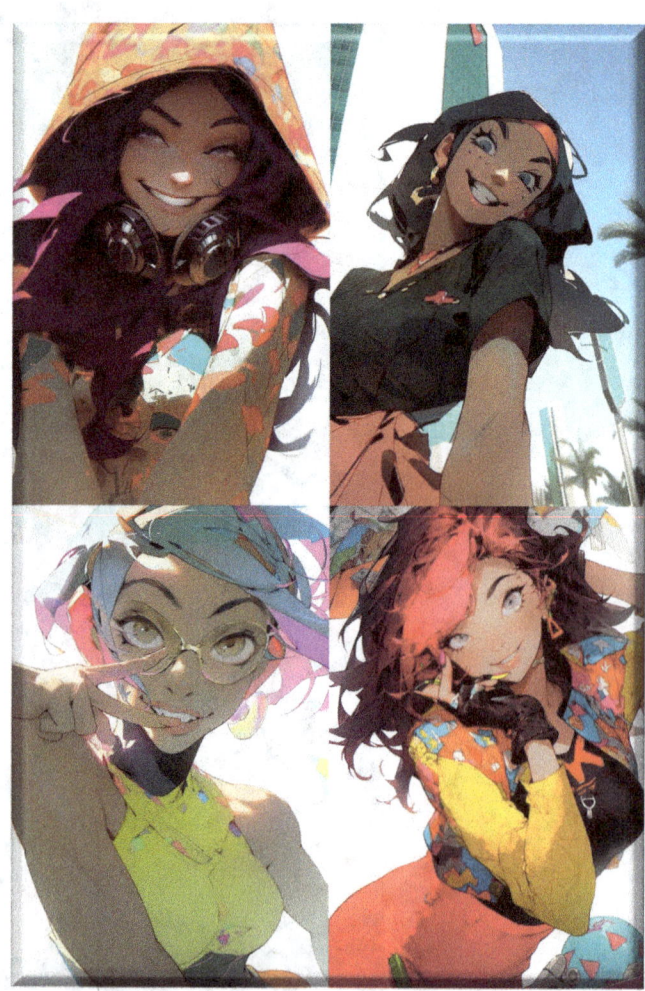

[DNA IV]

Established Character DNA Strands

The Comfortable Approach: Feel free to make profit-free fanart of established characters for yourself, but be a bit more careful when you're thinking of profiting or sharing widely.

The Careful Approach: Inevitably, people want to make images of characters that are currently popular and are owned by profiting corporations. I cannot encourage you to do so without a significant amount of blending. I would recommend that you use at least two established characters, and then blend them with two or more characters in the public domain (below).

In particular, keep in mind that celebrities own the rights to their own imagery and appearance, and making quasi-realistic AI "art" of recognizable people doing bad things that they didn't actually do is a colossally inept no-no. I recommend against it.

FOLIO IMAGE 026

/imagine   **Moonlight rakes across Times Square in NYC, a romantic evening --ar 9:16 --style expressive --niji 5**

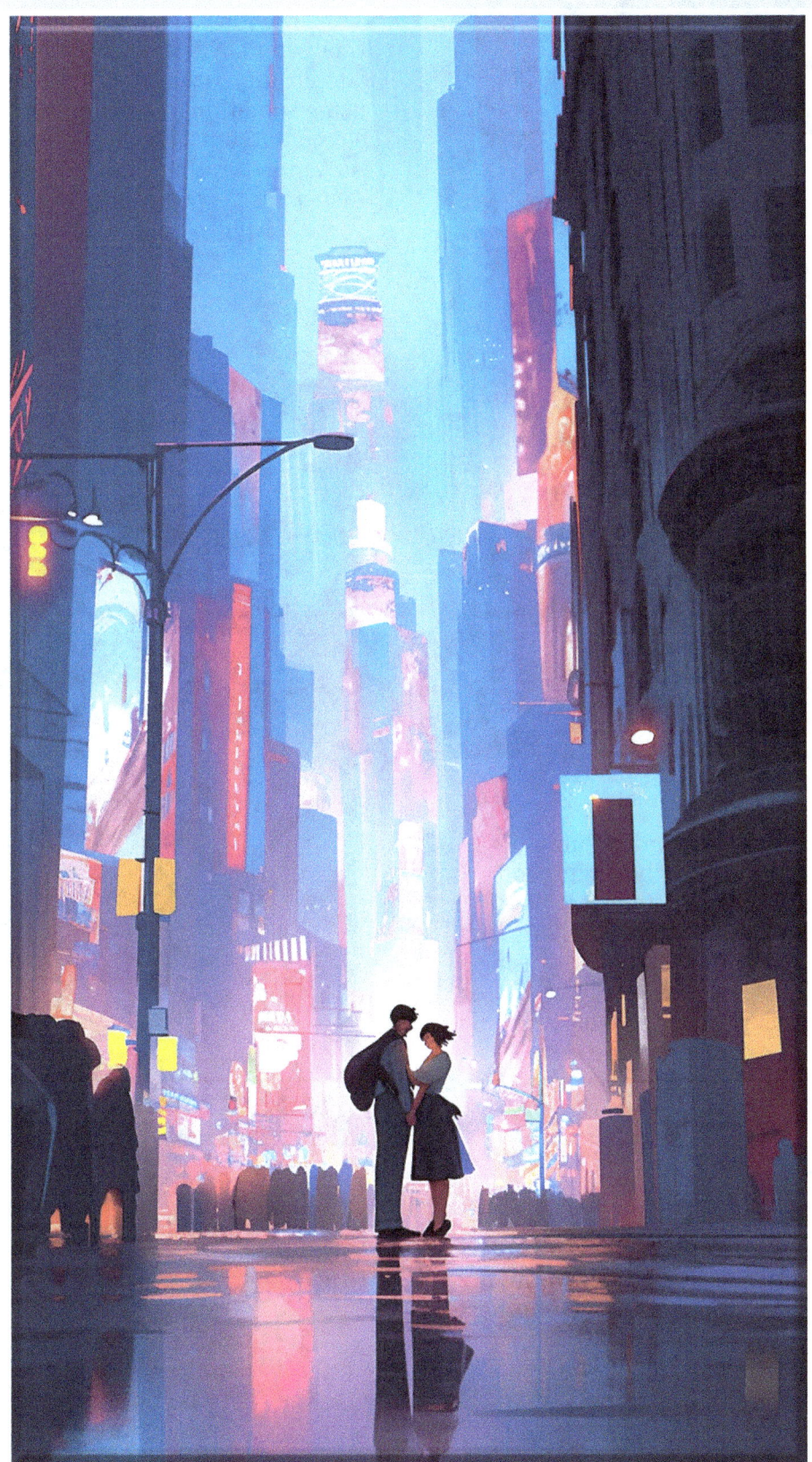

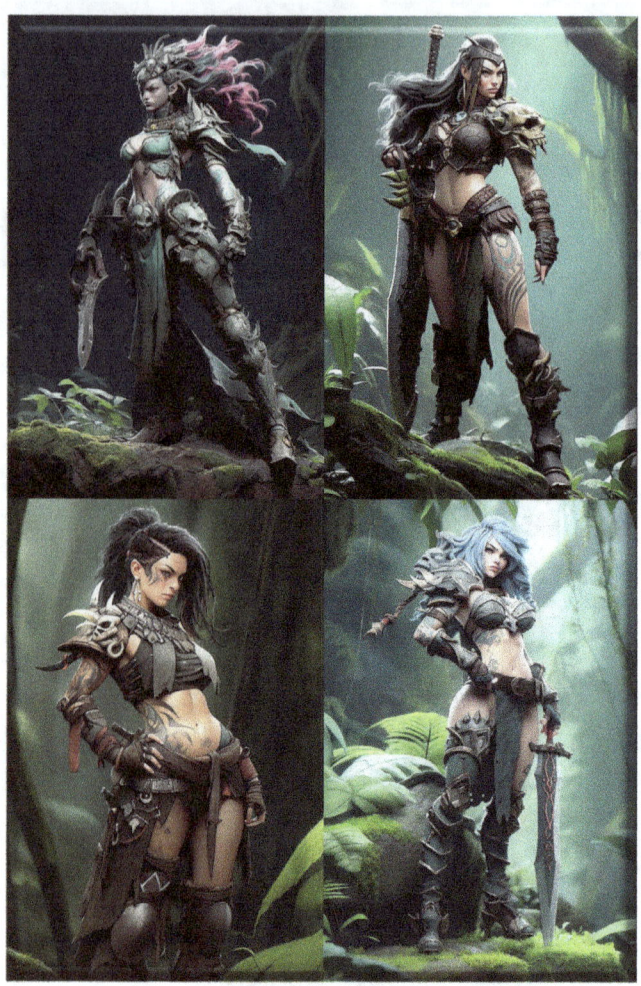

Just think of the fandom and enthusiasm surrounding your own favorite videogame, comic, book, show, or movie, and you will know what I mean. I recommend treating these entities in the same way that you would an Established Character DNA Strand: use either two or more in you prompt, or none, but never one. And try using something like "similar to inspirational elements from *League of Legends* and *Fullmetal Alchemist*," rather than "art by *Fullmetal Alchemist*" as one example.

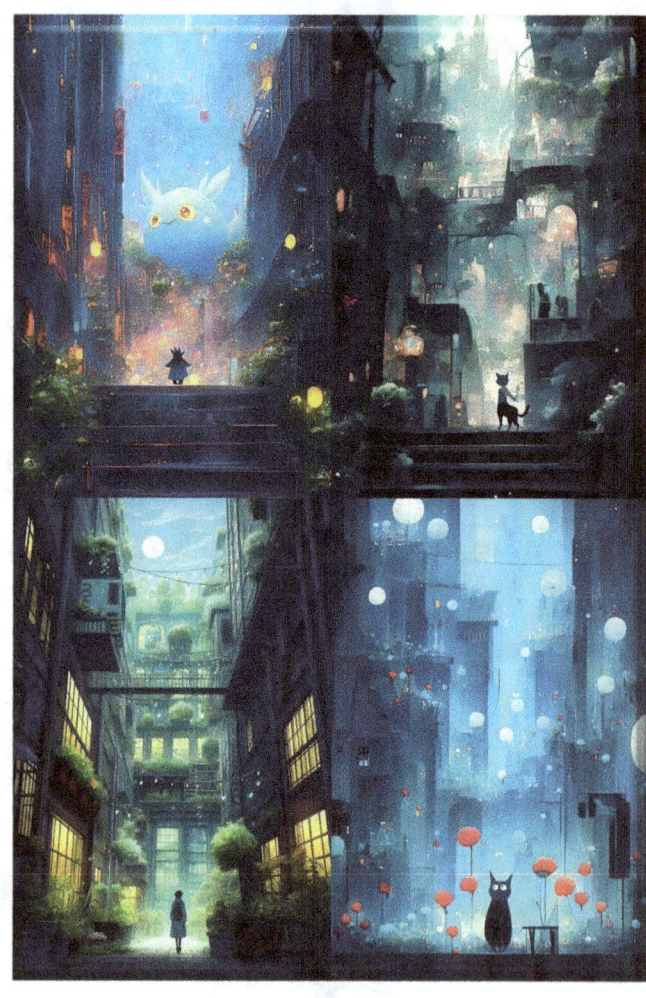

Be careful using heavily guarded public domain characters, particularly belonging to litigious and vampiric estates. While it is not to my advantage to name them all for you here, you can find the identifies of many of them by using a Google search such as "fictional character estates that like to sue," which you might want to do from time to time, as a cautionary measure.

[DNA VI]

Anime Product DNA Strands

The Comfortable Approach: If your research shows that the product's fan community is thriving, relaxed, and approved of, do as others do without seeking profit.

The Careful Approach: In a manner similar to established characters, people always want to create art that is a direct and recognizable tribute to an established persona.

[DNA VII]

Public Domain Product DNA Strands

The Comfortable Approach: Use any public domain franchise in your non-profit fan art. Keep in mind however that the public domain can be a bit more complicated than you might expect.

FOLIO IMAGE 027

/imagine   **The face of cyberpunk woman in neon lit dress, in the style of graphic design - inspired illustrations, futuristic robots, Argus c3, beautiful soft colors and pastels, futuristic Victorian, oil portraitures --ar 9:16 --style expressive --niji 5 --q 2**

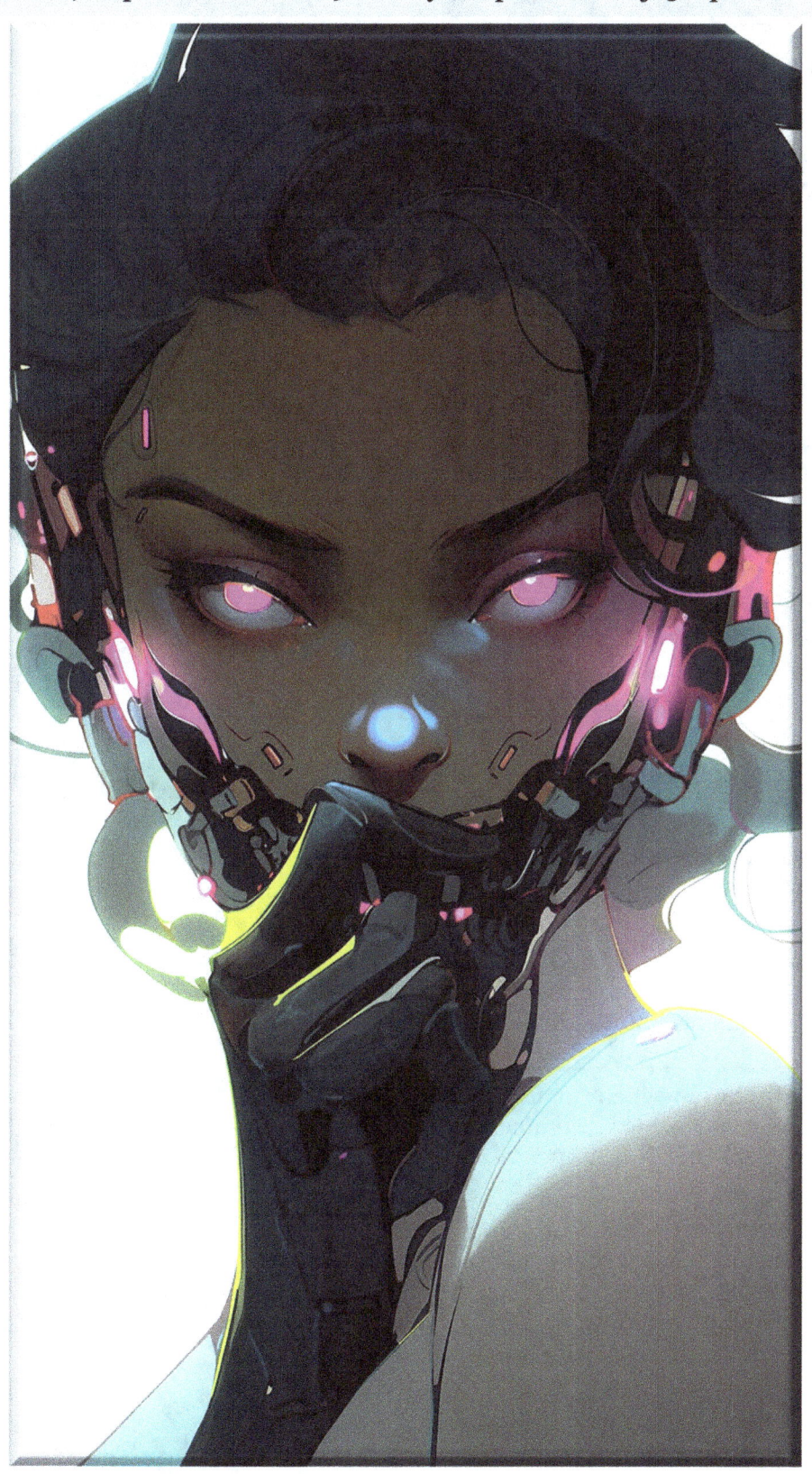

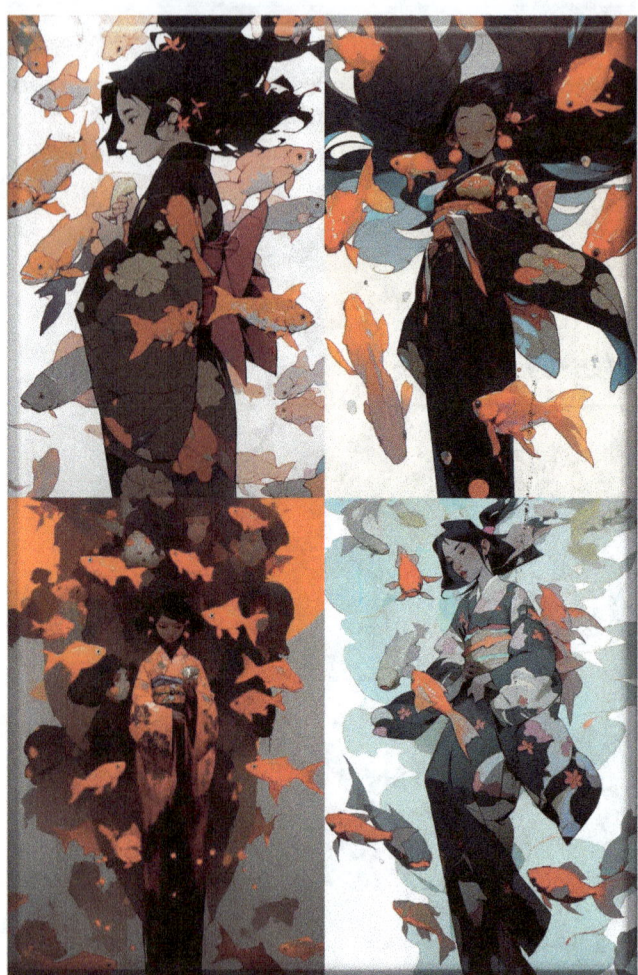

Inferno, Dracula, Edgar Allan Poe, Frankenstein, Greek Mythology, Jekyll and Hyde, The Lost World, Paradise Lost, Phantom of the Opera, Shakespearean, Three Musketeers, The Time Machine, Treasure Island, Voyages Extraordinaires, The War of the Worlds, The Wind in the Willows, and *The Wonderful Wizard of Oz.* You will find that Monte Christo brings in swashbuckling elements that influence your designs, Cthulhu invites cosmic horror, Dracula gives elements of gothic and Victorian horror, and so forth.

[DNA VIII]

Core and Punk Aesthetic DNA Strands

The Comfortable Approach: Go crazy with these terms and have fun. These are youth movements and Internet-age inspirational subcultures, for the most part, along with some conceptual cultures that don't really exist (yet).

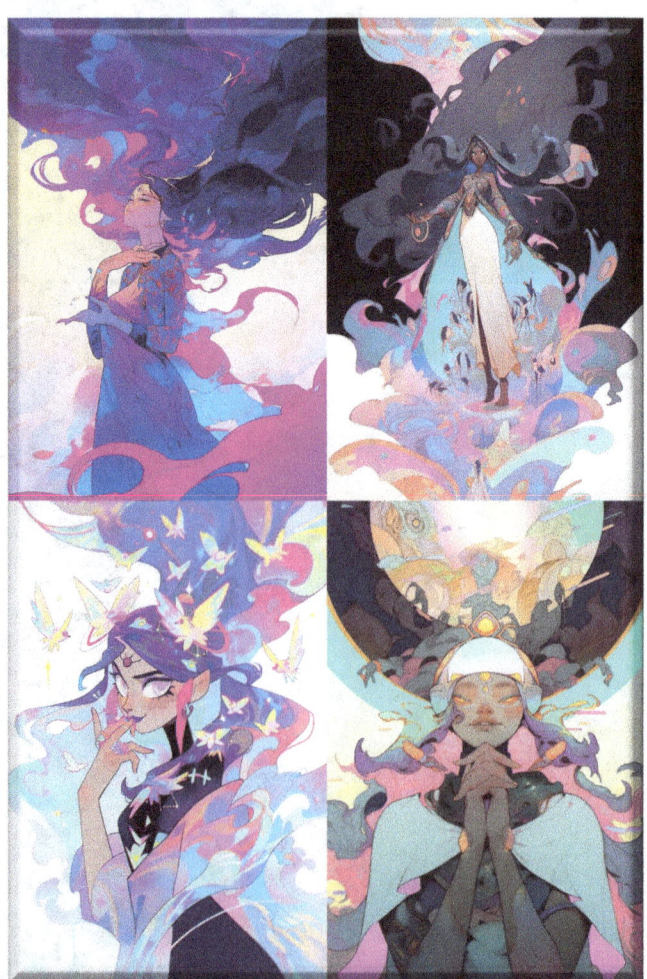

Be a bit more careful with franchises that are partly in the public domain (with some books) but not all the way (with some books still under copyright, and expression of the character perhaps trademarked).

For example Barsoom, Conan the Barbarian, Grimm princesses (Snow White, Rose Red, etc.), Peter Pan, Professor Challenger, and Winnie the Pooh are all in this "be a bit careful" category.

The Careful Approach: When you use Anime Product DNA Strands, I also recommend using Public Domain Product DNA Strands.

This can be a bit difficult, because most popular products are still copyrighted and/or trademarked. But when we consider the worlds of books and authorial bodies of work, we can come up with many examples. Some of my favorites to use include the following:

Alice in Wonderland, Beowulf, Brothers Grimm, Childe Roland to the Dark Tower Came, The Count of Monte Christo, Cthulhu, Dante's

FOLIO IMAGE 028

/imagine   **Super cool wise owl, incredibly high detail, octane rendering, no background, psychedelic style --ar 9:16 --style expressive --niji 5 --q 2 --niji 5**

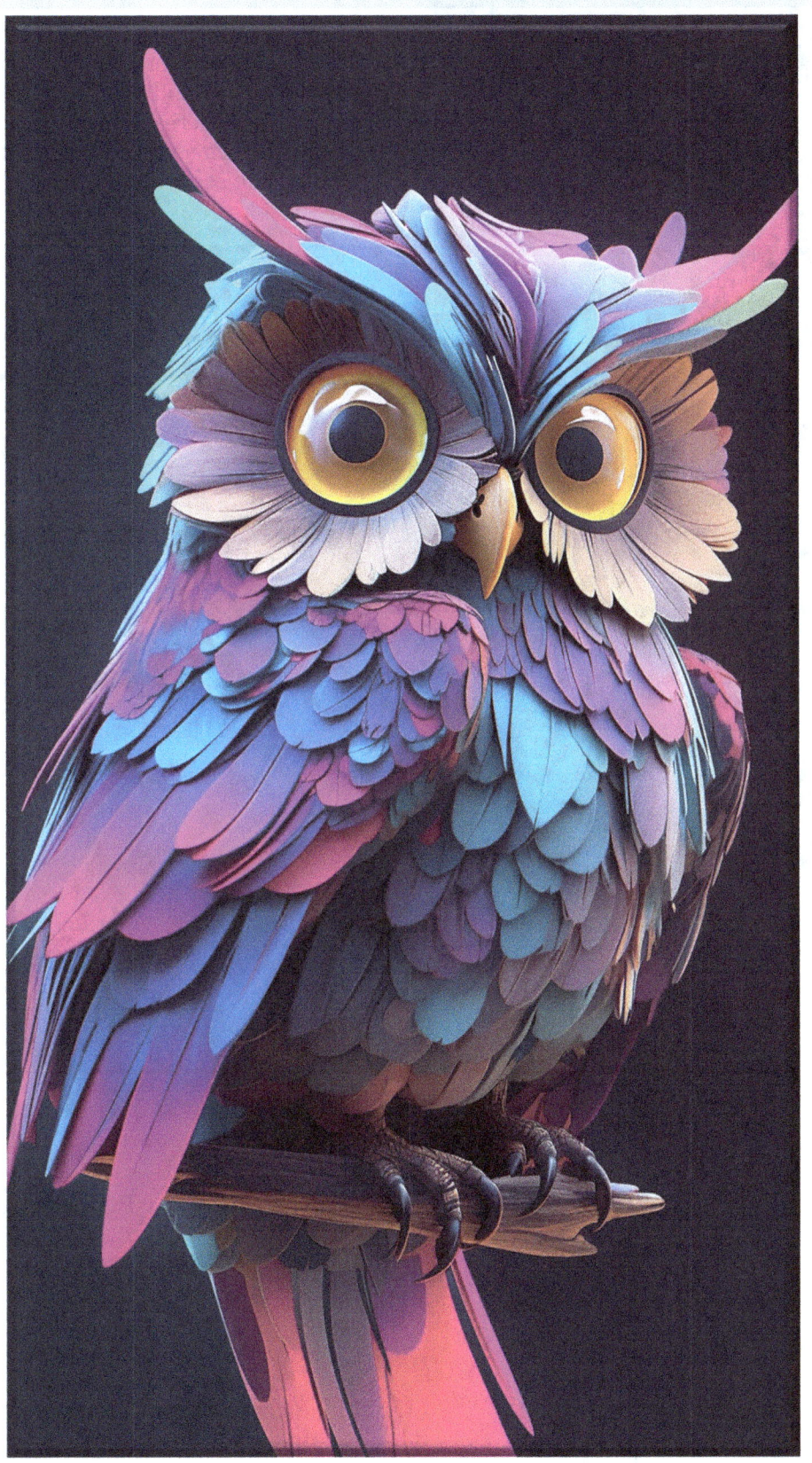

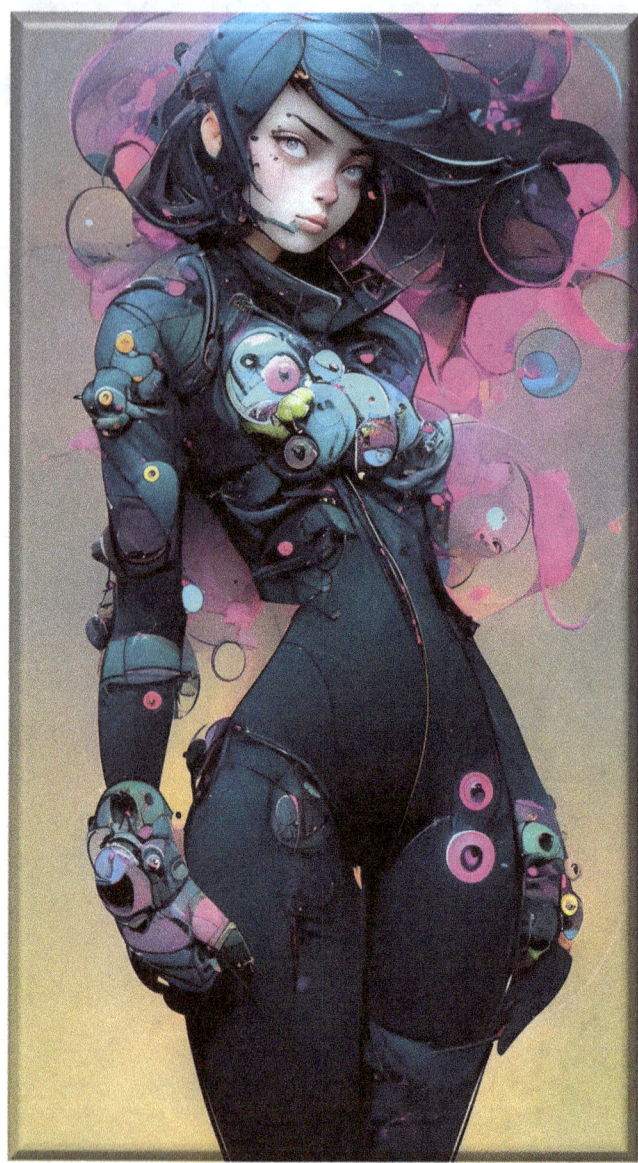

Core is the center, Punk is at the edges, and all of it is very useful in blended Midjourney prompting whenever you want to find something new.

Here are some partial lifts of Cores and Punks for your amusement, which are not copyrighted in any way (nobody owns them) and which Midjourney increasingly recognizes. Feel free to use these terms in Midjourney prompts with wild abandon to see what they do.

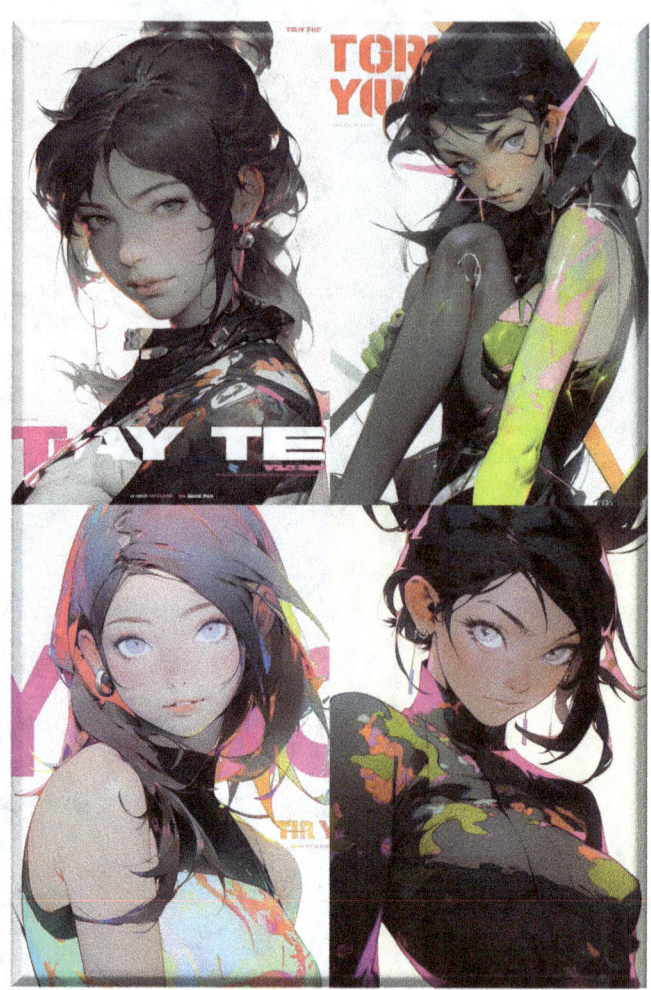

The Careful Approach: You can still pretty much use these terms with abandon, so long as the "-core" or "-punk" doesn't include a copyrighted name.

These are current terms for grassroots genres. Older people don't really understand these fandoms of things and concepts, but younger people will latch onto them immediately.

Basically, a "Core" is the imagistic "heart" or elemental essence of something, which means that its integral imagery is passionately celebrated in the art.

Similarly, "Punk" is the rebellious spirit or edge of something, which means that it has a specific aesthetic as an artistic statement. So the

Influential or Promising Cores:
Androidcore, Angelcore, Animecore, Cabincore, Carnivalcore, Cottagecore, Cutecore, Dreamcore, Fairycore, Gamercore, Goblincore, Gothcore, Mushroomcore, Nerdcore, Nightcore, Nintencore, Rainbowcore, Spacecore, Sparklecore, Technocore, Traincore, Urbancore, Villaincore, Weirdcore, Wetcore, Wizardcore, Zombiecore, and you can create your own.

FOLIO IMAGE 029

/imagine   **Stars, planets, stars in water on canvas art print, Ukai, in the style of Synthwave, fantasy landscapes, detailed background elements, lens flare, sea and coast painter, panorama, scattered composition --ar 9:16 --style expressive --niji 5**

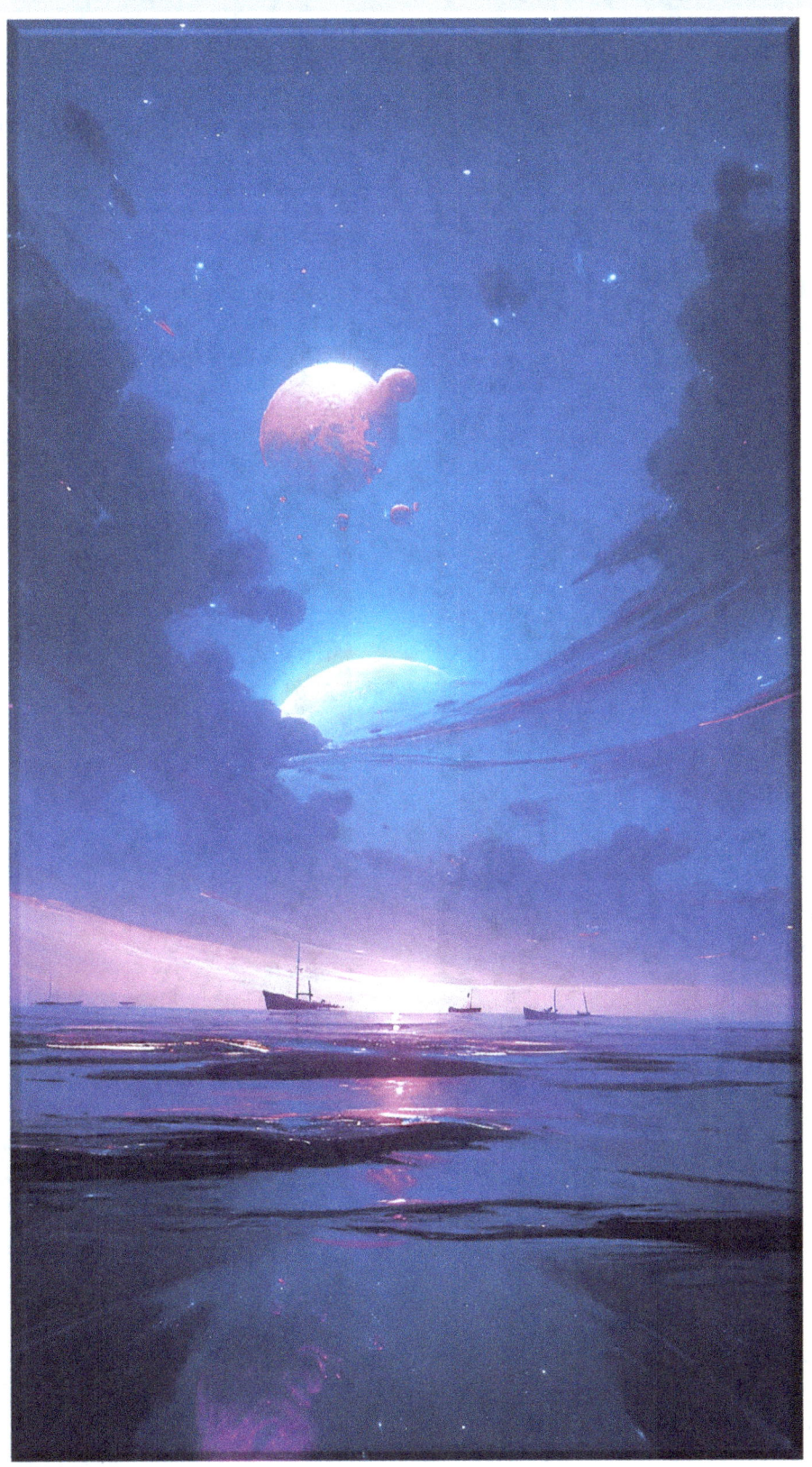

Influential or Promising Punks: Here's just a few. Afropunk, Atompunk, Clockpunk, Cyberpunk, Decopunk, along with Dieselpunk, Dungeonpunk, Gothpunk, Piratepunk, and also Postcyberpunk, Rococopunk, Steampunk, not to mention Vintagepunk, and you can create your own. And sometimes, if you turn any word into something more edgy by adding "-punk" to the end, Midjourney will move with you!

Although technology is moving at the speed of light and legislation is moving at the speed of snails, eventually the snails are going to get where they intended to go ... and when they arrive, everyone else might have forgotten they were even there.

All of these preceding techniques are perfectly legal and reasonable at the time that I am writing this book (April 2023). Inspiration is never illegal, especially when it is disparate and many-formed.

Being a savvy veteran Midjourney art crafter involves knowing just how far you can push things, as well as knowing when you have "struck gold" into a vein of creativity that no one has ever deeply mined before.

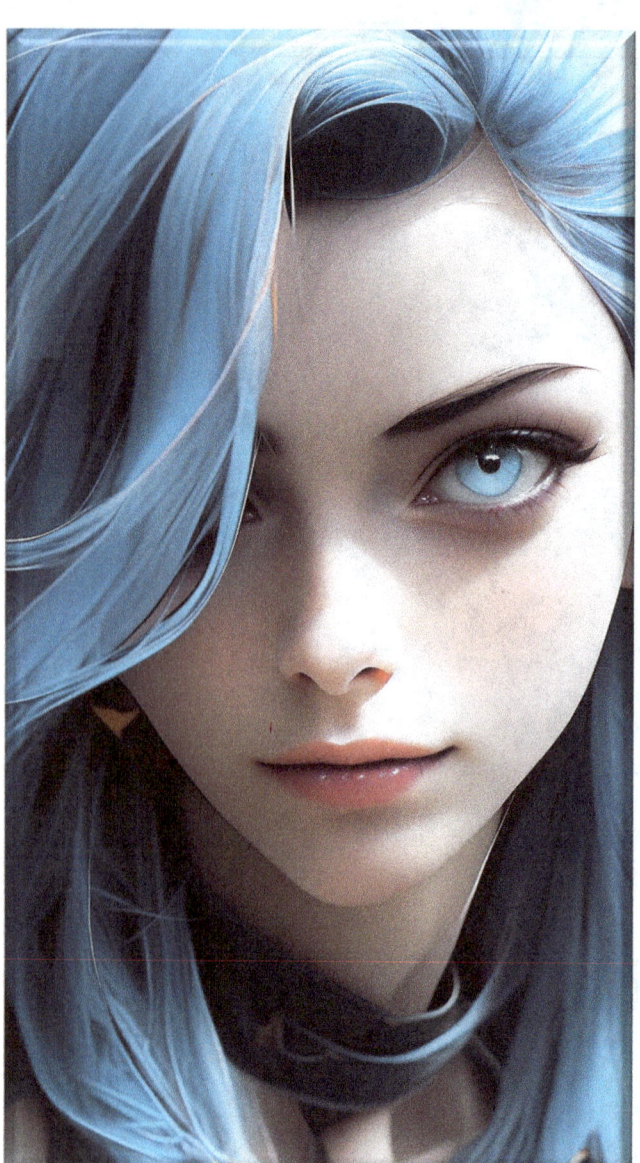

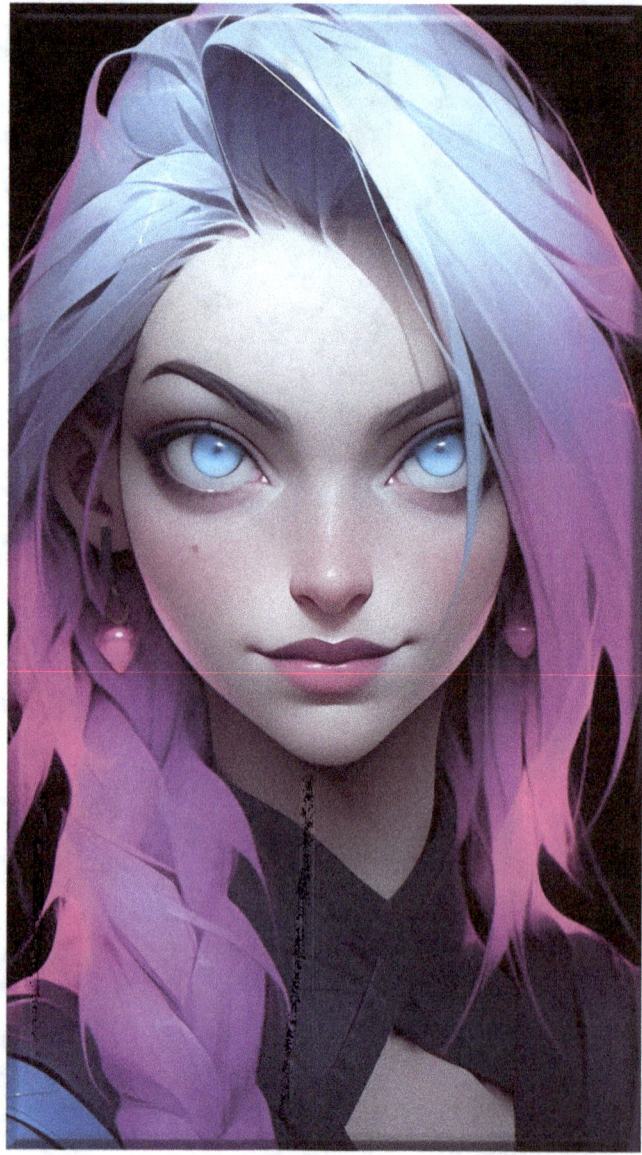

Keeping DNA Strand Mixing in Mind

Always feel free to use my DNA Mixing technique, but be aware of any changes in copyright law or rulings by high courts that filter down into business and/or the public idea.

FOLIO IMAGE 030

/imagine   **A person is sitting on a bus in subway station, in the style of reflective surfaces, dark indigo and silver, like Peter Sculthorpe or Victor Horta, glass as material, manapunk, mirrored --ar 9:16 --style expressive --niji 5**

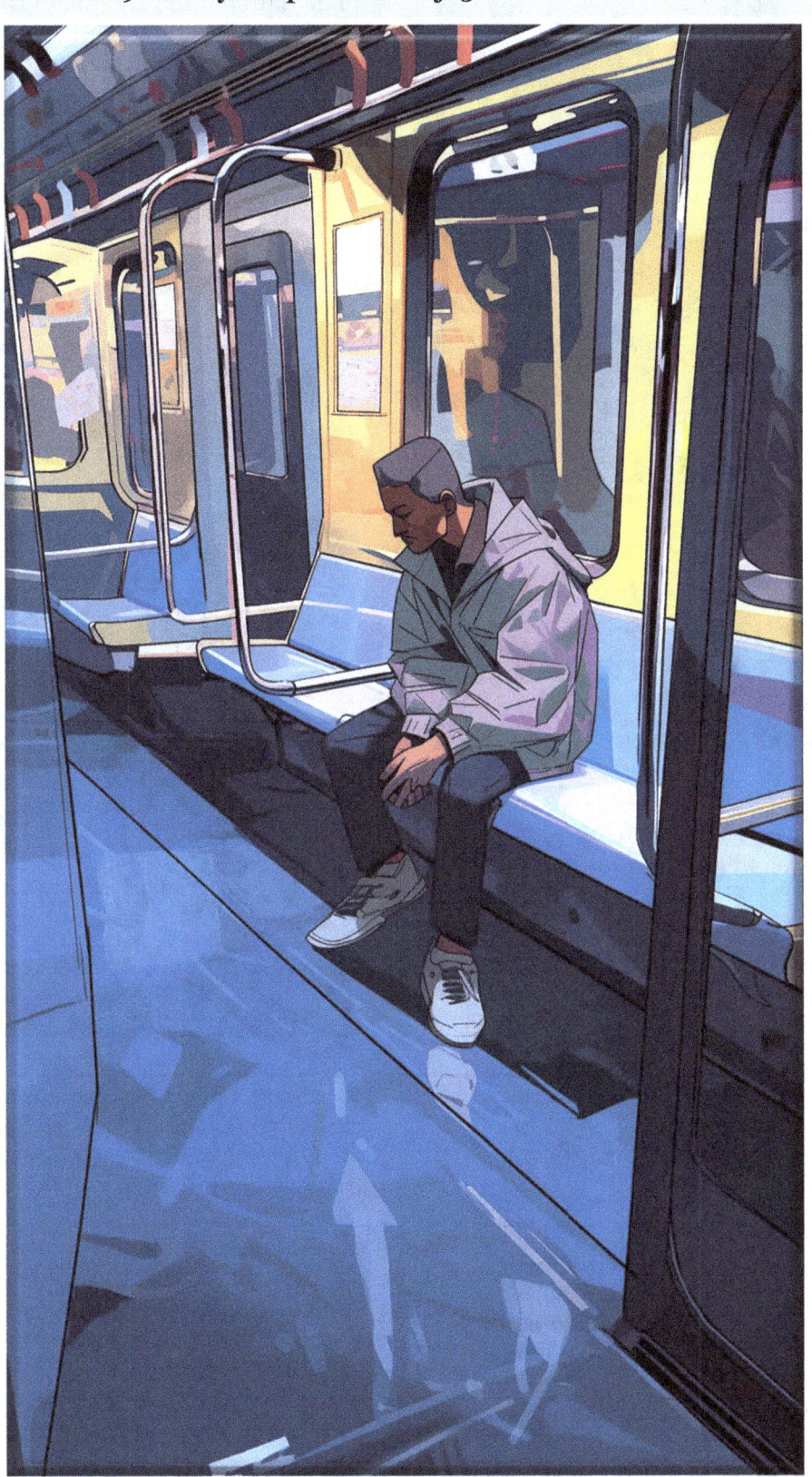

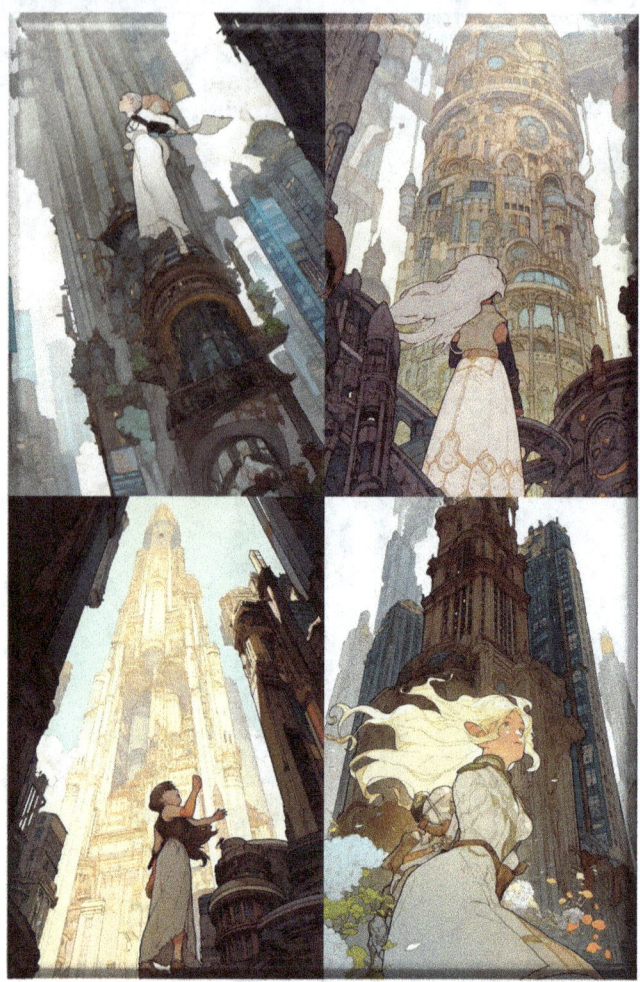

in the original artist's name. They call this "learning from the masters." You can remind "real" artists of such if they try to give you any heat for using Midjourney to envision your own imagination. They might angrily try to disprove your factual statement at length, using emotional angles and hairsplitting, which in itself is a rather intriguing thing.

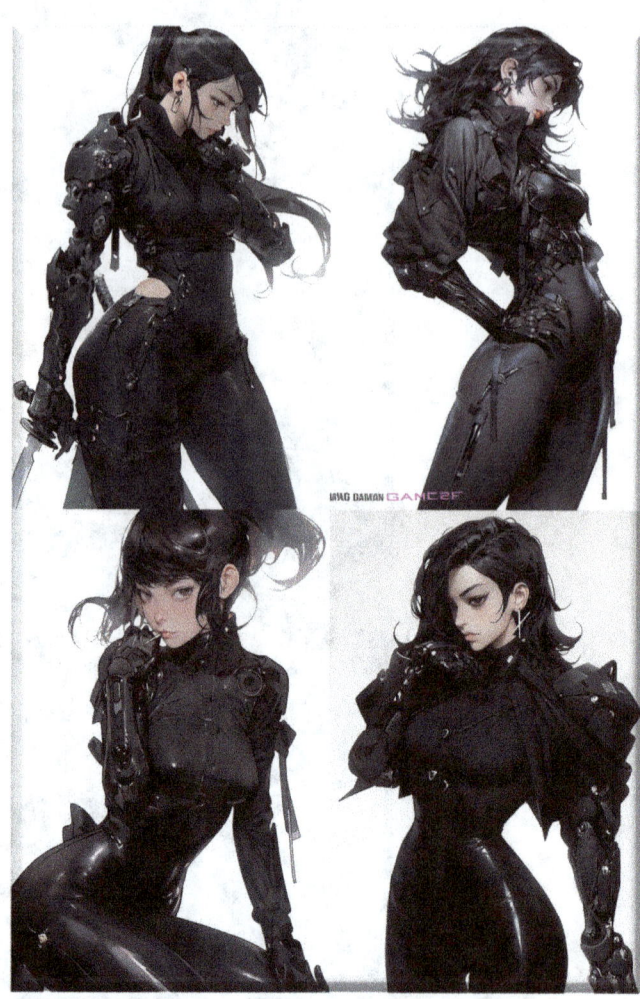

But whenever you are looking for more inspiration, the mainstream does have its charms. You can learn to intelligently sidestep copyrighted franchises whenever you like. You might not want to make *a Star Wars*™ character with a light saber, but why not make a sci fi character with a laser sword? Energy swords were conceptualized by Isaac Asimov in 1944.

And you might not want to make a *Harry Potter*™ character named Hermione Granger casting Wingardium Leviosa, but why not make a wizardcore image of a cute young wizarding girl using a wand to levitate a feather?

Keep in mind too that emulating an idea is not the same as copying a creation. And as an interesting aside, you will find that artists are literally taught to learn – throughout history, in classes, online, from mentors, and from books – by directly copying the works of past artists, by name, with the specific intent of emulating not only the style, but also the specific work in question, without signing the newly copied work

Final Thoughts on the Matter: The more closely your art looks like or directly references an older piece of artwork, the more likely it is that you are infringing on the original work.

Contrariwise, the more you blend your own ideas and the public domain with others' ideas, the more likely it is that you have created something unique. Whether you choose Comfortable or Careful, stay intelligent, informed, reasonable, and mindful of the ever-changing world. We're in the midst of an AI revolution, for good and ill omen, so expect a wild ride!

FOLIO IMAGE 031

/imagine   **Female Samurai cyberpunk cyborg art poster by Michaeld or Winslow Home or He Jiaving, in the style of japanese - inspired motifs, dark white and light red, cardboard, rtx, cross - hatching --ar 9:16 --style expressive --niji 5**

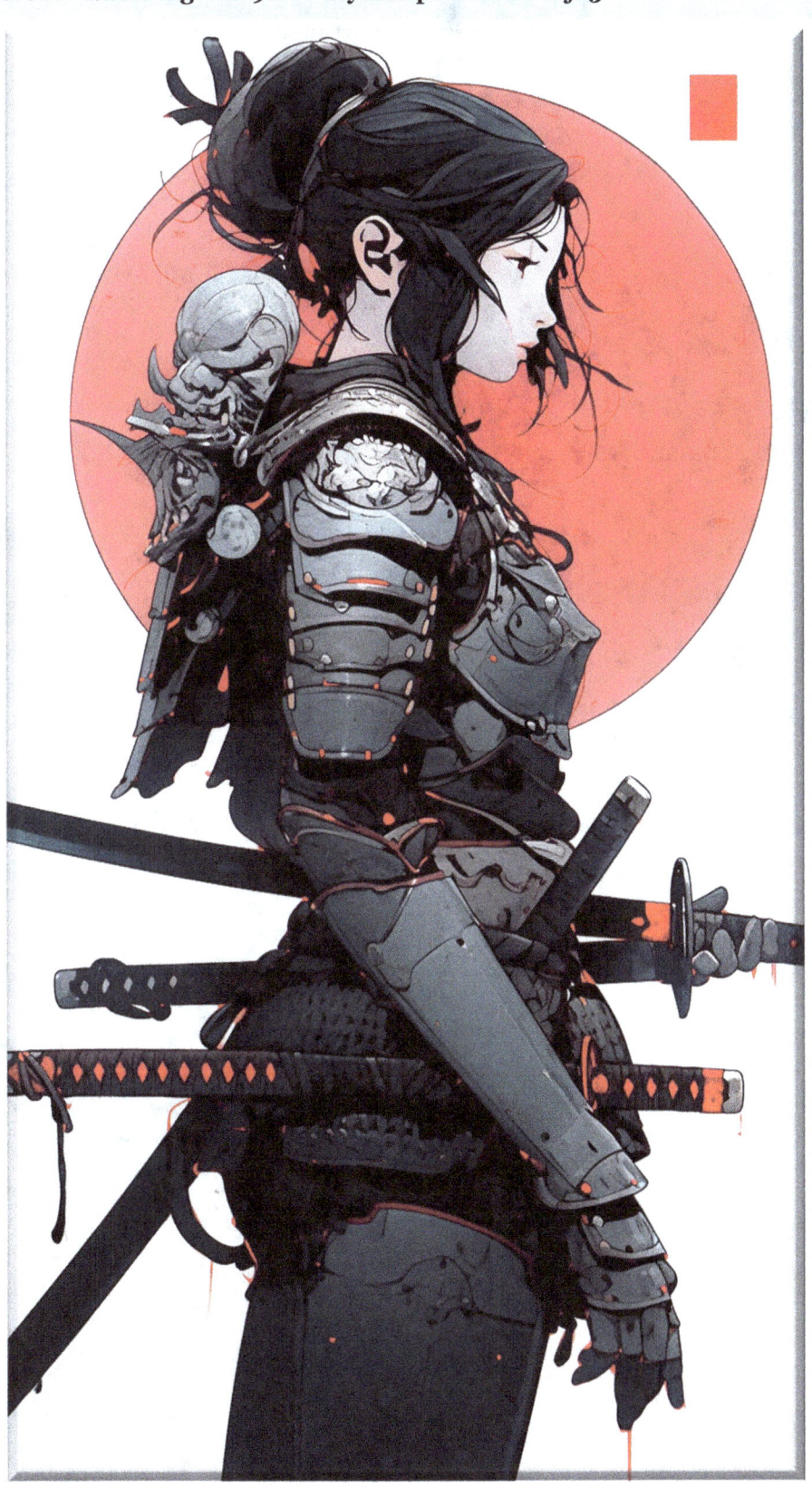

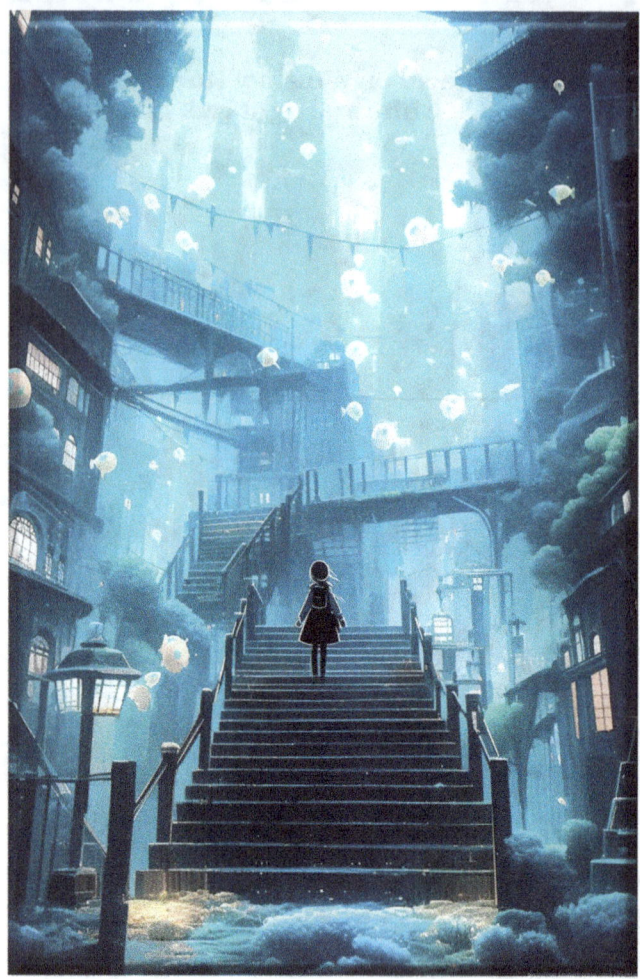

reasons – individuality, uniqueness of expression, detail, coherence, and user control being several – I recommend beginning your idea with a long prompt, and then whittling it down until you get to something that works perfectly without taking up a lot of space.

The reason for this is that if you ever want to repurpose one of your prompts for a new subject or project, it's much easier to recode if the prompt is proven, versatile, descriptive, and relatively short.

Necessarily, you will need to deviate from this depending on what you are trying to create. Feel free to study the prompt language that I have used throughout this book, which varied wildly from subject to subject in the final iterations.

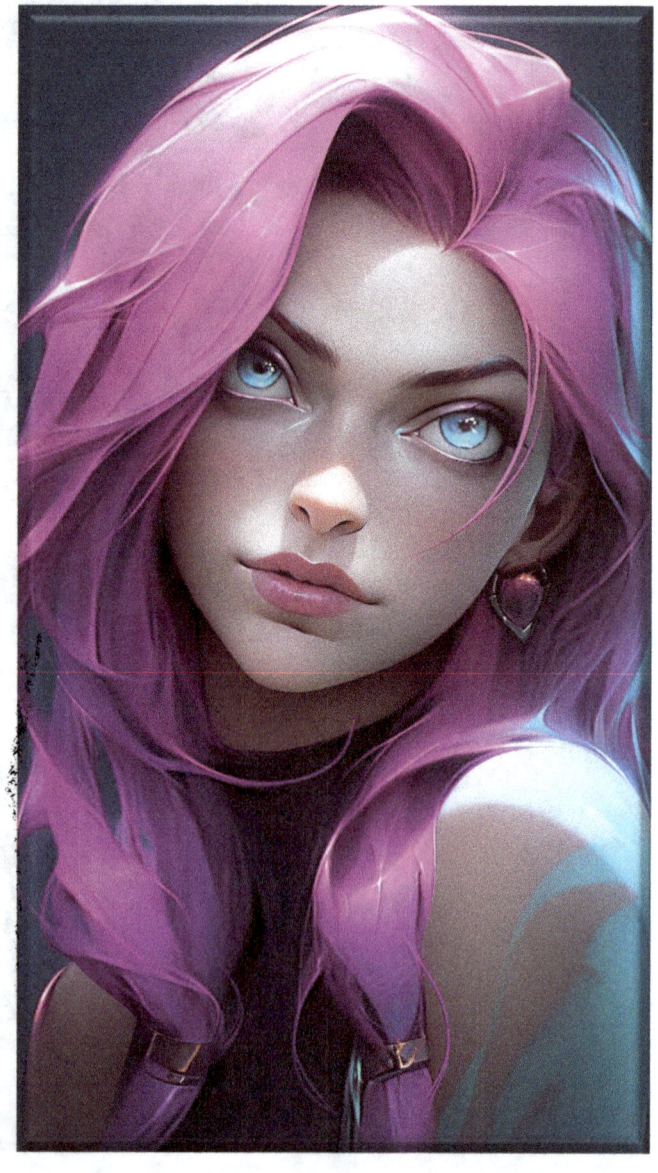

Creating DNA-Driven Niji Prompts

If you want to create your own prompts using this guide as inspiration, I recommend the following format.

Please remember that the closer words are to the beginning of your prompt, the more weight and importance Midjourney gives them. Similarly, the farther are words toward the end of your prompt, the more likely it will be that they are downplayed or simply nonexistent in the results.

You can remove any words you like, but if you change the double hyphen codes at the end (--ar 2:3, --niji, etc.) you are changing coding, and not just the image description.

Depending on the complexity of the image you are going for, you will find through trial and error that there is a definite sweet spot for each composition. Sometimes, a short prompt will work better than a longer one. But for many

FOLIO IMAGE 032

/imagine   **Wonderment, in the mixed styles of Martiros Saryan and Masaaki Sasamoto, embroidered art, elaborate, elegant, space opera scenery, a long sandy coastline with coastal sand dunes covered in beach grass and ivy, a large windblown coastal cypress tree in the foreground, tumultuous ocean, alien planet, dynamic clouds, otherworldly, epic sci - fi fantasy, cinematic vibrant raking light, long shadows --ar 9:16 --style expressive --niji 5**

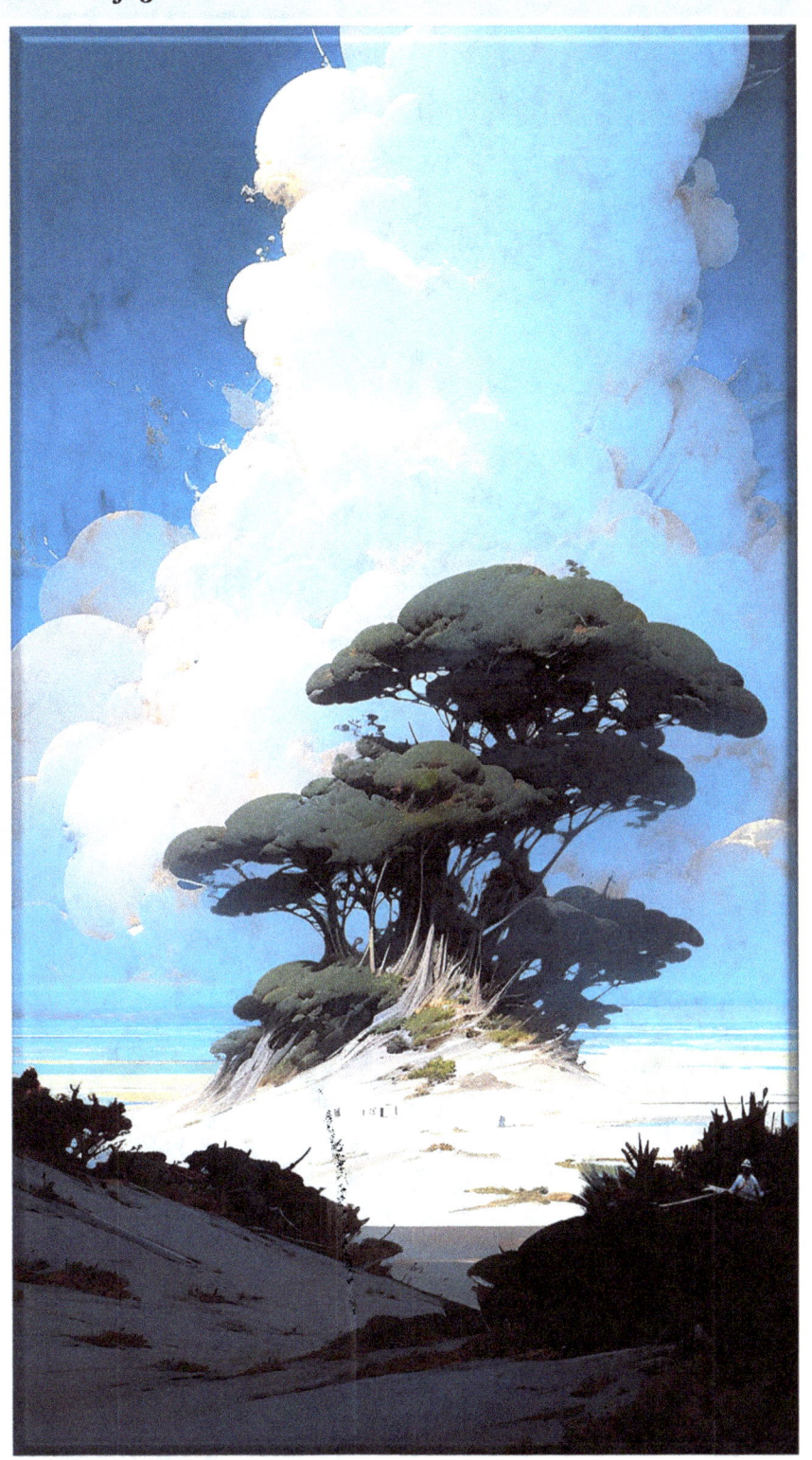

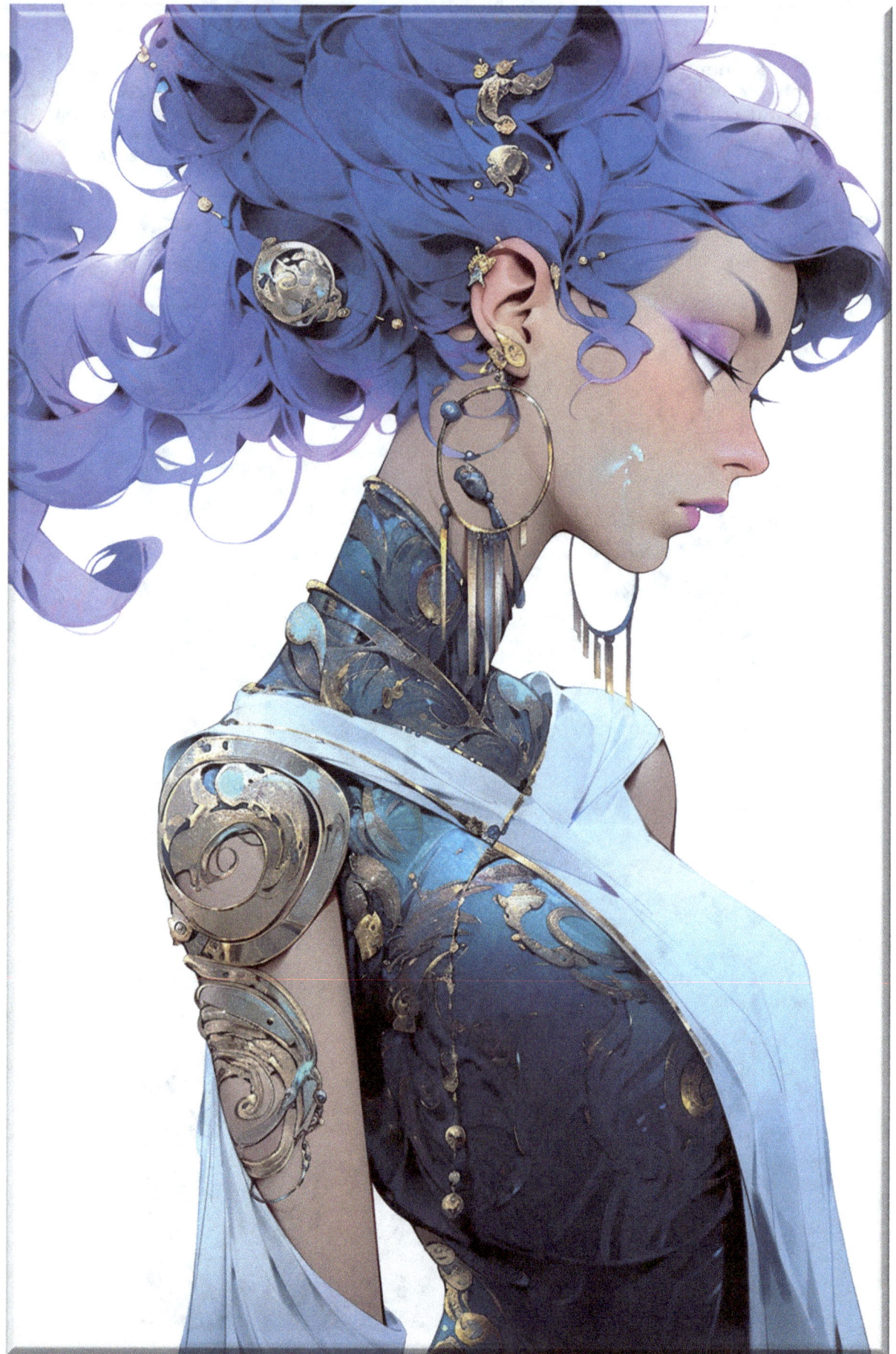

FOUR: SECRET PATHS

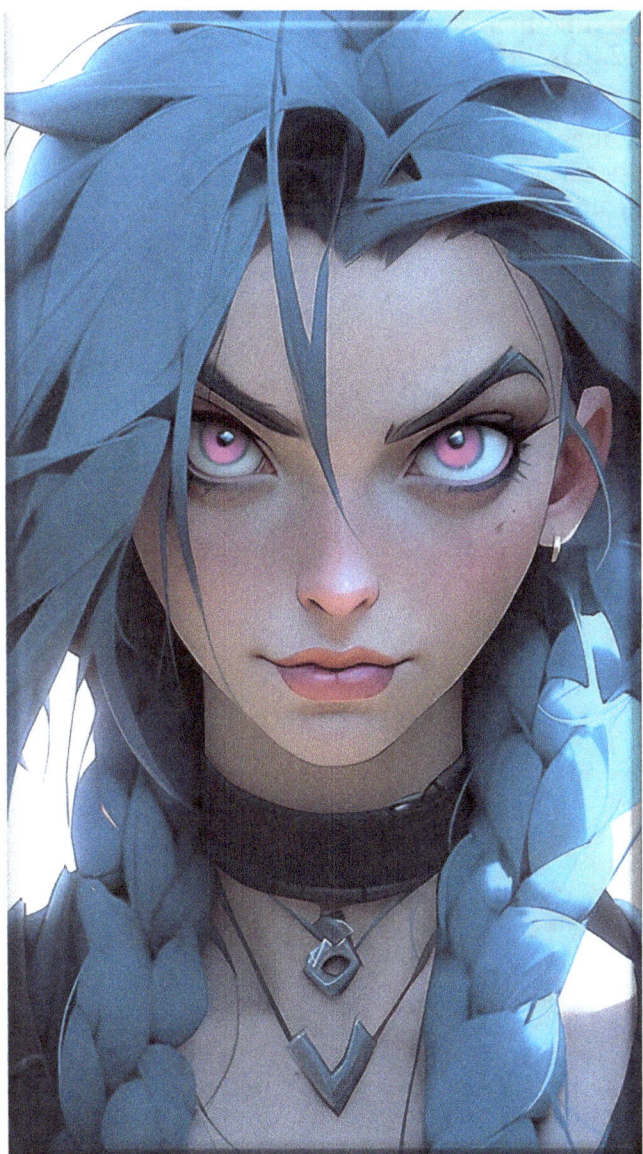

I cover all of the basics of Midjourney prompting and art composition – system strengths and weaknesses, messaging, prompt elements, prompt coding styles, keywords, subjects, perspectives, aspect ratio, stylization, prompt re-crafting, curating, journaling, rating, art styles, and rerolling – in my **Beginning with Midjourney** book.

Also, you will find many hundreds of specific keywords, ideas, and tricks listed in the right-hand rail next to each piece of art throughout this current book as well, as active demonstrations of all those key decisions in composition and execution. But if you are learning the core features, this succinct guide should help you out as figure out the additional tricks of using Midjourney and Discord to aid you in your art designs. **Note:** This chapter will be a bit technical by necessity.

The Niji Discord

Hidden away from the main Midjourney feeds, you can find the dedicated Niji servers. This place is quite a bit smaller than the main Midjourney Discord, but it is very international and multicultural which can lead you into discovering some surprising new techniques, anime releases, characters, and digital art tricks that often go by obscure names.

I found these for example by going into Google and searching for "Midjourney Niji Discord Server," which takes you to Niji | Journey. It should be a top result.

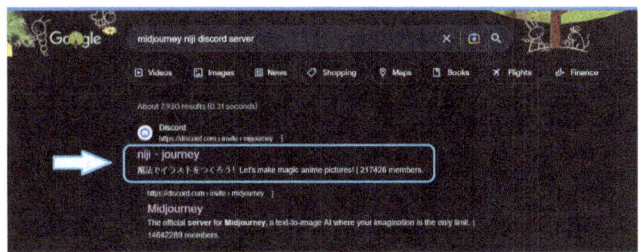

(Screenshot © Midjourney Inc., presented for educational and informative demonstration only.)

"Hidden" Core Features for MJ Niji

There are many secrets that you can learn to make your artwork generation even more informed and more powerful.

Some of my best tricks, over time, have come from watching the AI masters at work and not only copying them, but trying to figure out why their prompts and techniques and obscure keywords work so much better than those of other users.

Clicking there will take you to a screen inviting you to the separate Niji | Journey Discord. Click the Accept Invite button, and off you go!

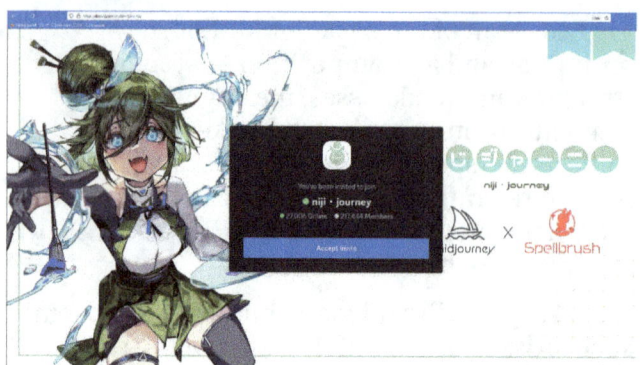

(Screenshot © Midjourney Inc., presented for educational and informative demonstration only.)

After you accept the invite, click on Continue to Discord. Then select your preferred language and click Finish. You're in the club now! I then recommend scrolling down your left-hand Niji | Journey column, until you find the Image-Generation rooms. In my current exploration, they are numbered, and I'm going to dive into "image-generation-4."

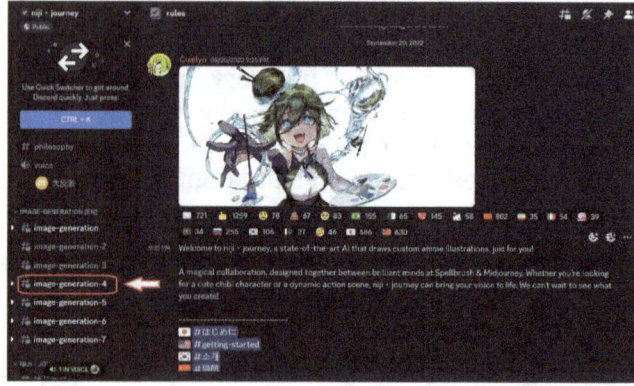

(Screenshot © Midjourney Inc., presented for educational and informative demonstration only.)

So what is so amazing about this? Basically, this gives you the keys to the kingdom. You can now scroll through the feed to see what everyone else is crafting. But instead of being stuck over in the chaos of the main Midjourney rooms, you are now surrounded by crafters who are working specifically and solely in the Niji and Anime styles.

Now, you can scroll down, see images that you like, copy and paste prompts from the masters, modify them to your own desires by changing keywords, and basically go crazy in a limitless world of inspirations. I would warn you

to watch the time, however, because it's easy to get swept away by all of the creative enthusiasm. Some of the works that people are putting on display here are simply incredible. But these aren't finished masterworks; you're literally watching "over the shoulder" as people craft and refine their prompts to make countless amazing things.

Don't forget that you can also click on the other image-generation-# rooms on the left, because each one has a totally different community group (which changes in the moment), and of course a new endless feed of generative outputs for you to browse.

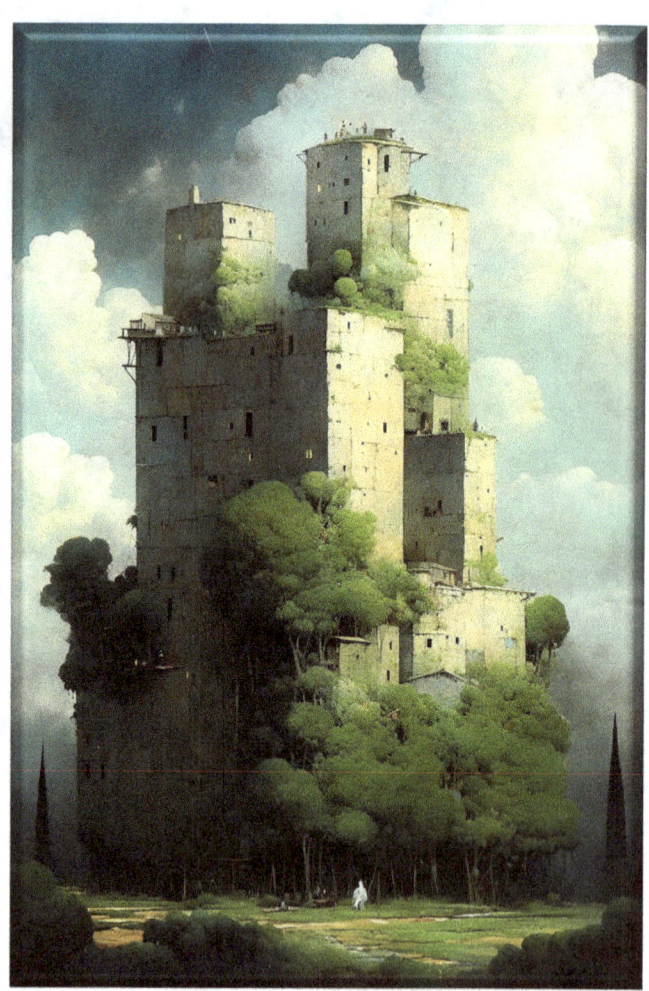

The Niji Showcase

While not as communal and inviting as the Niji | Journey discord, the Niji Showcase is also a tremendous help as you learn the true power of Midjourney's crafting ability in the anime field.

To get here, you need to be in the main Midjourney Discord feed.

But instead of going to a room like Newbies-56 or General-18, you're going to scroll on the left-hand panel until you find a little thing called "# niji-showcase." It's under the SHOWCASE tab and it takes a little digging the first time to find it.

Left click on "# niji-showcase," and you're there. These are pieces that are quite impressive, where you can see the some great art that other people are rating. This isn't a great place to look for prompt codes, but it is a good place to find great pieces, to open them in your browser, and to save them.

Remember that you can copy other people's images from Midjourney, but I strongly recommend that you do NOT claim others' work as your own. (Technically you could do so, but it would be very rude, and also dishonorable, in my opinion.)

Instead, I will teach you how to take someone else's image, and to learn from it. You have to be a bit tech savvy to get all of the steps here, but I try to make it as clear as possible. My apologies if anything is confusing, as there are a lot of steps.

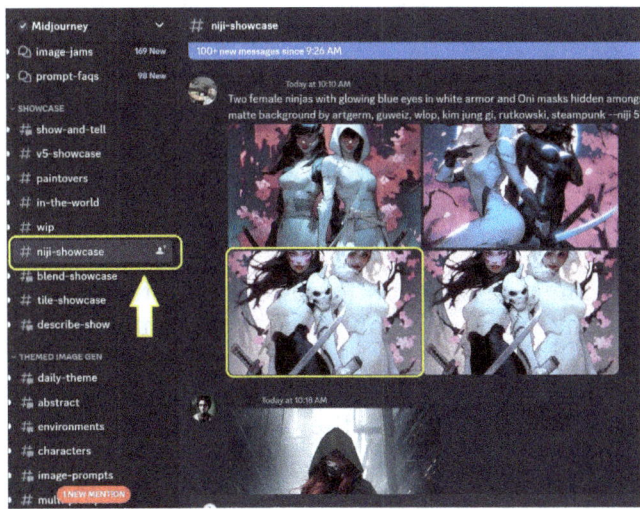

(Screenshot © Midjourney Inc., presented for educational and informative demonstration only.)

In this example, we are going to borrow another creator's "Two female ninjas" output and see what we can learn from its composition. You can see that the user kindly featured the code used, which is nice, but we don't learn much if all we ever do is copy other people's works. We also

need to learn about composition details and how Midjourney "thinks" so that we can add some more coding techniques to our personal repertoire. To do this, we're going to save the image I've shown above, and then have Midjourney analyze its own work.

Strange? It's actually very easy, and an extremely valuable tool. Just follow along when you want to try this for yourself using a different image.

First, left click on the image you want to store and analyze. Then, to expand it, click on Open in Browser. The image enlarges. Now, you right click on the image, select Save Image As, and save it (to your Desktop, for example). The other creator's image is now saved to your computer.

Now, we're going to have Midjourney consider the image. It won't give you the exact prompt that the user typed in; rather, it will show you how it thinks about image elements and some useful language that you can apply in your prompts. This form of "reverse engineering" is powered by the Describe feature of Midjourney.

Go into a Midjourney Discord room (General-12, or whatever else you prefer), and right click Midjourney Bot and select Message to get to a quiet space. In the cursor window at the bottom, type the command /describe and press the space bar. You will get a sub-window that says, "Drag and drop or click to upload the file."

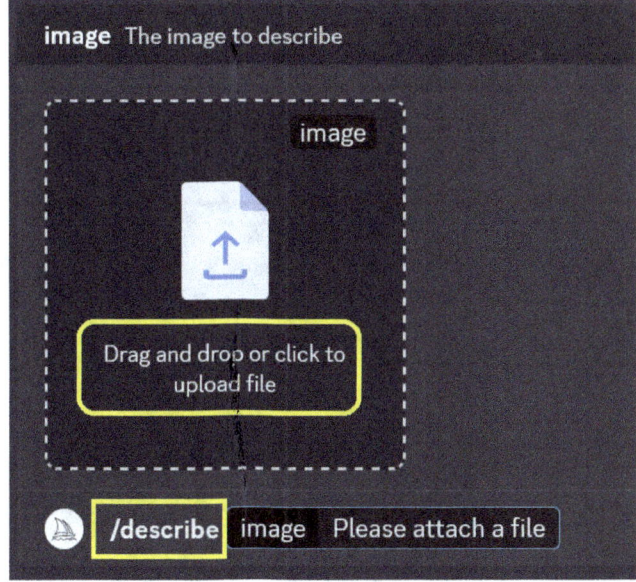

(Screenshot © Midjourney Inc., presented for educational and informative demonstration only.)

Left click on the paper icon with the up arrow on it, as shown above.

Navigate to the image you saved on your computer's Desktop.

Left click it, and then click Open. Now, your image is in Midjourney's /describe window. Press Enter to upload it.

Sometimes, you will get a false positive from Midjourney's "Banned image prompt" bot.

This bot upholds Midjourney's community standards, but sometimes it gets things wrong. If you get that screen, don't try to circumvent it by uploading similar images, because you might pull a ban. Instead, find another image that Midjourney will let you upload.

When it works, you will see the message "Midjourney is thinking …" for a while. Then, Midjourney gives you four examples of its image analysis process.

It will never get the exact prompt code that was used to create the image (if any), but it will give you four great examples of possible code that might lead Midjourney to generate a similar result.

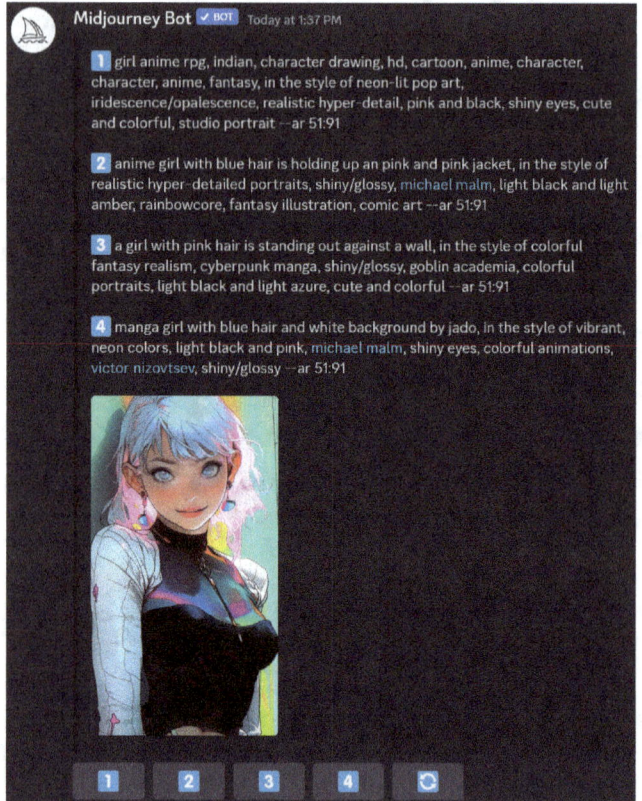

Here's a screenshot showing what Midjourney thinks of one of the prompt outputs I've featured in this book.

Now there are quite a few things we can learn from this. First, you will see that we might want to add the artists Michael Malm and Victor Nizovtsev to our list of inspirations, and this is a great way to find artists whose works you enjoy.

Secondly, we learn some new terms that we might want to use not just in this image series, but in all prompts. Here, I'm seeing helpful descriptive terms such as "neon-lit pop art," "iridescence," "opalescence," "realistic hyper-detail," "rainbowcore," "goblin academia," "background by Jado," and "shiny eyes."

These are all valuable terms for prompt coding, because we already know that Midjourney responds well to them and understands them! Even though these aren't the terms we used originally, this adds lots of tools to the toolbox.

I recommend that you keep a list of such terms for later use (refer to the "secret sauce" section of my Beginning with Midjourney book, where I discuss the importance of these types of data gems). But there's more here to consider. Looking back at the screenshot, do you see the buttons at the bottom? We can click on 1, 2, 3, or 4 to have Midjourney generate a piece using it's own guess prompt. Or, we can click on the blue circle button.

The blue circle button here is extremely valuable, although you wouldn't know it unless you pay close attention to the experimental results. This causes Midjourney to make four new analysis guesses using the same image. For example, when I do this, it tells me about some more artists I might want to research (Nikita Veprikov, Natalia Rak, Krenz Crushart, and Lois Van Baarle). It also gives me some great new prompt wordings to try out, like "colorful Moebius," "metallic ethomerealism," "vibrant neo-traditional," and – you will have seen me using this to create some of the art in this book – "I can't believe how beautiful this is." More treasure and magic words for us to add to our secret hoard!

FOLIO IMAGE 033

/imagine **Minimalistic retro 80s Japanese album art, Formicapunk, cassette futurism, digital painting featuring a woman with a helmet --ar 9:16 --style expressive --niji 5**

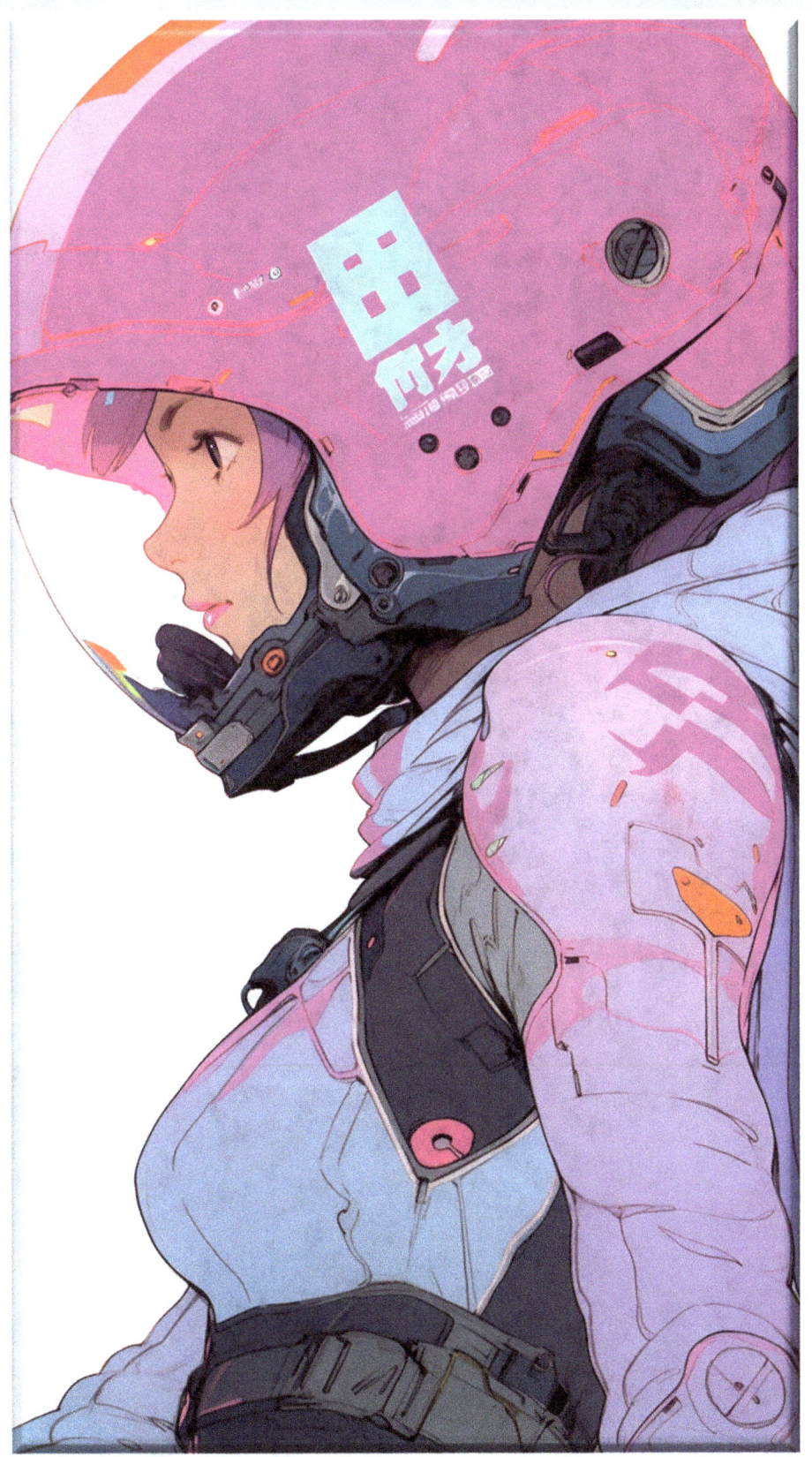

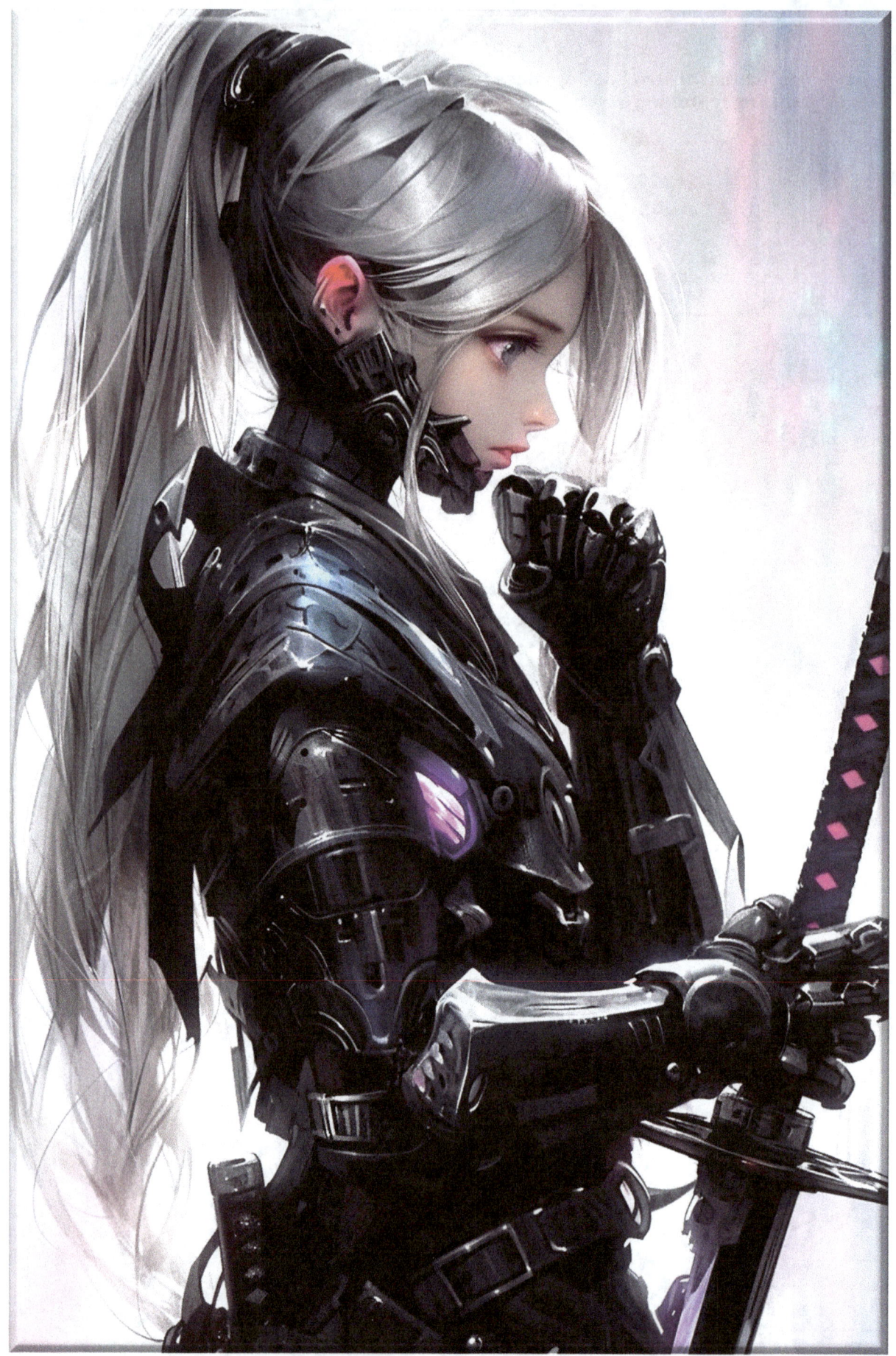

FIVE:
MOVING FORWARD

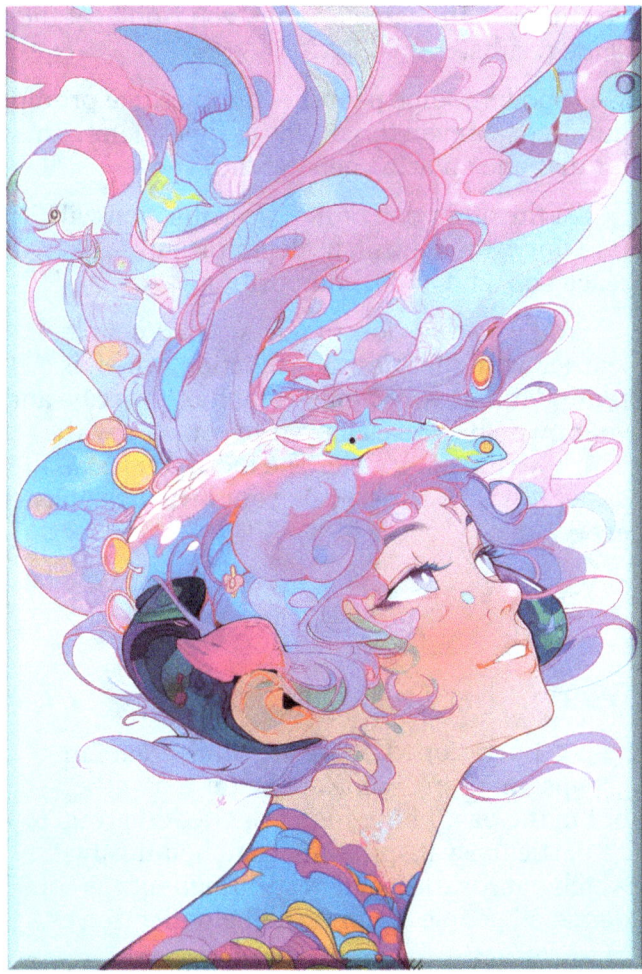

Where to Go from Here

I have only touched the surface of the depthless topic of anime in Midjourney throughout this introductory guide.

There's much more that you can learn, so much so in fact that it can be overwhelming when you're trying to get started and to swim with the tide. To help you in learning more, I've put some of the most useful places to look at here. Don't forget to use the Niji | Discord and Niji Showcase for all of the inspiration that they can provide as well.

I recommend checking the Showcases daily.

Moving On with --Describe

And now, you're ready to upload some more images, and to have Midjourney analyze them. They can come from any source in the public domain, and you can use /describe to study old Renaissance paintings, modern art, and even your own saved digital artwork for key insights. It's a really powerful tool that – due to it endless AI learning – is getting greater all the time. But when you're uploading images for /describe, always keep Midjourney's rules in mind and be sure to follow them. Examples of rules and ideals from Midjourney – not from me – include "Don't be a jerk," "Keep it PG-13," "No gore," "No sex," "Don't try to sneak around subjects that we have banned for various reasons," and "Don't harass other people." I recommend keeping up with their Community Guidelines to always be aware. Whether you like all of the rules is a matter beyond other people's concern. Whether you follow the rules, which I strongly encourage, is a matter between you and Midjourney. But please do so, you don't want to get yourself in trouble.

Midjourney Online Guides

If you Google search for "Midjourney Documentation and User Guide," you'll find another treasure trove of technical information. As of this writing, the main sub-areas are Using Discord (Discord tricks and tips), Getting Started (current Midjourney features and subscription options), and User Guide (a massive compendium of tech info on commands, parameters, models, bots, upscalers, reaction options, and much more).

If you want to continue your learning there, I recommend starting with "Getting Started," then "Next Steps," then "Prompts." It's not very well organized I'm afraid, but if you start there you'll find some very good information that you can build your ongoing learning upon.

The Midjourney Official Facebook

There are many Midjourney and AI social media groups that you can join, but they vary wildly in purpose, membership, goals, and posting rules. But the most consistently helpful, fun, and friendly place I have found so far is the Midjourney Official public group. It's very welcoming, and you will see some great prompting and composition ideas from other members. People don't always post their full prompts or techniques, but they are friendly and helpful with few exceptions (and the place is quiet carefully moderated as well, if you do find any troublemakers).

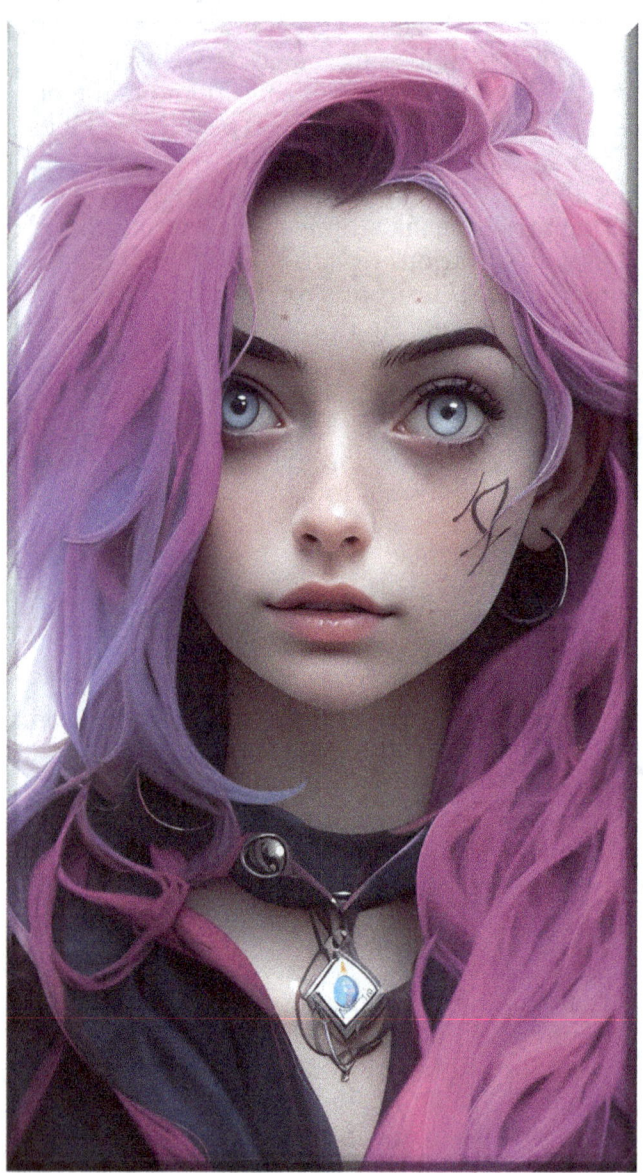

The Midjourney Showcase

Over on the Midjourney website, the Showcase is a never-ending feed of the current hot art – not just anime – that people are creating through the Midjourney Discord app. You can vote on your favorites, scroll for inspiration, and have some great laughs as well.

If you're logged into your Discord, you can also click on images and pull the full prompt code that was used too. This does not mean that the prompt will always be helpful, however. Sometimes, people use one-word prompts and hit the absolute jackpot with a gorgeous image; but if you enter in the same prompt, you won't get the same results.

(Spoiler: Some people enter the same prompt hundreds or even thousands of times before they hit that one amazing generation.)

At the other end of the spectrum, you will find huge, thoughtful, in-depth prompts that will teach you a lot about composition.

You'll also see lots of phrases that people learned with the /describe function, which is a reminder that you should combine /describe and your own Showcase analysis to come up with your own amazing style. The more you learn, the easier it will be to generate your own amazing art every time.

Midjourney on Reddit

(And Other Social Media)

As I mentioned, there are some great fan groups out there. Some are better than others, but in the past I have found the Reddit group to be particularly inspirational and helpful. Just watch out for the usual nasty arguments as some damaged people simply can't help themselves.

My Own Casual Hangouts

Companies do not always like it when I put in detailed links to my own materials, books, and art. But I will say that you can always find me and my new books at Amazon, Facebook, Itch, and DriveThruRPG. I hope to see you soon!

Cliffhanger

There will many more Midjourney books to come, if they are wanted. Thank you for reading. If you enjoyed this and found it helpful, please consider sharing with your friends and writing a review. I write better when I survive. Stay tuned.

Your journey has just begun!

SIX:
THE FOLIO GALLERY

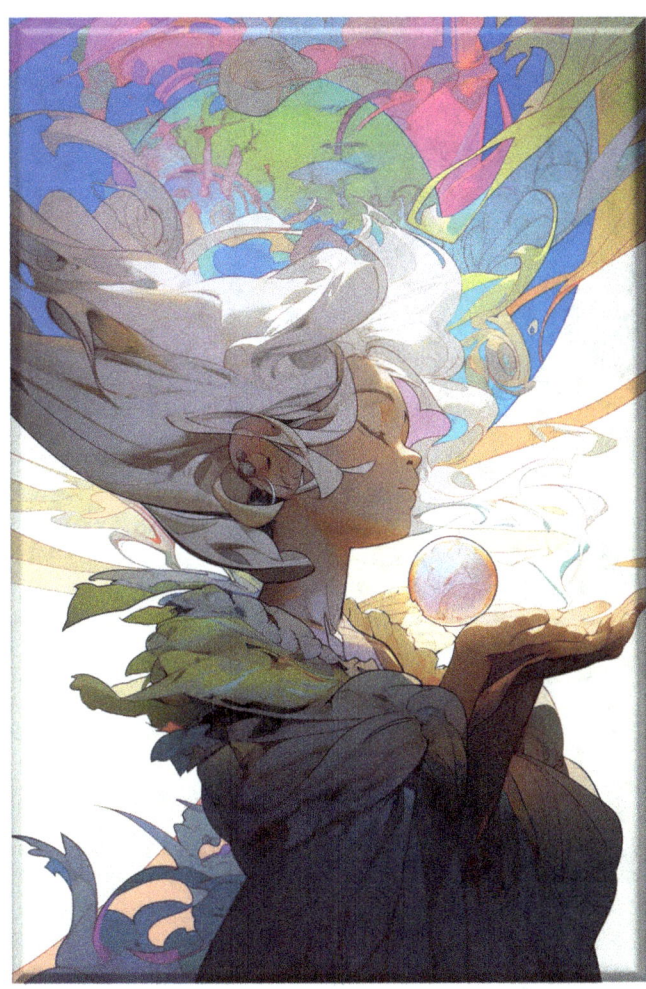

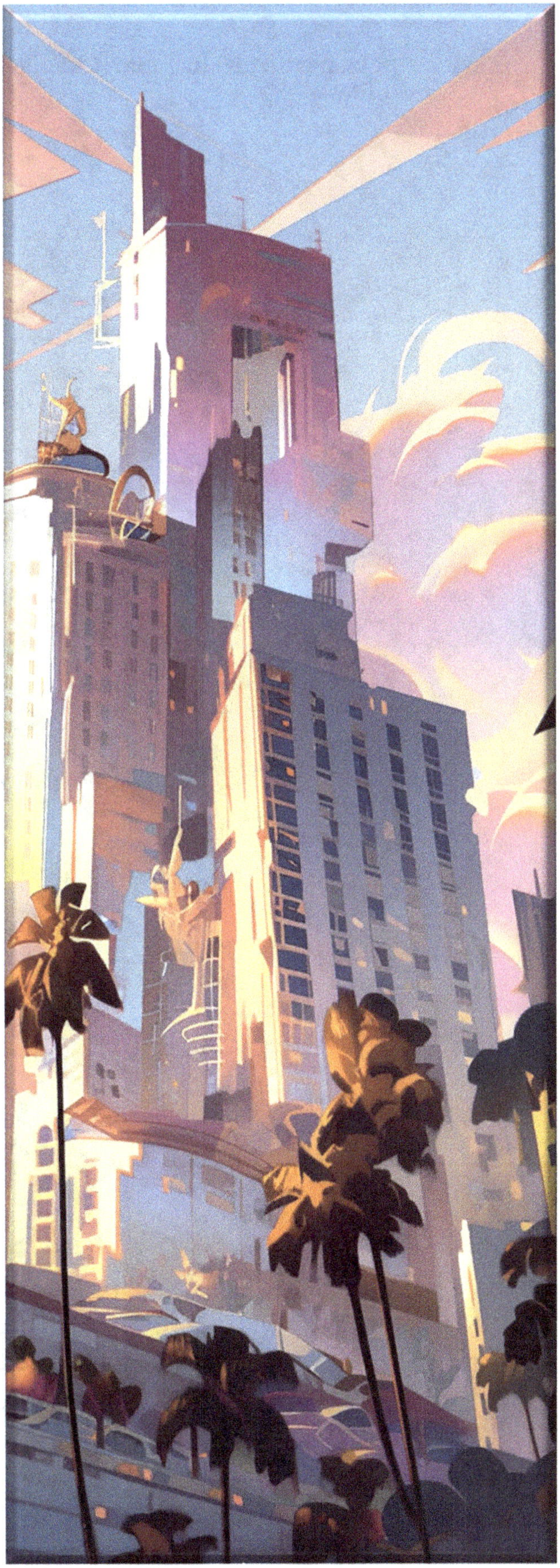

This section is just filled with nonstop prompts and images for your inspiration. Find your dream and make it your own!

I encourage you to analyze the prompts, and to dissect the pieces that you like. Cut away the parts that you don't think are worthwhile, and add in your own special keywords and scenes that you want to see. Try to generate a prompt's output at least two or three times before you give up on it, unless the generations are truly horrid. (Which does happen, from time to time. Or, on rare occasions, Midjourney breaks and gives you very weird things that have nothing to do with the main idea.)

Let's go!

FOLIO IMAGE 034

/imagine　　A beautiful girl like Lum Chan, drifting in the star world --ar 9:16 --style expressive --niji 5

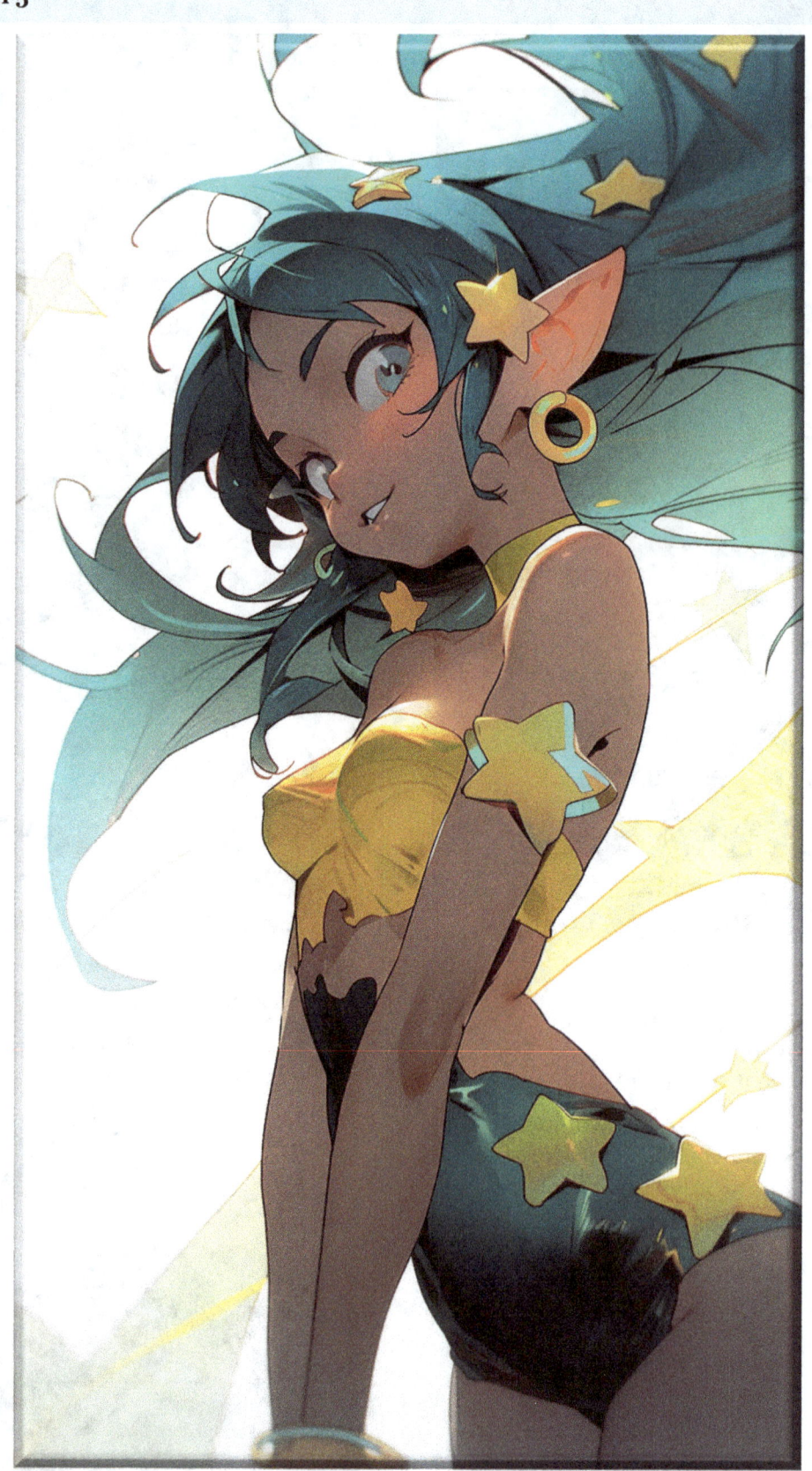

FOLIO IMAGE 035

/imagine   **Alternate reality, like a weirdpunk art deco steampunk Disneyland, colorful surrealism --ar 9:16 --style expressive --niji 5**

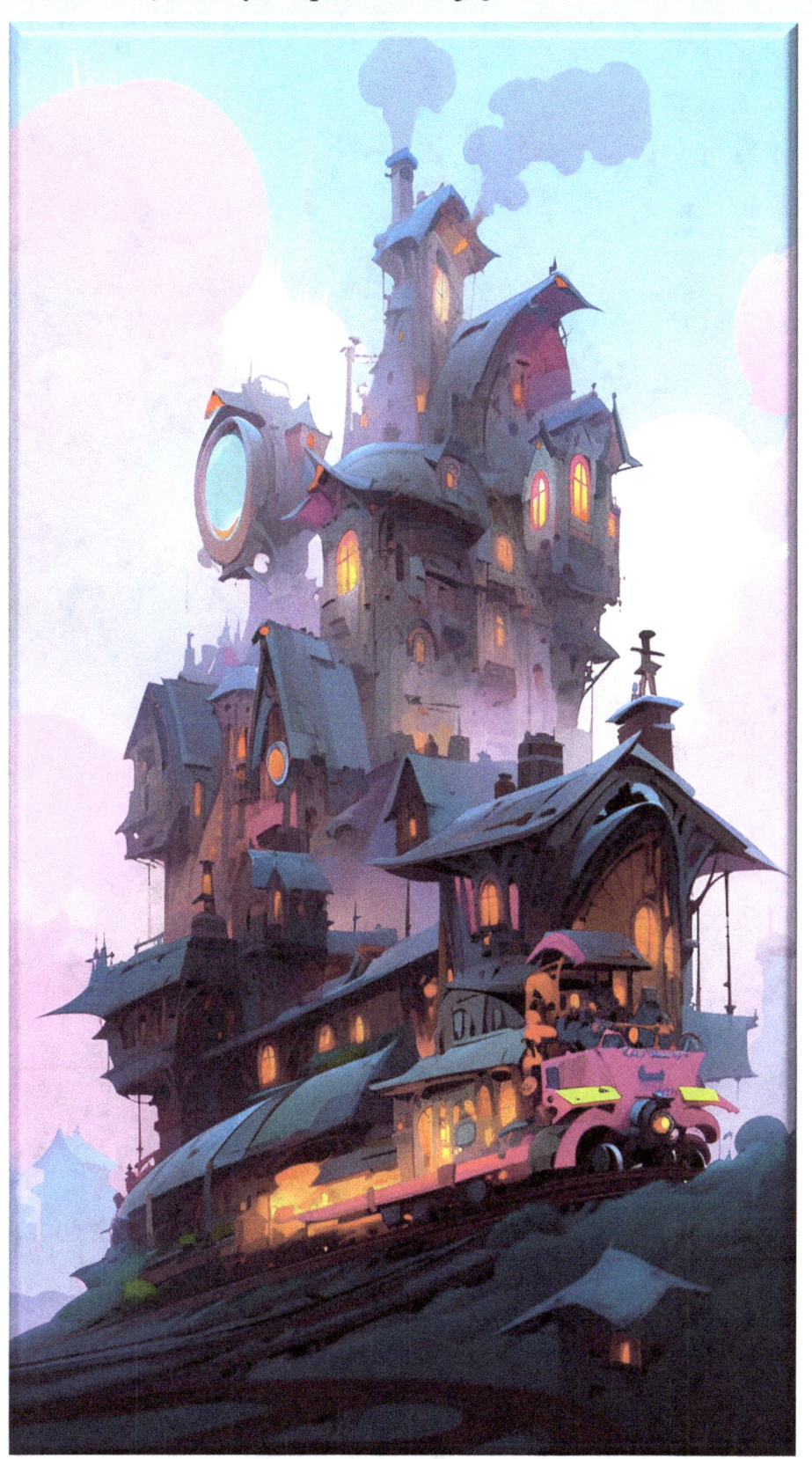

FOLIO IMAGE 036

/imagine   **An anime girl with blue hair is holding up an pink and pink jacket, in the style of realistic hyper-detailed portraits, shiny/glossy, Michael Malm, light black and light amber, Rainbowcore, fantasy illustration, comic art --ar 51:91 --q 2 --niji 5**

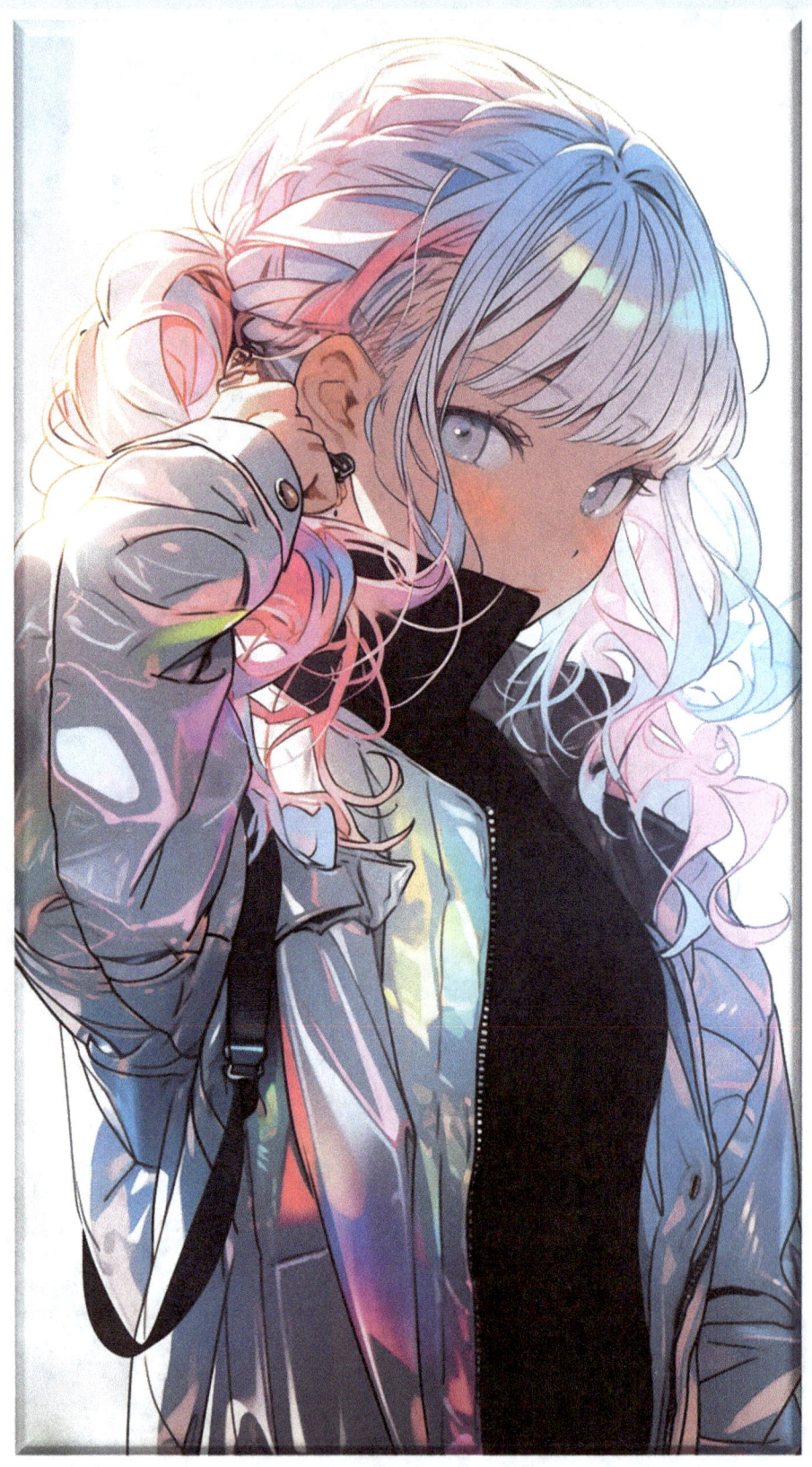

FOLIO IMAGE 037

/imagine   **A beautiful and highly detailed character sheet, tribal girls of the wolf tribe, intricate design, multicolored background, in the mixed style of Katsyuya Terada and the Pre-Raphaelites --ar 2:3 --niji 5 --style cute --s 300**

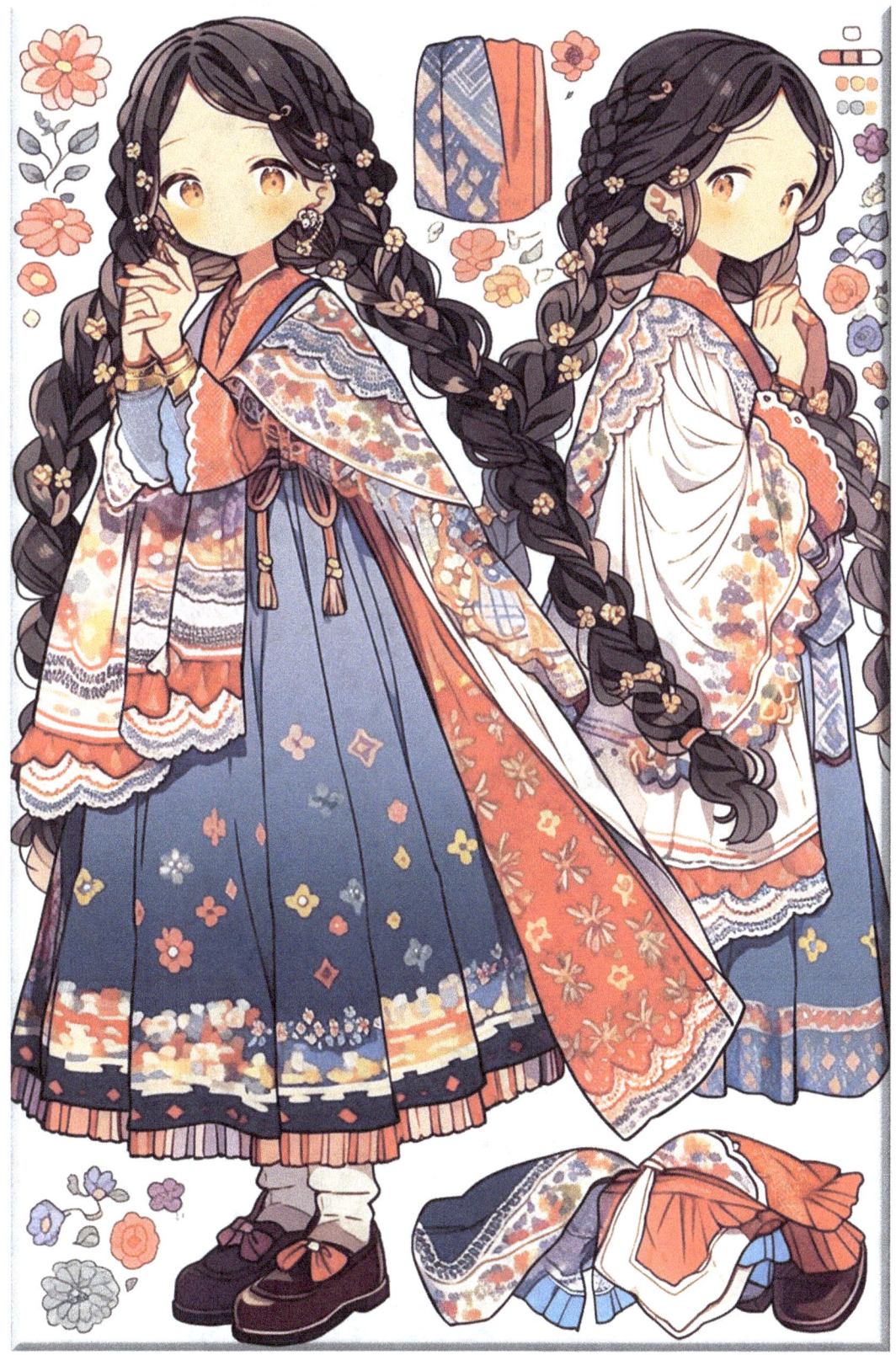

FOLIO IMAGE 038

/imagine   **A masterpiece lithograph, realistic game concept art, a gorgeous cyberpunk girl, dramatic pose, full body, wearing black opaque and opalescent glass armor, industrial design, in the style of Kim Jun Gi or Artgerm or Rossdraw or Yoji Shinkawa --ar 2:3 -- niji 5 --style expressive**

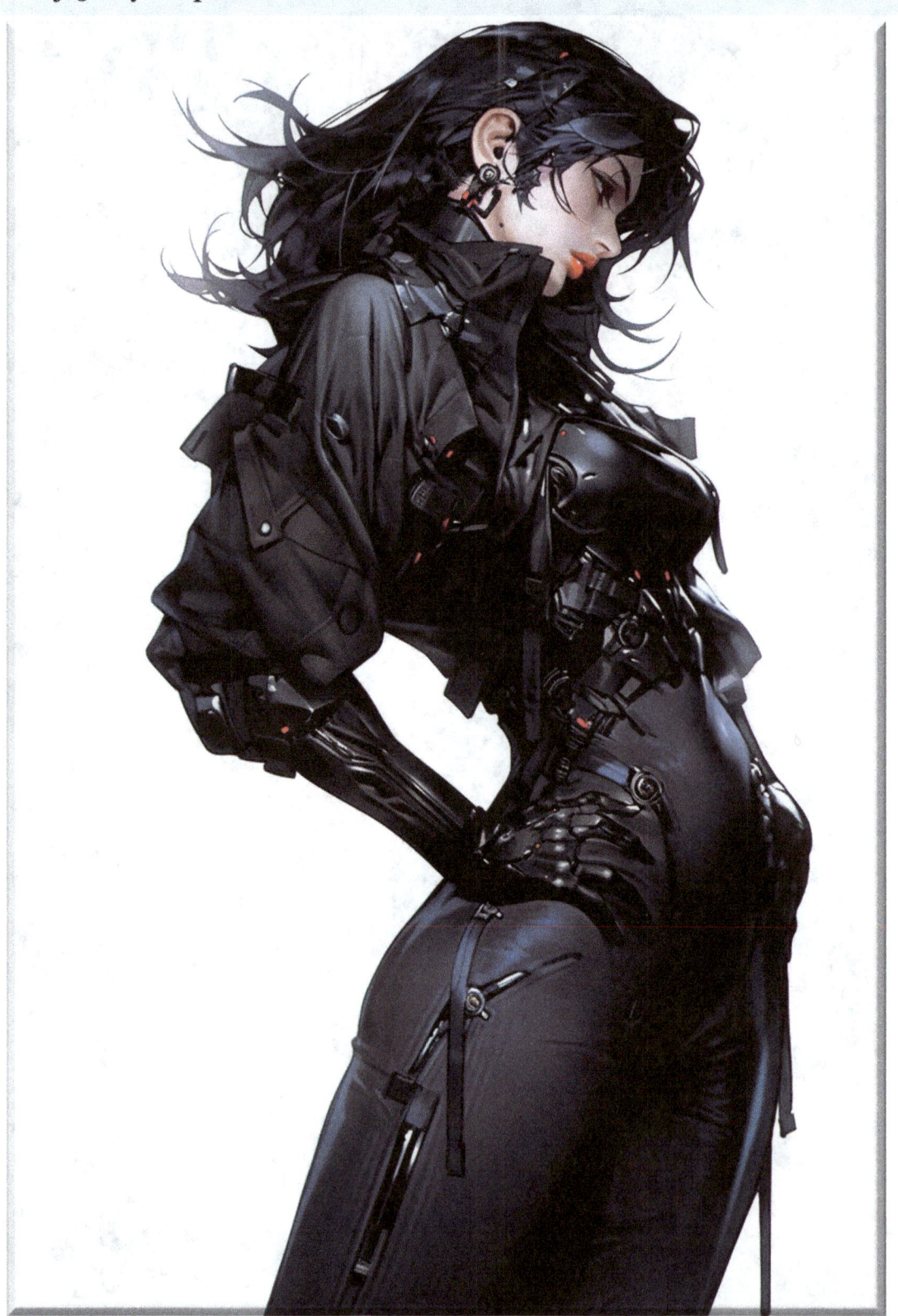

FOLIO IMAGE 039

/imagine   **A cute girl, OMG, looking through the fisheye lens, big colorful eyes, grinning, playful --ar 2:3 --niji 5 --style expressive**

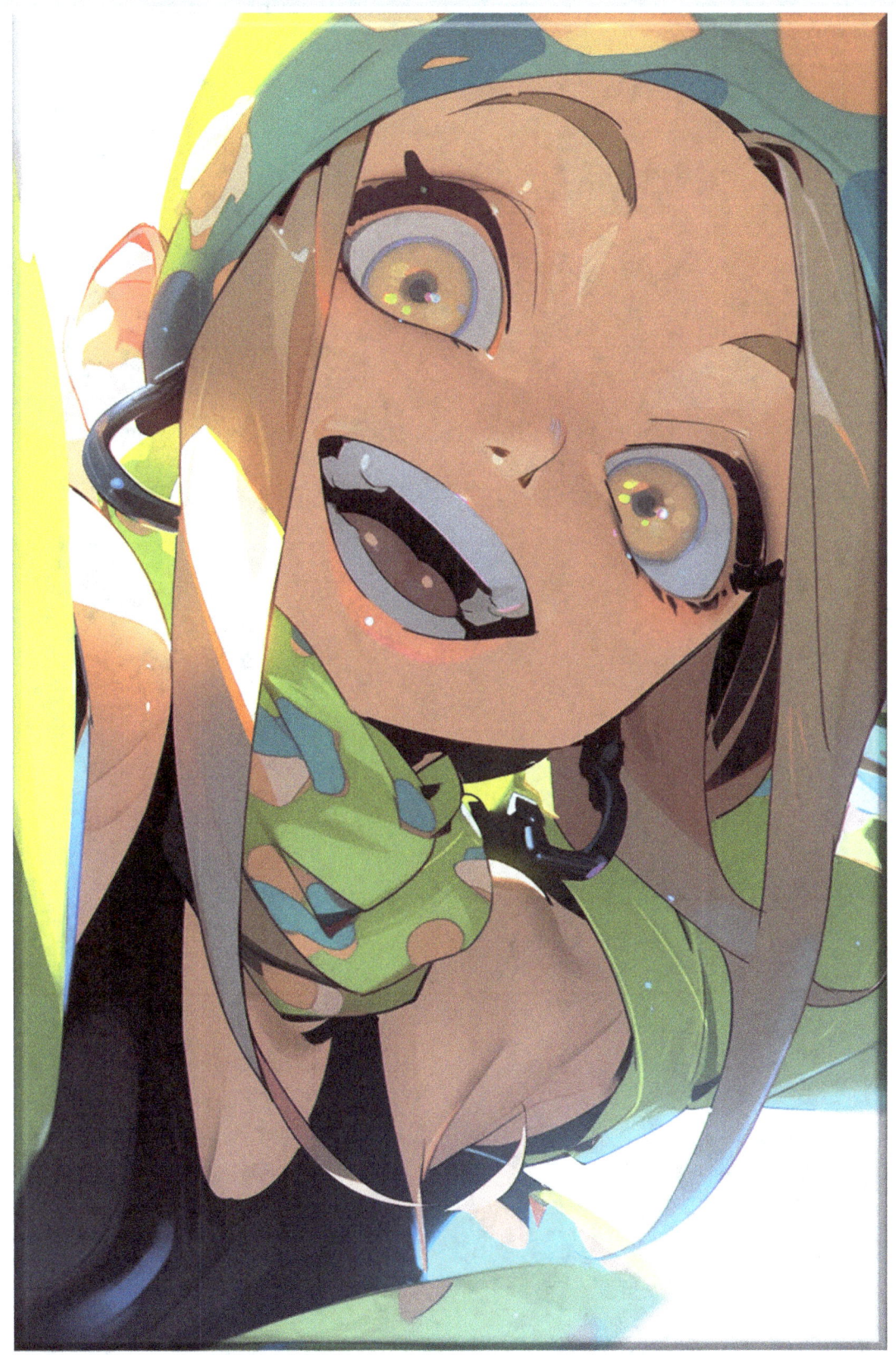

FOLIO IMAGE 040

/imagine   **A fierce armored fantasy warrior woman, standing on a mossy boulder, in a lush and misty temperate rainforest, beautiful colors, jewelry, tattoos, great hairstyle, leather, strong and beautiful, fitness, jungle, intense, determined --ar 2:3 --niji 5 --style expressive**

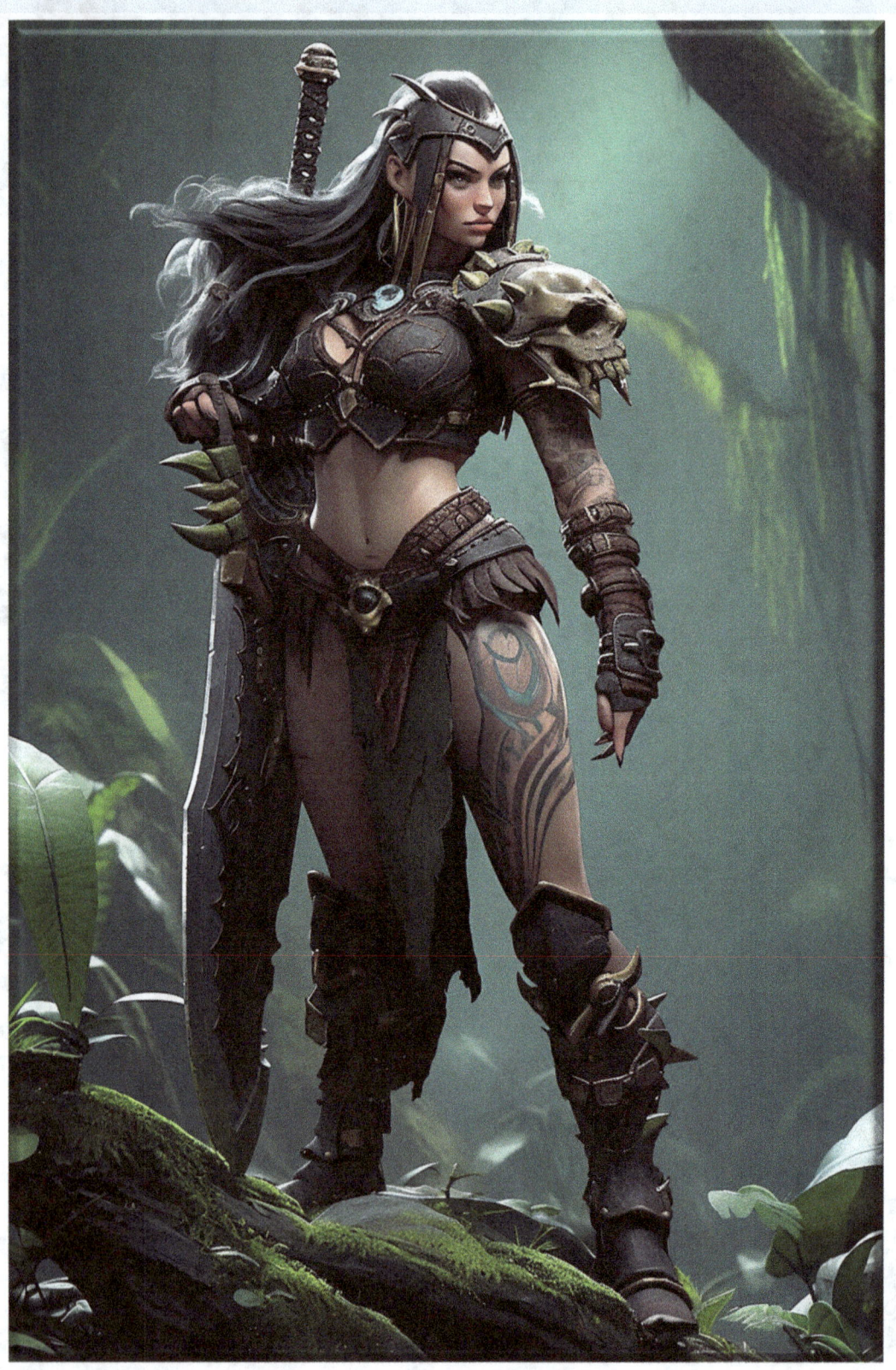

FOLIO IMAGE 041

/imagine · **A scene from a scary Jim Henson movie, group of goblins, goblin princes, in the style of Wendy Froud or Rob Liefeld, distinctive noses, green and brown and yellow, dusty piles, kid's closet, grotestque --ar 2:3 --niji 5 --style expressive**

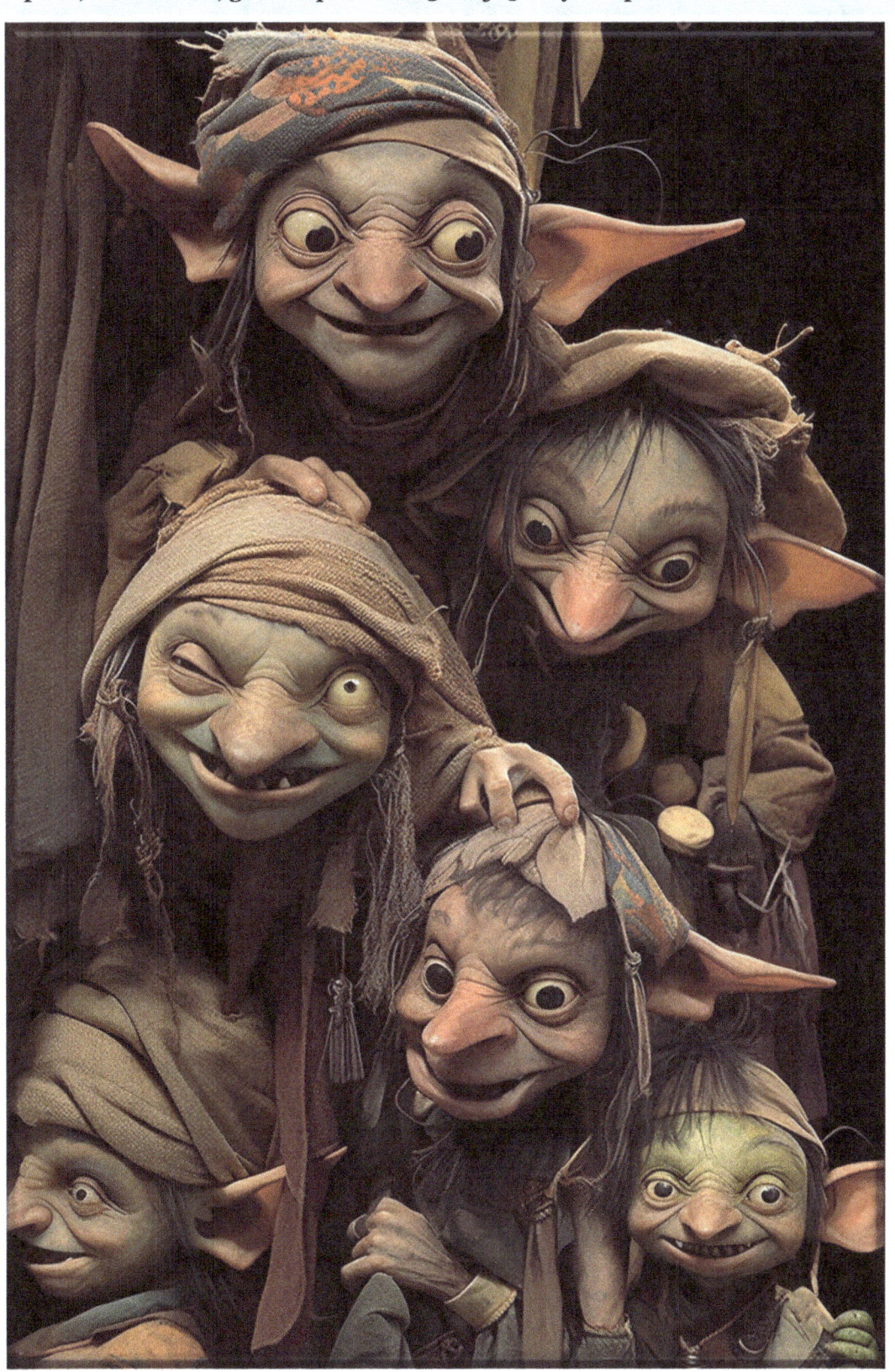

FOLIO IMAGE 042

/imagine   **A girl exploring New York City, wow skyscrapers, a beautiful detailed comic cover illustration, viewed from below, crowded, fantasy steampunk world, in the style of Love Kakao mixed with Mucha, intricate design --ar 2:3 --niji 5 --style expressive --style 300**

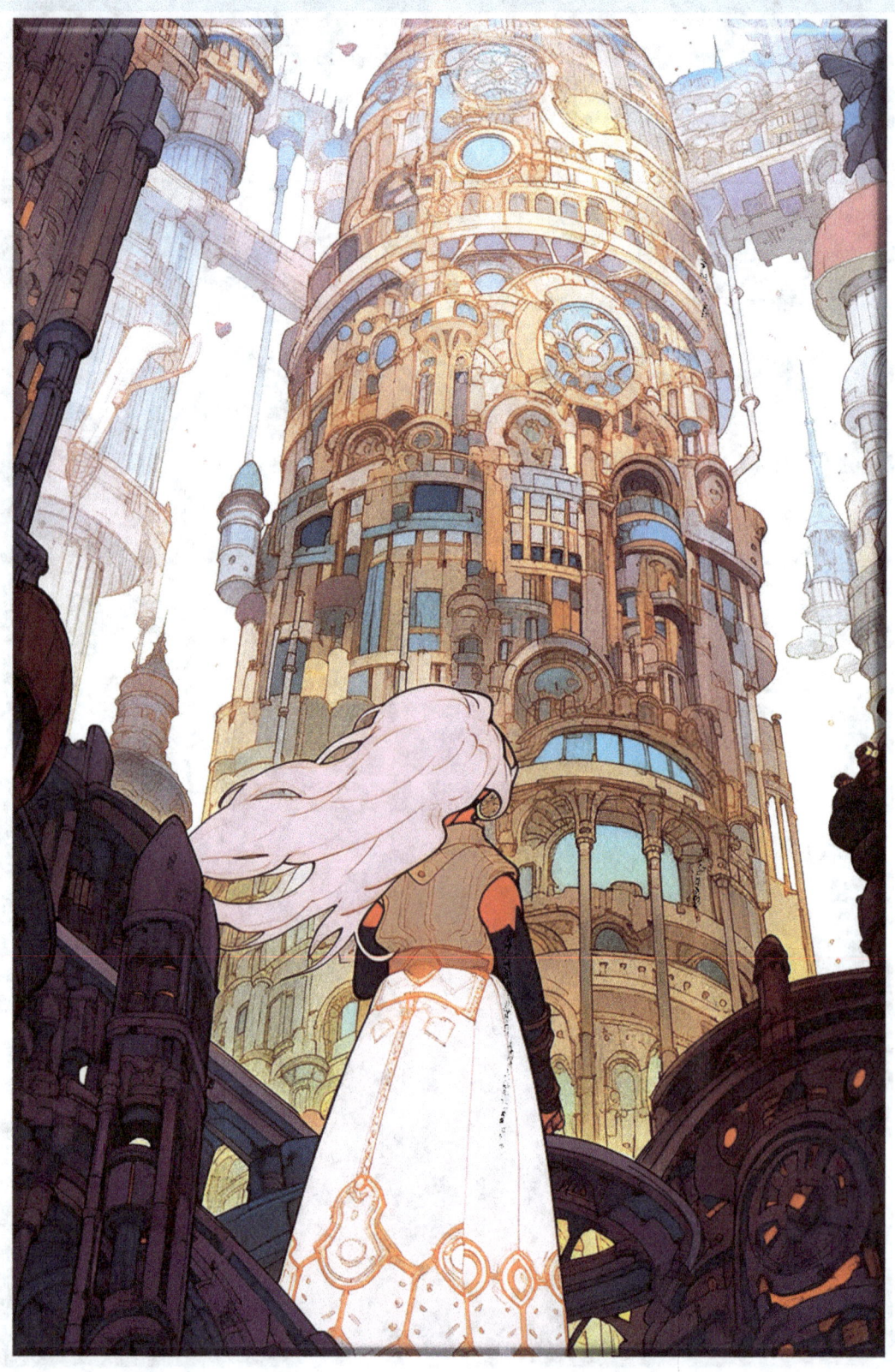

FOLIO IMAGE 043

/imagine   **Warrior of the future past, a samurai or jedi or bounty hunter, in a Samuraipunk city, illustrative styles of Raimonds Staprans and Pascal Campion and Beksinski, reflecting water puddles, bonsai, bamboo, neon at night --ar 2:3 --niji 5 --style expressive**

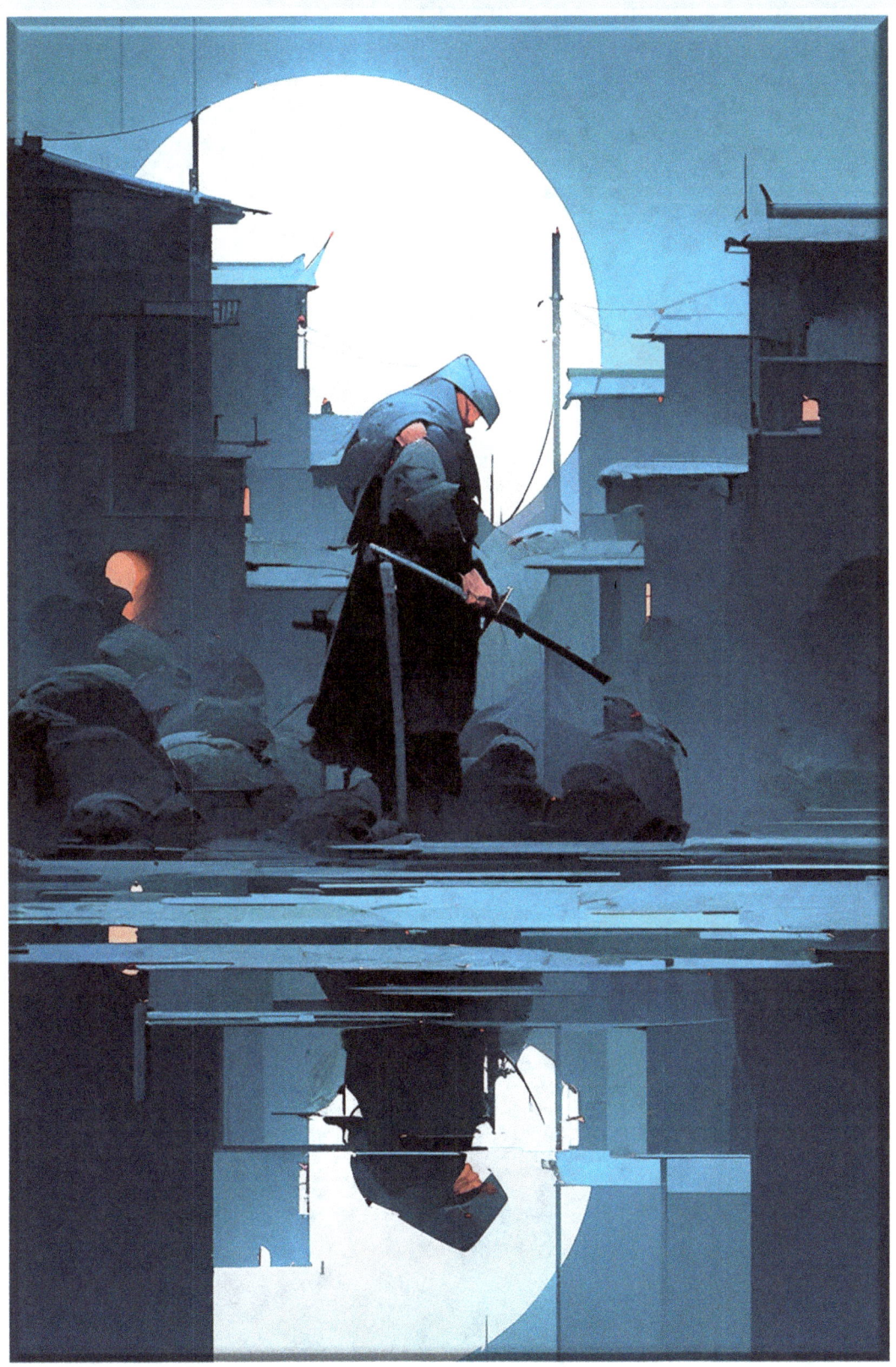

FOLIO IMAGE 044

/imagine   **A towering pyramid, colorful, hypnotic, mesmerizing, stretching high into the sky, the portal radiates an otherworldly energy, unknown, hyper-realistic, wonder, trepidation, secrets, mysteries of the other side, vastness, infinite possibilities of the universe --ar 2:3 --niji 5 --style expressive**

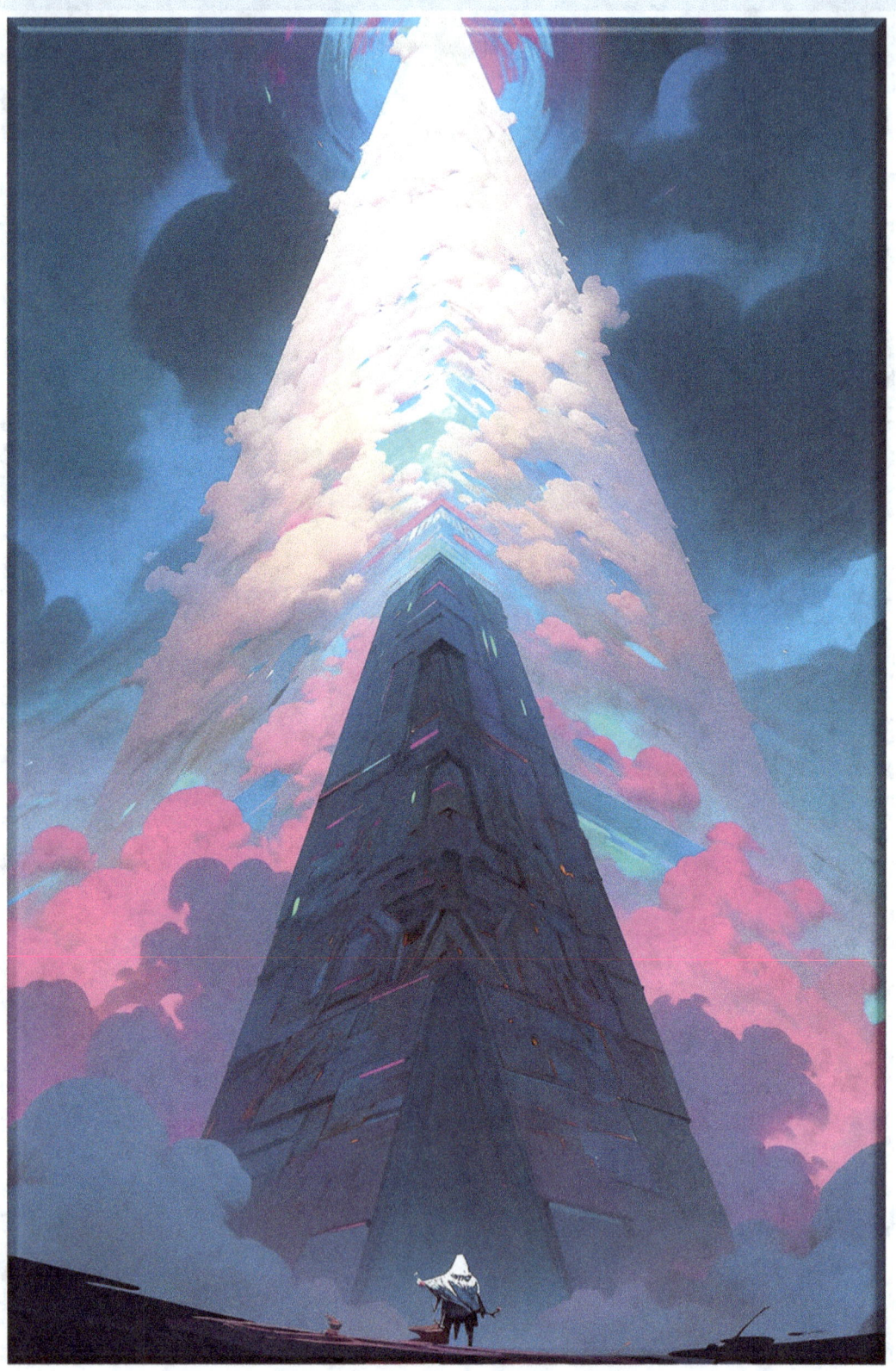

FOLIO IMAGE 045

/imagine   **a series of buildings on the hill in front of a sunset, in the style of outsider art, dark silver and yellow, enchanting watercolors, haunting houses, nightmarish visions, ashcan school --ar 2:3 --niji 5 --style expressive**

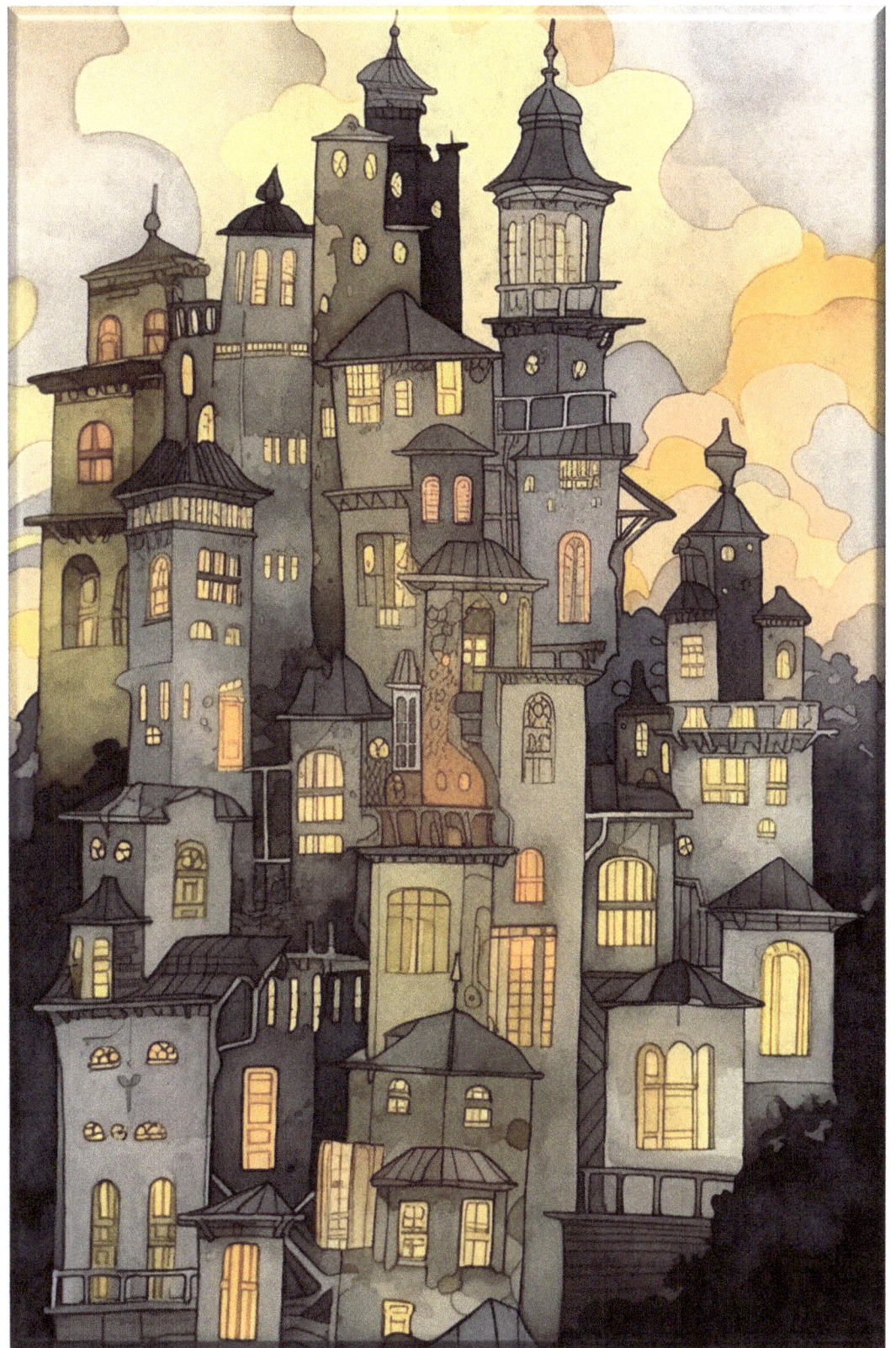

FOLIO IMAGE 046

/imagine   **An anime character in a kimono, floating amongst a group of fish, in the style of Iryna Vermolova or Marko Manev or Clayton Crain, gorgeous, eerie --ar 2:3 --niji 5 --style expressive**

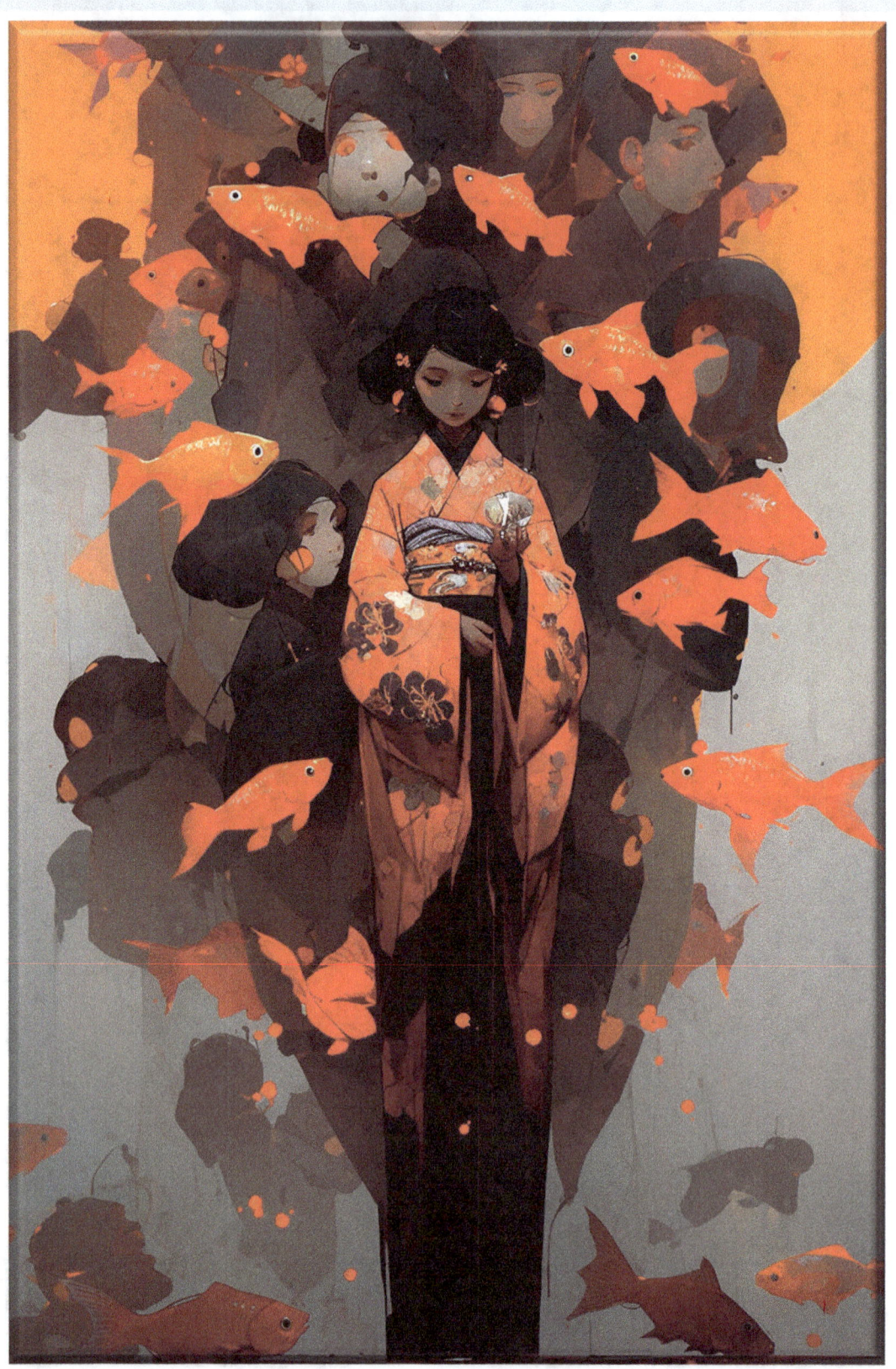

FOLIO IMAGE 047

/imagine Dangerous girl trio, like Ahri, Harley Quinn, Tifa, friends joking around, style of Luis Royo mixed with Donato Giantola, Hearthstone or Overwatch feel, embers in the air, something might be burning, low angle --ar 2:3 --niji 5 --style expressive

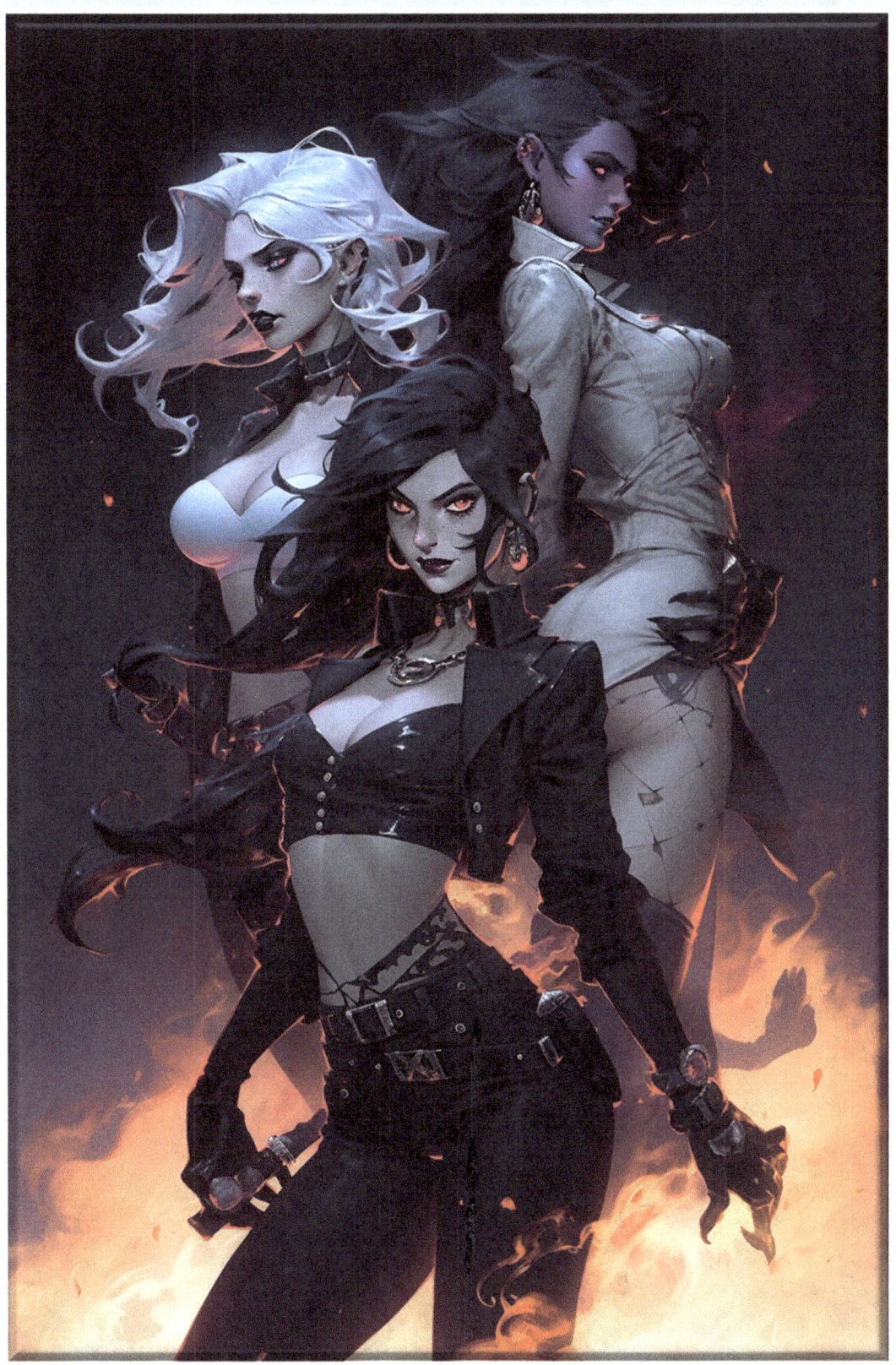

FOLIO IMAGE 048

/imagine   **The city of sunsets and destiny, Miami or LA, modern city shaped into a heart dream, in the style of MC Escher or Artgerm, dream it, nostalgia, sports cars, emotion over realism, astonishing, creative, relaxing, magical, ultra clear textures --ar 2:3 --niji 5 -- style expressive**

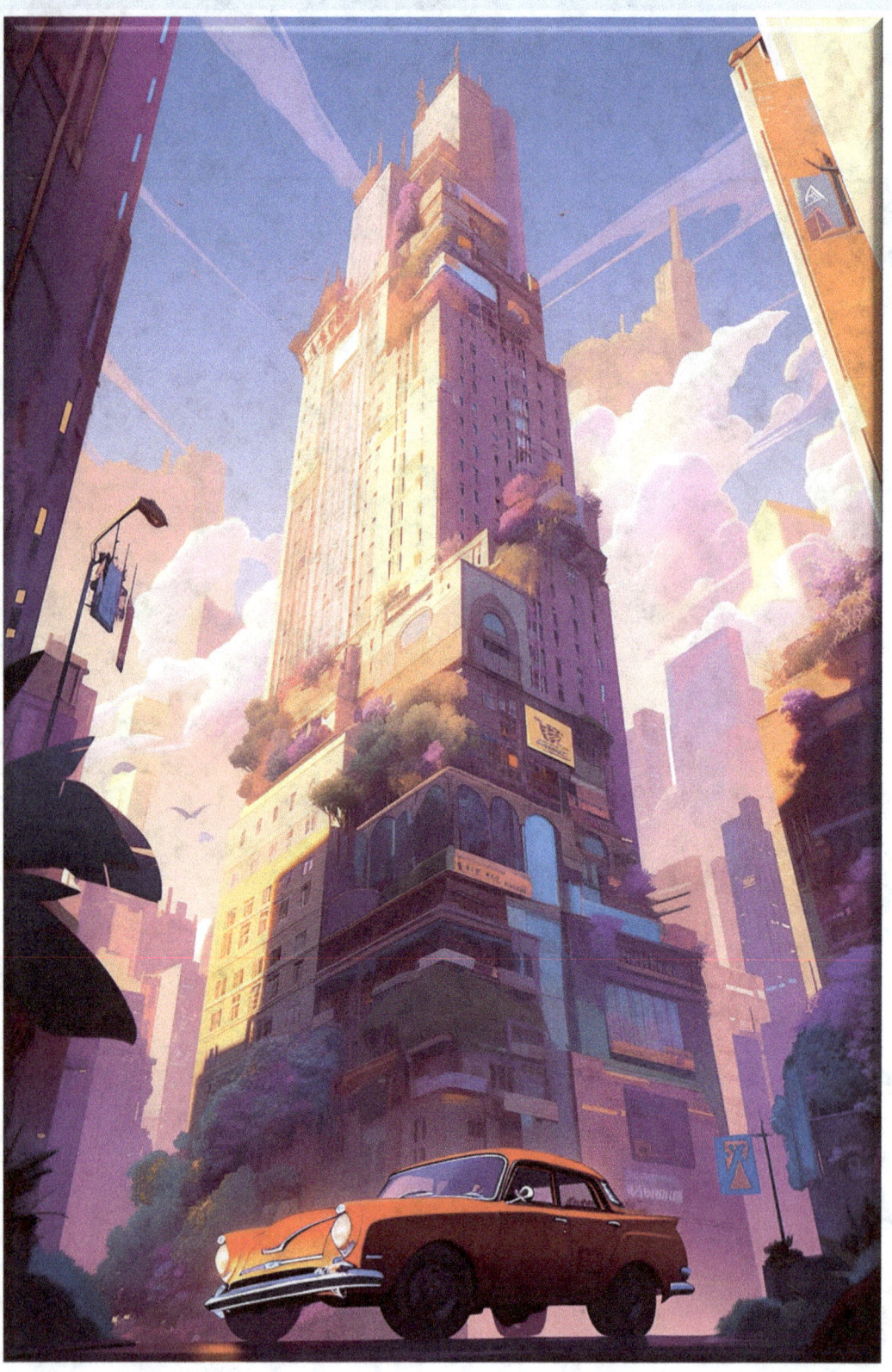

FOLIO IMAGE 049

/imagine   **Do you really think so, young woman in a flirty expression, mix up of Tsutomu Nihei, Atey Ghailan, FAILE, Krenz Cushart, ultra detailed illustration, official game poster, attractive face, colored street Manga style, neon and chrome clothing, cute and exaggerated facial features --ar 2:3 --niji 5 --style expressive**

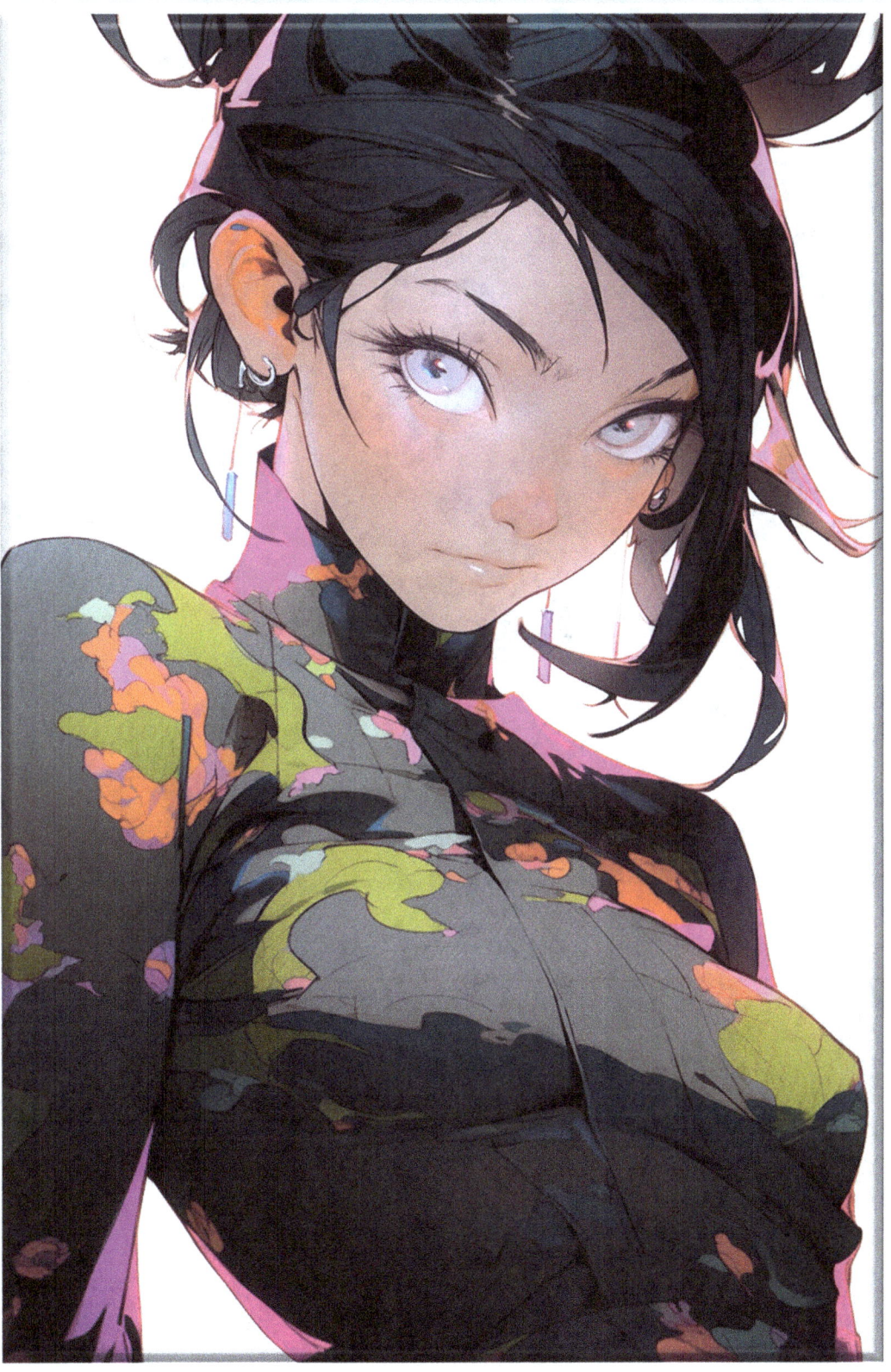

FOLIO IMAGE 050

/imagine   **Drop it hit it 321, a silhouette of an amazing techno cyberpunk DJ wearing headphones, one with the machine, the human element behind the machine must, vibrant and colorful background, geometric light rays, reflections, dancers, dynamic lighting --ar 2:3 --niji 5 --style expressive**

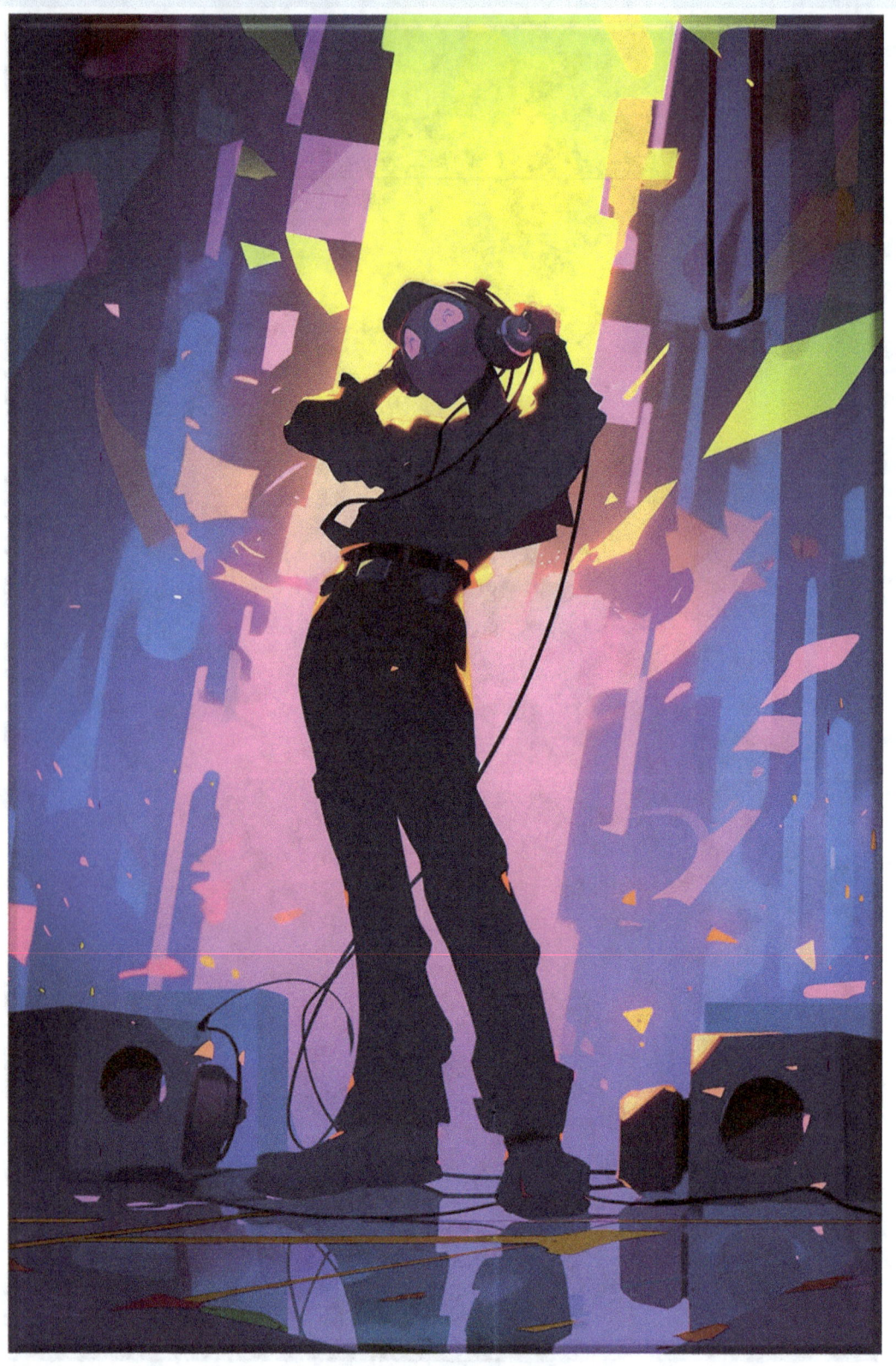

FOLIO IMAGE 051

/imagine   **Mushroom underworld of the drow, come hither only once, eerie light, netherworld Wonderland, 16k anime photo full body realistic dark elf female, ateletic --ar 2:3 --niji 5 --style expressive**

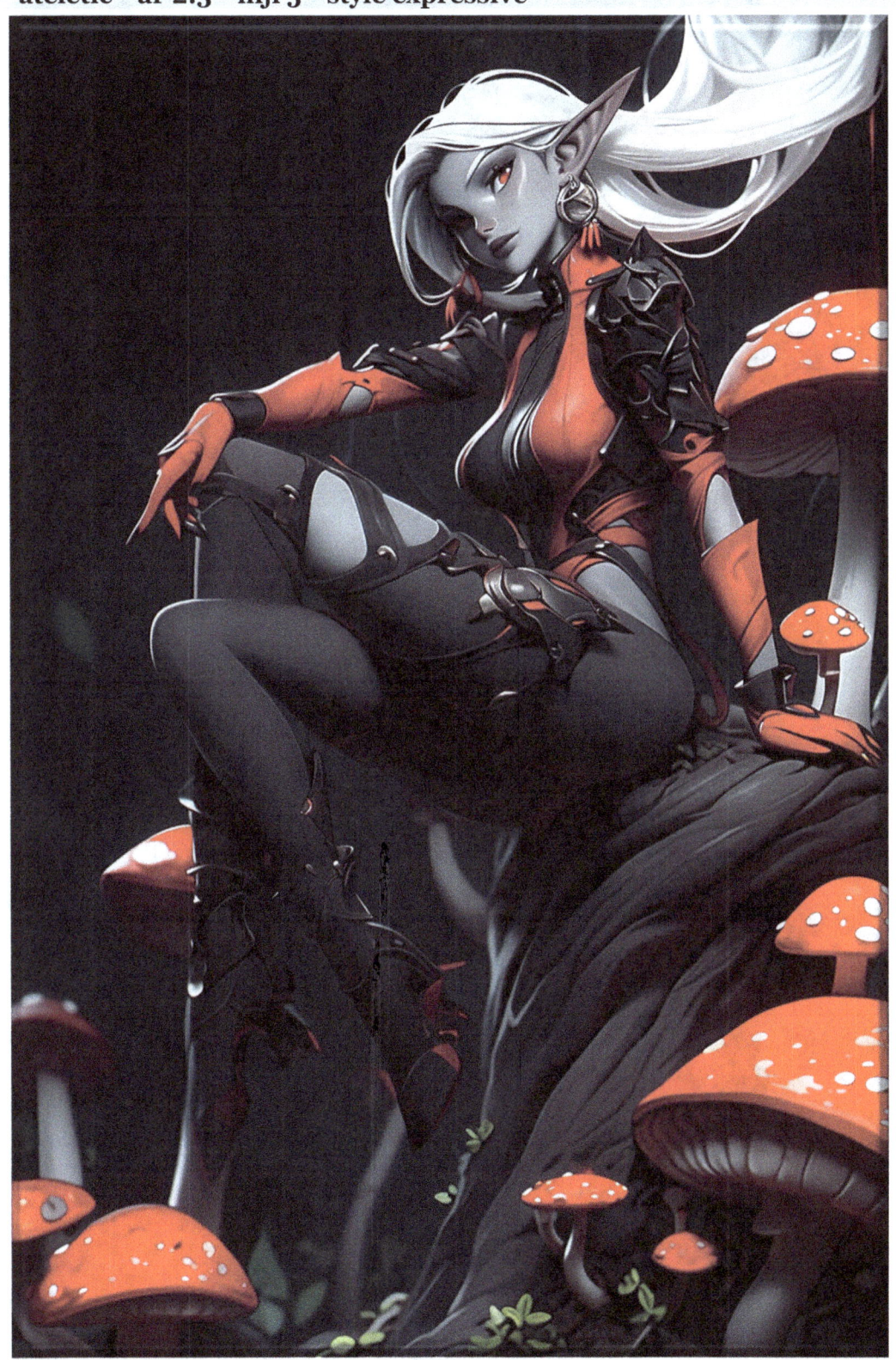

FOLIO IMAGE 052

/imagine   **The most beautiful look of the future, save the planet, cyberpunk and zoopunk, half animal sanctuary and half night glass city, elegant black and red fashion, inspired in part by Anna Dittmann and Tristan Eaton --ar 2:3 --niji 5 --style cute**

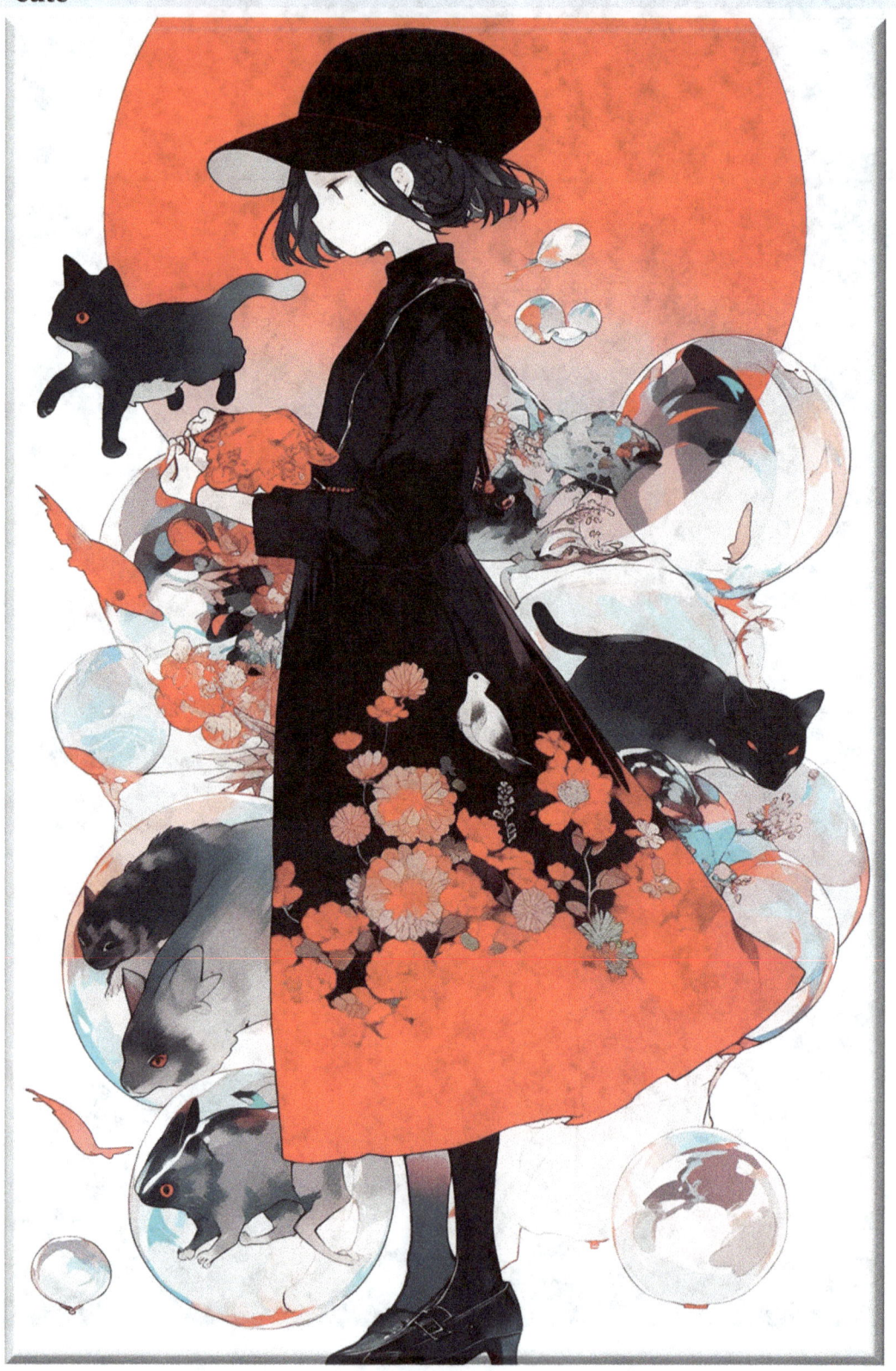

FOLIO IMAGE 053: STRIKING GOLD, SUPER PROMPT (ITERATION #01)

/imagine   **We have arrived, take me to your Eden, tiny alien in the night city, where are all the plants, realistic photography, dynamic background, intricate details, rich colors, realistic style --ar 2:3 --niji 5 --style cute**

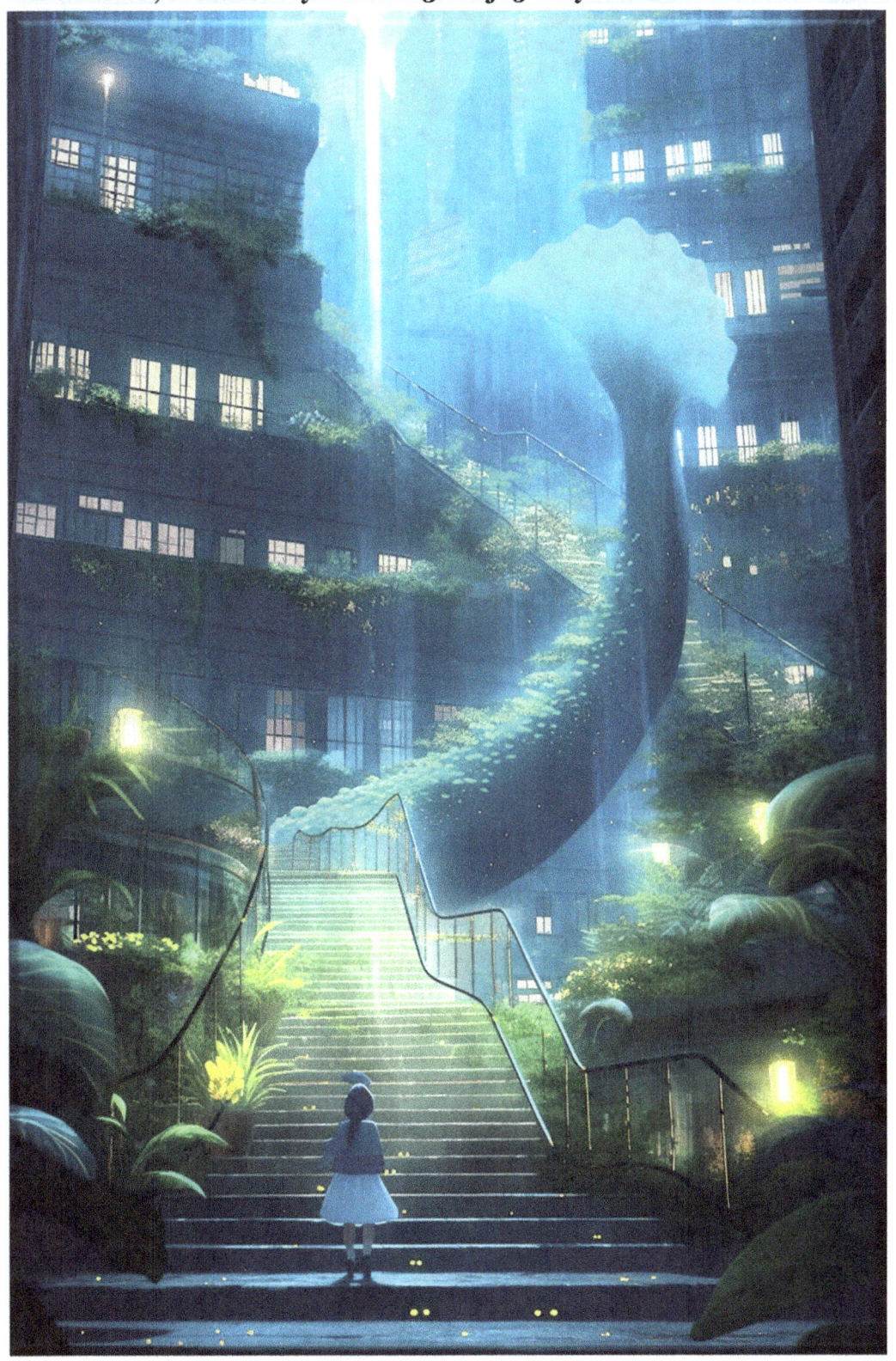

FOLIO IMAGE 054: STRIKING GOLD, SUPER PROMPT (ITERATION #02)

/imagine   **We have arrived, take me to your Eden, tiny alien in the night city, where are all the plants, realistic photography, dynamic background, intricate details, rich colors, realistic style --ar 2:3 --niji 5 --style cute**

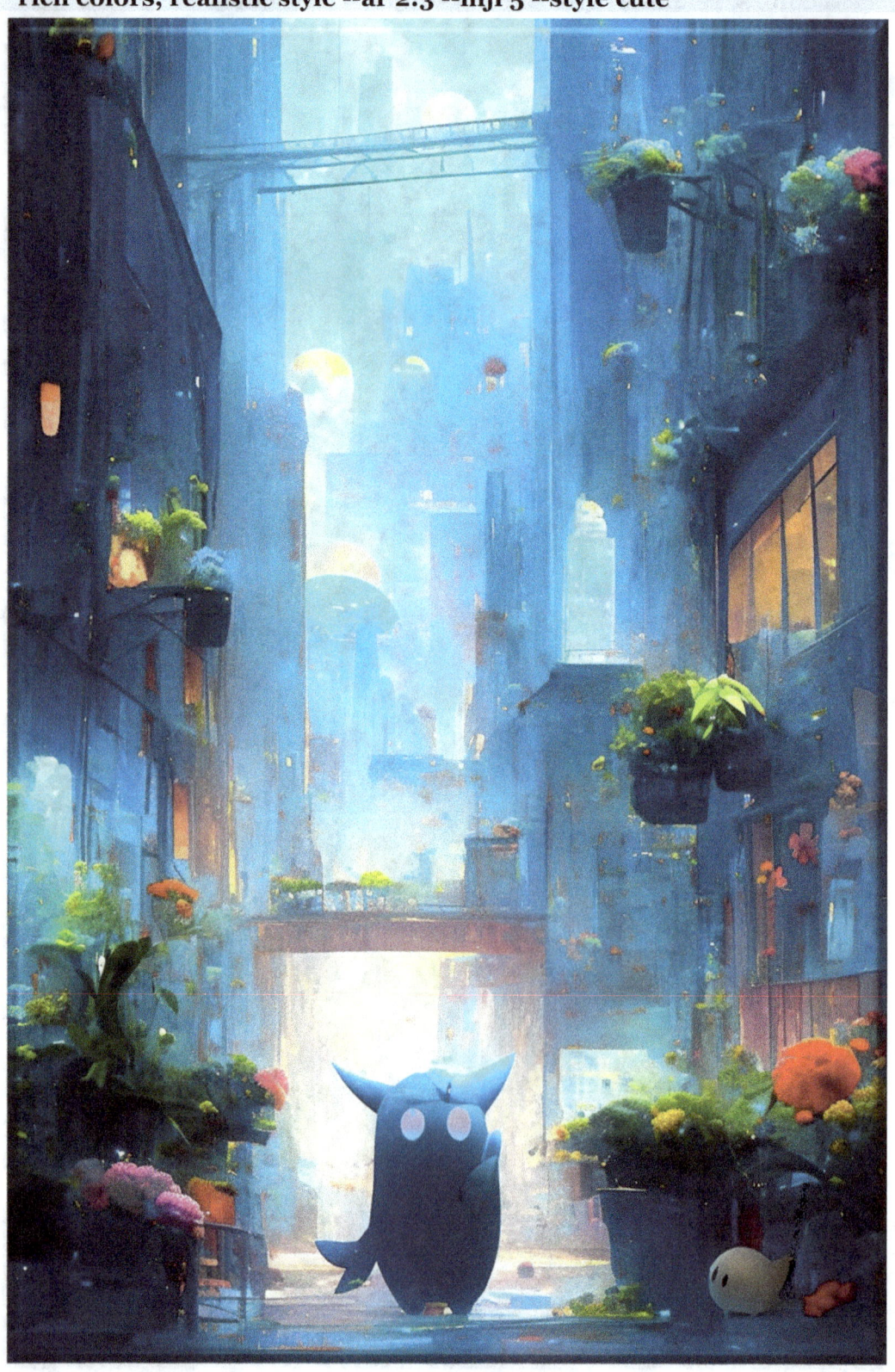

FOLIO IMAGE 055: STRIKING GOLD, SUPER PROMPT (ITERATION #03)

/imagine   **We have arrived, take me to your Eden, tiny alien in the night city, where are all the plants, realistic photography, dynamic background, intricate details, rich colors, realistic style --ar 2:3 --niji 5 --style cute**

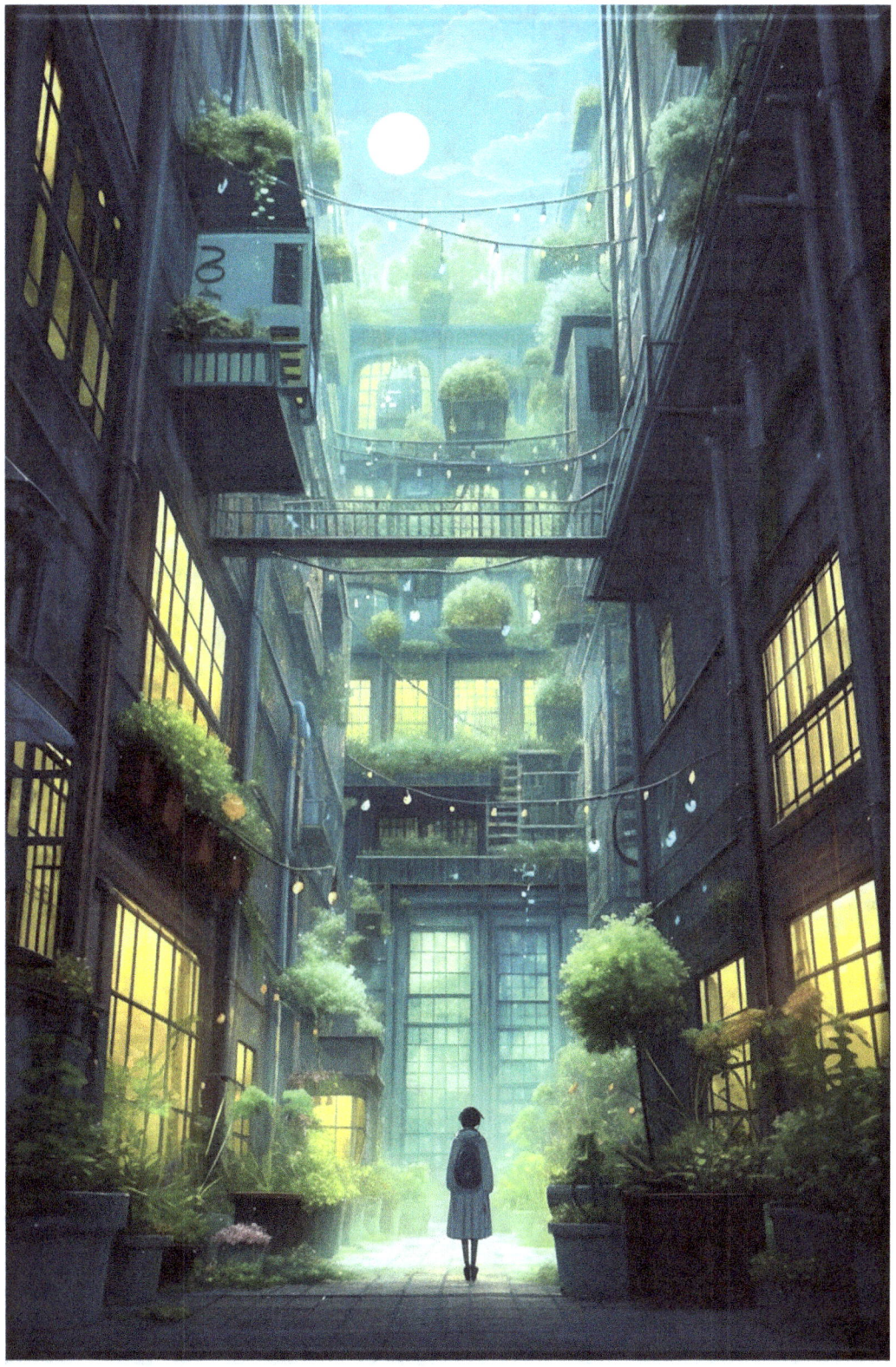

FOLIO IMAGE 056: STRIKING GOLD, SUPER PROMPT (ITERATION #04)

/imagine   We have arrived, take me to your Eden, tiny alien in the night city, where are all the plants, realistic photography, dynamic background, intricate details, rich colors, realistic style --ar 2:3 --niji 5 --style cute

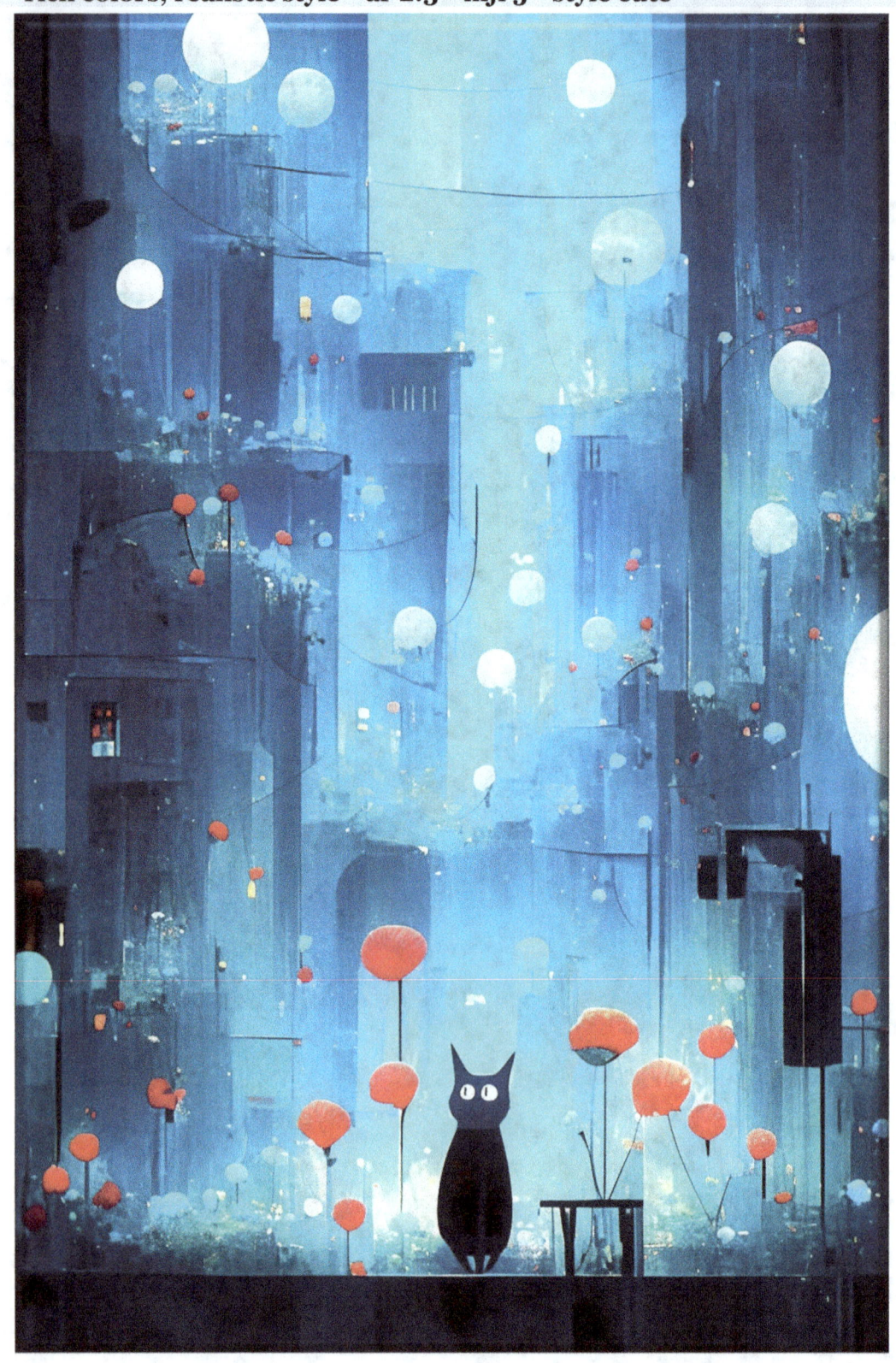

FOLIO IMAGE 057: STRIKING GOLD, SUPER PROMPT (ITERATION #05)

/imagine   **We have arrived, take me to your Eden, tiny alien in the night city, where are all the plants, realistic photography, dynamic background, intricate details, rich colors, realistic style --ar 2:3 --niji 5 --style cute**

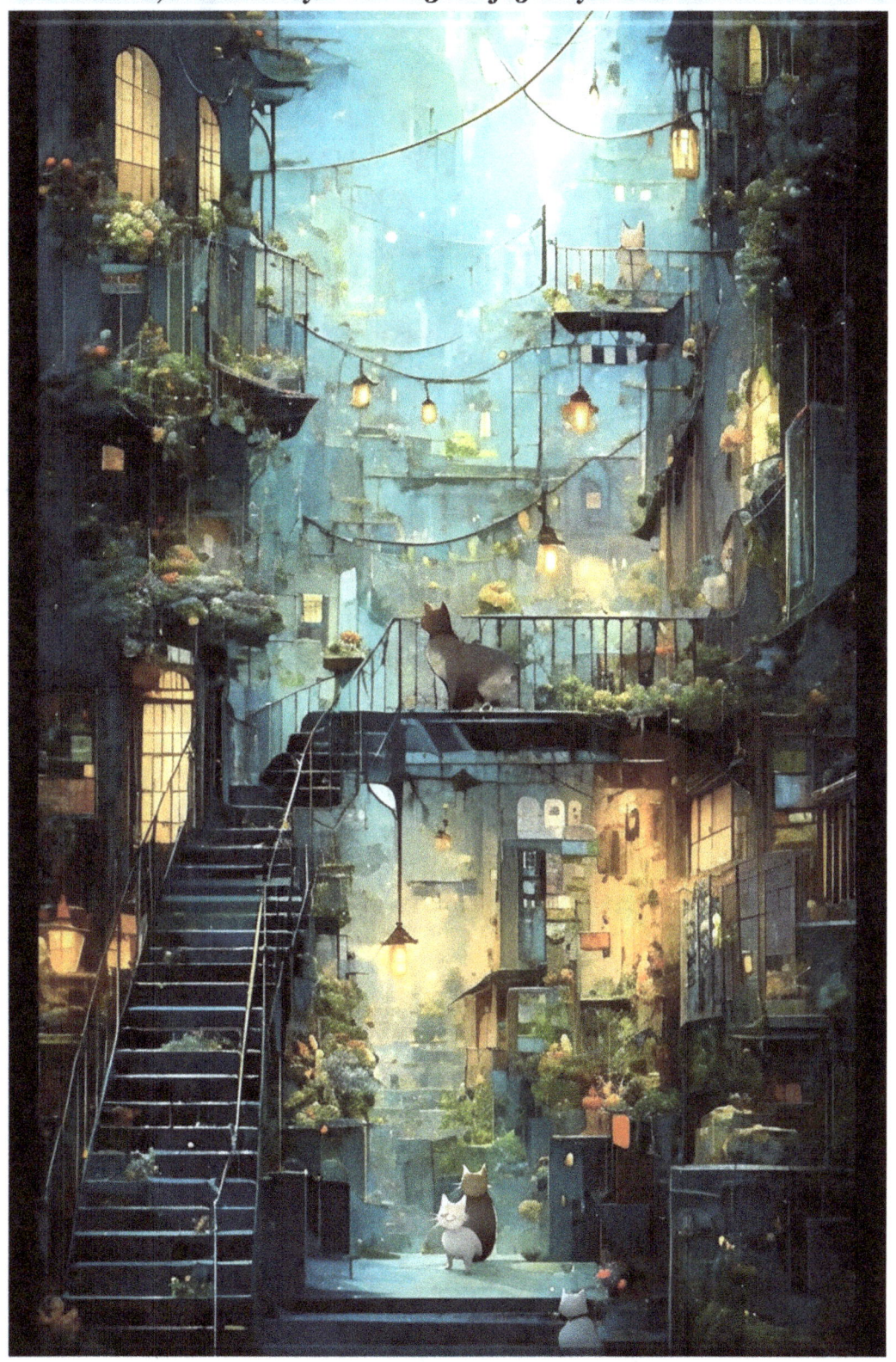

FOLIO IMAGE 058: STRIKING GOLD, SUPER PROMPT (ITERATION #06)

/imagine   **We have arrived, take me to your Eden, tiny alien in the night city, where are all the plants, realistic photography, dynamic background, intricate details, rich colors, realistic style --ar 2:3 --niji 5 --style cute**

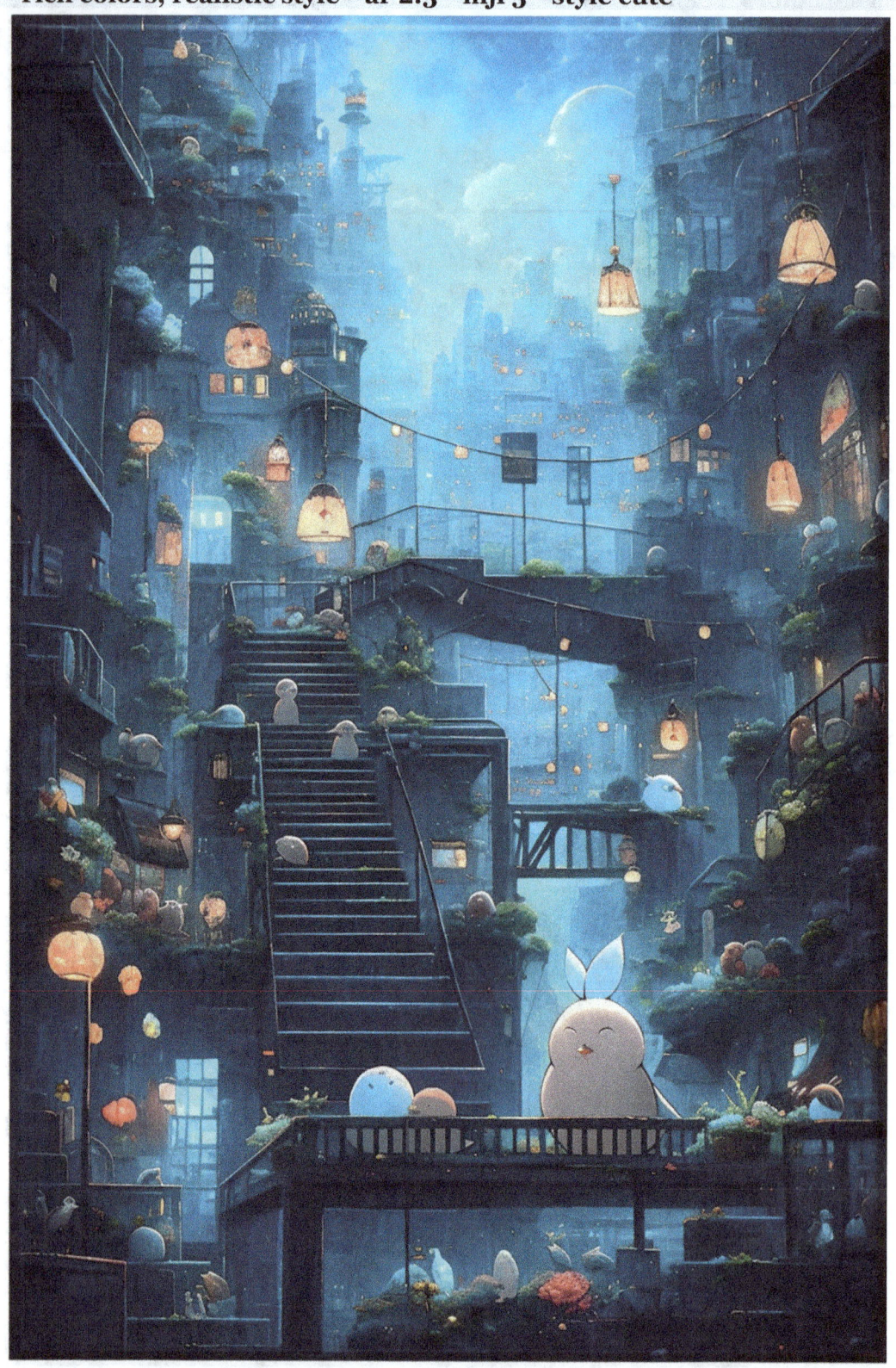

FOLIO IMAGE 059: STRIKING GOLD, SUPER PROMPT (ITERATION #07)

/imagine   **We have arrived, take me to your Eden, tiny alien in the night city, where are all the plants, realistic photography, dynamic background, intricate details, rich colors, realistic style --ar 2:3 --niji 5 --style cute**

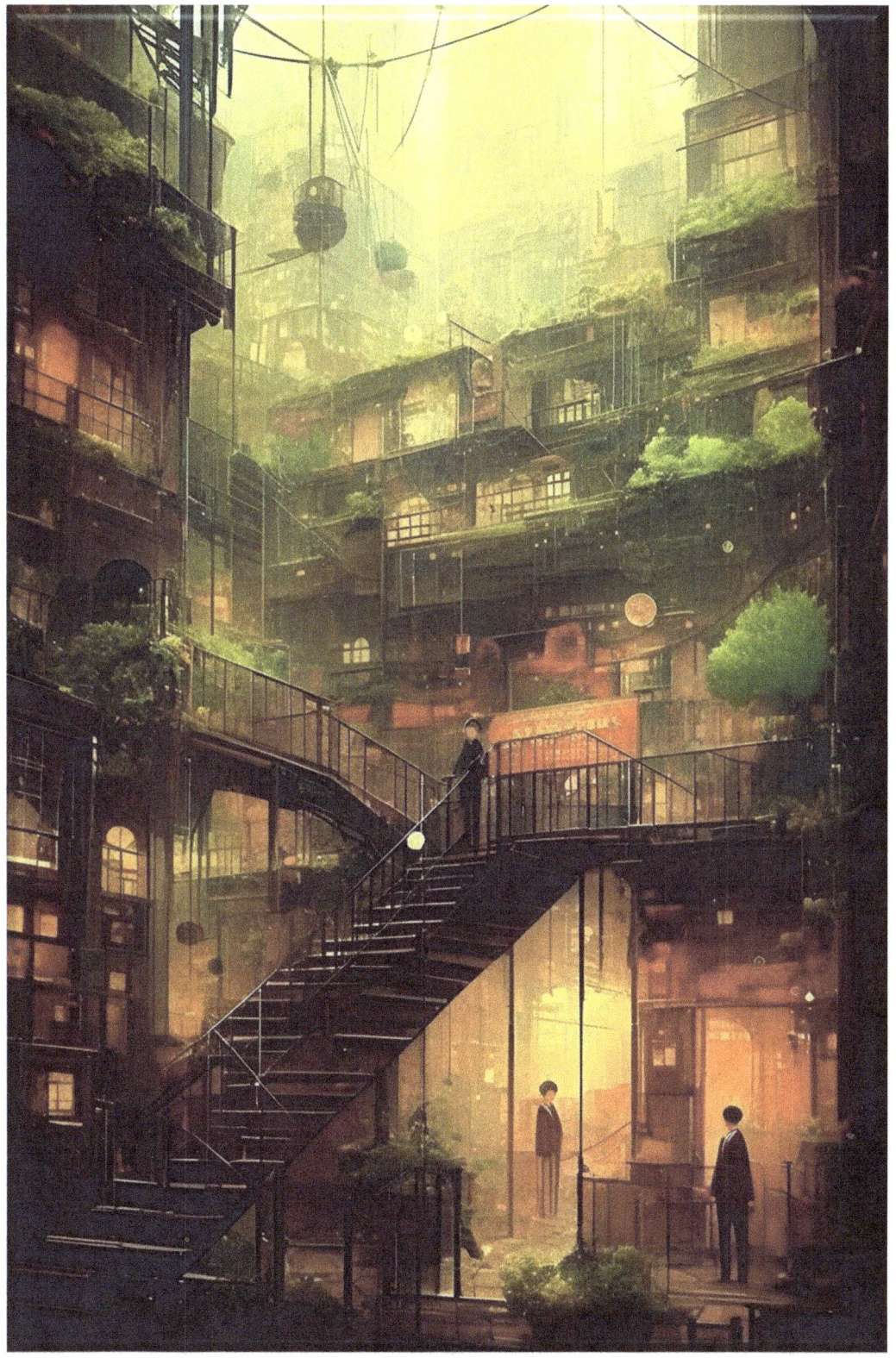

FOLIO IMAGE 060: STRIKING GOLD, SUPER PROMPT (ITERATION #08)

/imagine   **We have arrived, take me to your Eden, tiny alien in the night city, where are all the plants, realistic photography, dynamic background, intricate details, rich colors, realistic style --ar 2:3 --niji 5 --style cute**

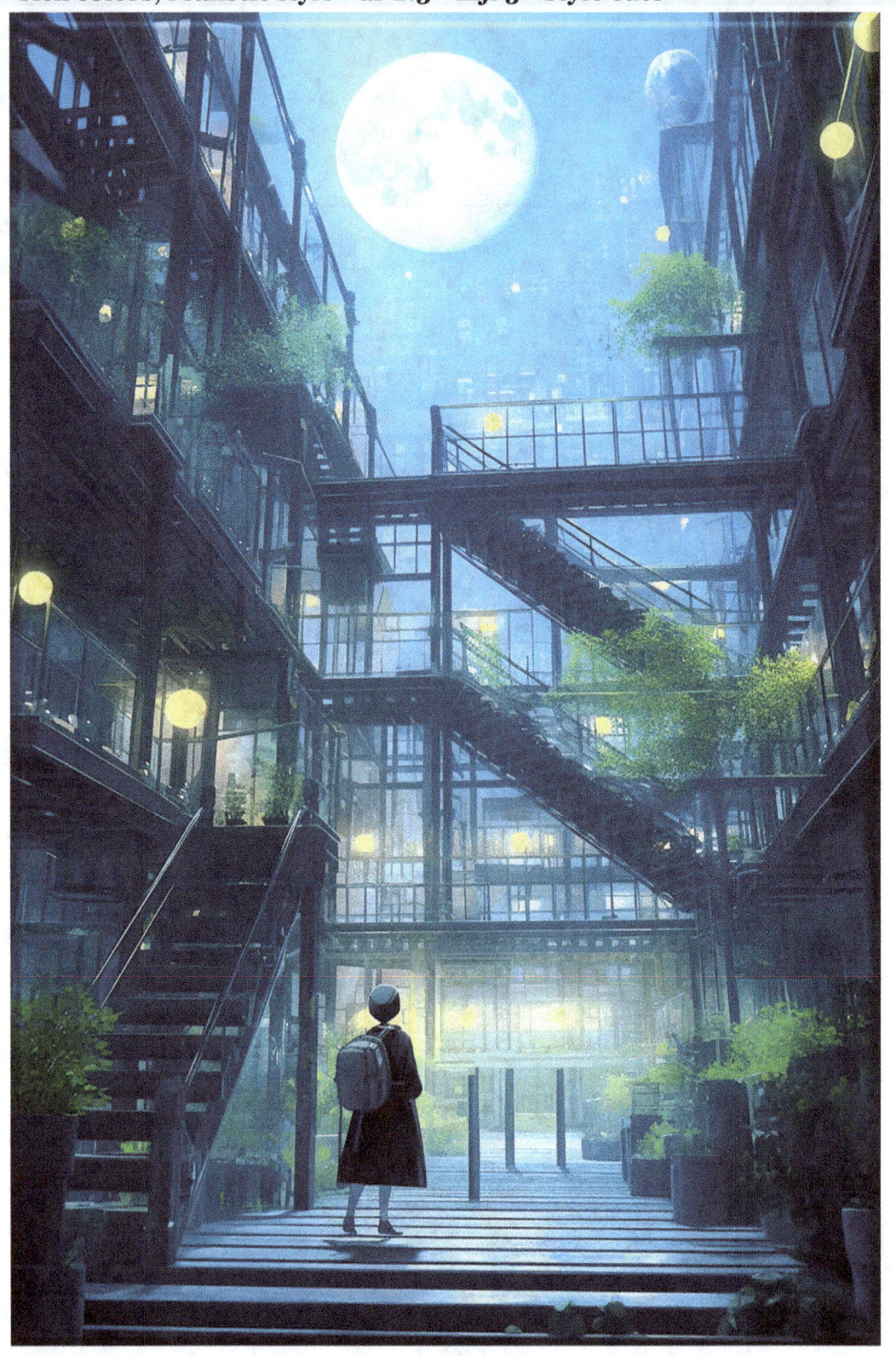

FOLIO IMAGE 061: STRIKING GOLD, SUPER PROMPT (ITERATION #09)

/imagine   We have arrived, take me to your Eden, tiny alien in the night city, where are all the plants, realistic photography, dynamic background, intricate details, rich colors, realistic style --ar 2:3 --niji 5 --style cute

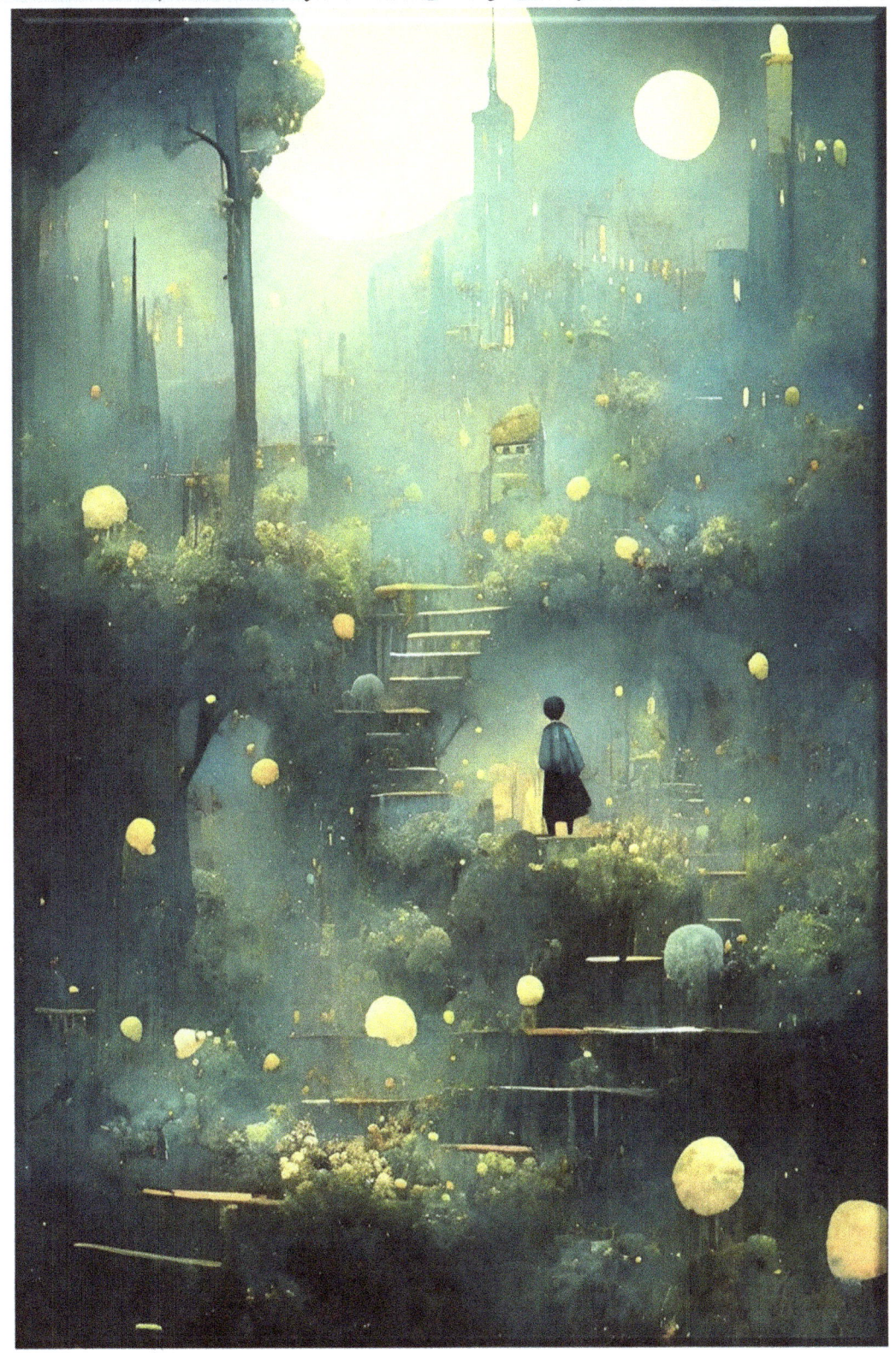

FOLIO IMAGE 062: STRIKING GOLD, SUPER PROMPT (ITERATION #10)

/imagine   **We have arrived, take me to your Eden, tiny alien in the night city, where are all the plants, realistic photography, dynamic background, intricate details, rich colors, realistic style --ar 2:3 --niji 5 --style cute**

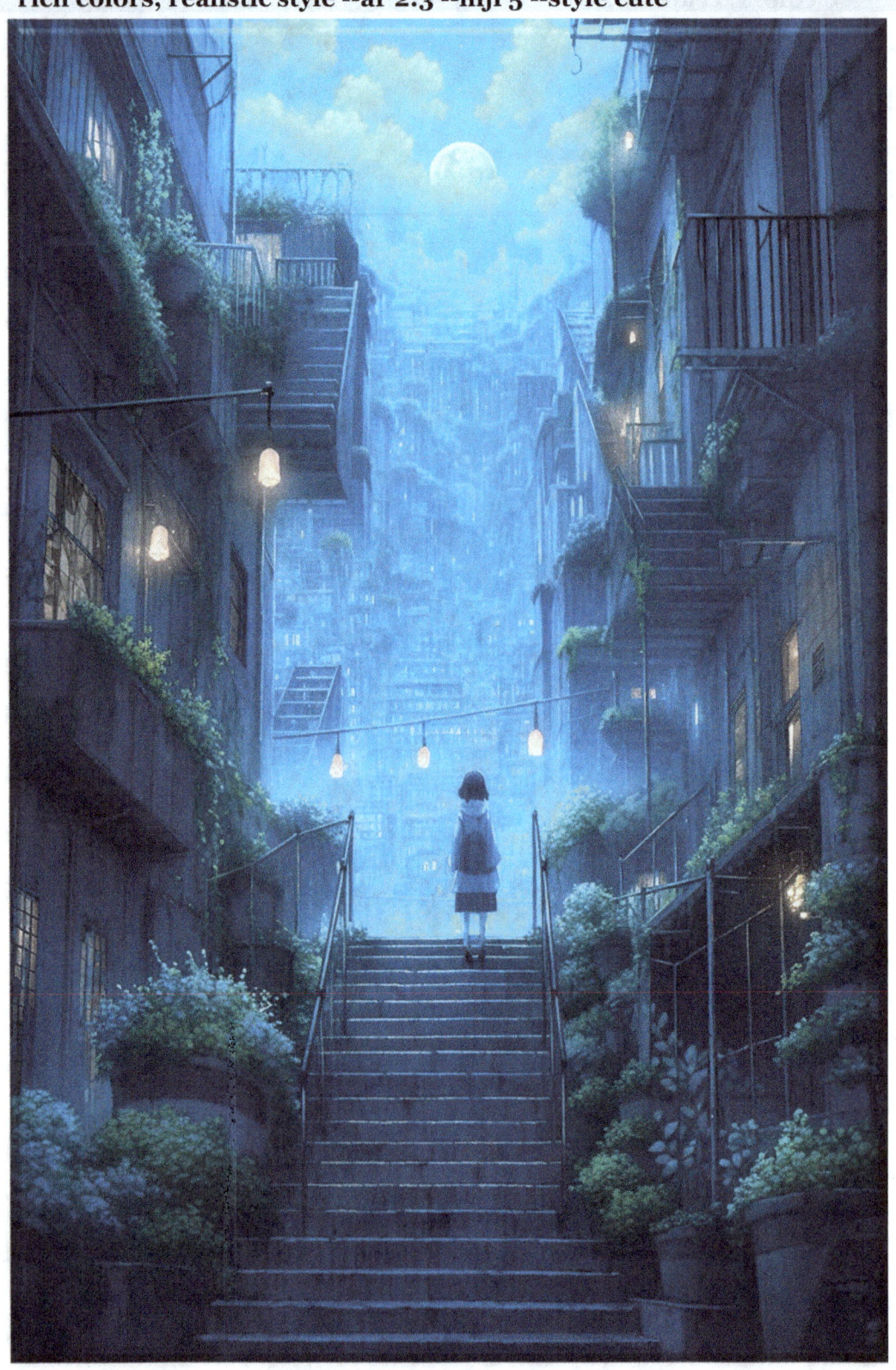

M-Discord Commands

/ask - Need an answer to a burning question? Just type /ask and let our bot provide you with the information you need.

/blend - Want to easily blend two images together? Our /blend command makes it a breeze to create stunning visual combinations.

/daily_theme - Don't miss out on the latest updates in the #daily-theme channel! Toggle notification pings with our /daily_theme command.

/docs - Need quick access to our user guide? Just type /docs and our bot will generate a link to the topics covered.

/describe - Looking for inspiration? Upload an image and let our bot write four example prompts based on it to kickstart your creativity.

/faq - Have questions about prompt crafting? Our /faq command generates a link to our FAQ channel for quick answers.

/fast - Need faster results? Switch to Fast mode with our /fast command and unlock the full power of our bot's upscaling capabilities.

/help - Need some basic information and tips? Type /help and our bot will provide you with helpful guidance on how to make the most of Midjourney.

/imagine - Want to generate an image based on a prompt? Our /imagine command lets you do just that, and brings your ideas to life.

/info - Want to view information about your account and job status? Type /info and our bot will provide you with all the details you need.

/stealth - For our Pro Plan Subscribers, switch to Stealth Mode with our /stealth command and enjoy a seamless experience with added privacy.

/public - Pro Plan Subscribers can also switch to Public Mode with our /public command, allowing for easy sharing and collaboration.

/subscribe - Generate a personal link for your account page with our /subscribe command and keep track of your settings and preferences.

/settings - Want to view and adjust the bot's settings? Type /settings and our bot will provide you with options to customize your experience.

/prefer option - Create or manage a custom option with our /prefer option command, and tailor the bot's performance to your liking.

/prefer option list - View your current custom options with our /prefer option list command and stay in control of your settings.

/prefer suffix - Add a suffix to every prompt for a unique touch with our /prefer suffix command and make your images truly your own.

/show - Need to regenerate a job within Discord? Just use our /show command and provide the Job ID for quick results.

/relax - Want to switch to Relax mode for a more laid-back experience? Our /relax command lets you enjoy Midjourney at your own pace.

/remix - Toggle Remix mode on and off with our /remix command and experiment with different styles and variations.

Anime in Midjourney, by Kent David Kelly, © *2023. V1.0*

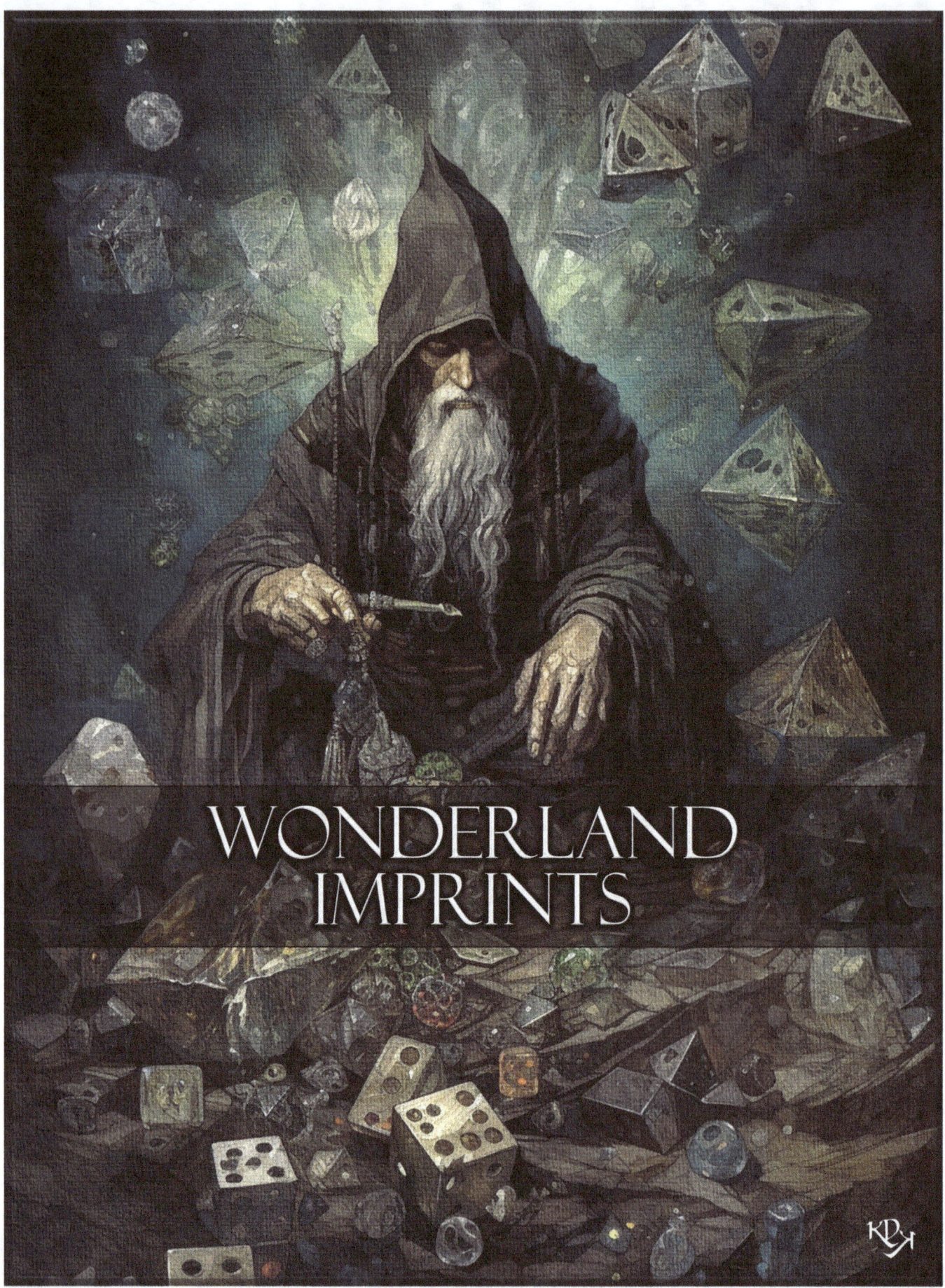

WONDERLAND
IMPRINTS